BUILDING
THE
SUCCESSFUL
THEATER
COMPANY

Lisa Mulcahy

ALLWORTH PRESS
NEW YORK

07 06 05 04 03 02   5   4   3   2   1

Published by Allworth Press
An imprint of Allworth Communications, Inc.
10 East 23rd Street, New York, NY 10010

Cover design by Leah Lococo Ltd.
Page composition/typography by Integras Software Services, Pvt Ltd., Pondicherry, India

ISBN: 1-58115-237-X

Library of Congress Cataloging-in-Publication Data: Mulcahy, Lisa.
Building the successful theater company / Lisa Mulcahy.

p. cm.
ISBN 1-58115-237-X
1. Theatrical companies—United States—History—20th century. I. Title.
PN2297.A2 M85 2002
792'.0973'0904—dc21

2002010822

Printed in Canada

FOR MY FATHER, WILLIAM MULCAHY

ACKNOWLEDGMENTS

I want to thank the following wonderful people for helping me invaluably during my work on this book:

First of all, at Allworth Press, Tad Crawford and Nicole Potter for their support of me as a writer and their tremendous guidance, trust, and encouragement. Thanks to Kate Lothman for her professionalism, warmth, and assistance as well.

To all of the amazing artists and administrators who participated in interviews for this book, I give my utmost gratitude. Your honesty, the generosity you show in sharing your wisdom, and your immense skills inspire me and will no doubt inspire scores of readers. Terrence Dwyer, Sheldon Epps, David Fuller, Corey Fischer, Michael Gennaro, Leslie B. Jacobson, Dona Lee Kelly, Susan Kosoff, Rick Lombardo, Susan Albert Loewenberg, Susan Medak, Ralph Remington, Jack Reuler, Mitzi Sales, Harriet Sheets, David Zak, and Paul Zuckerman—each of you provided me with your valuable time, insight, and memories, and I'm honored to be able to pass on what I learned from you to others.

I also wish to thank the following theater personnel for their specific assistance in helping me arrange the logistics of interviews and for providing me with supplementary materials: Ellen Bailey, Sheila Boyd, Brian Colvern, Peggy Ebright, Kay Elliott, Emily Lister, Stacey Moore, Jason Raitt, Jane Staab, Sara Truog, Shay Wafer, and Helene Sanghri York.

I would like to give a very special thank you to Molly Smith, Artistic Director of Arena Stage.

For special technical assistance, I would like to thank Johanne Cimon of The Most Office in Fitchburg, Massachusetts, whose work is excellent. I would also like to give a special thank you to my uncle, Gary Porter, who provided additional technical guidance to me on this project.

To my entire family, thank you for your support. To my posse of friends, you know who you are. To all of phenomenal artists I've encountered throughout my long life in the theater, thanks for great times.

To the Brandeis University theater community, especially Ted Kazanoff, thanks for a great education. Thank you also to Edward Albee for giving me a wonderful break.

To my aunt, Judith Porter, a very special expression of my love and gratitude for all of your devotion, enthusiasm, and unconditional love. I am so proud to be your niece.

To my mother, Joan Mulcahy, you mean the world to me, and I can't believe I am lucky enough to be your daughter. Thanks, Mom, to you and Dad for instilling me with strength and confidence and standing by my side every minute. You're the greatest.

—LISA MULCAHY

CONTENTS

INTRODUCTION

WHAT MAKES A THEATER COMPANY SUCCESSFUL?

Passion. Blind faith. Talent. Naiveté. Focus. A burning desire to say something important.

These are some of the qualities possessed by those brave individuals who enter the incredibly challenging field of professional theater. It's been said by many, including me, that in order to take on a career in the dramatic arts, your need to do it must supersede virtually every other desire you could possibly have. To make it, you must make sacrifices: of your time, of your financial security, of your personal life, and many times, of every last shred of your peace of mind.

You must also be a very tough cookie. Your self-esteem had better be bulletproof, and not simply in terms of the numerous professional rejections and the struggle you will invariably face. You also need to know who you are and like who you are, 24/7, because you can't measure success in the theater by any conventional business model yardstick. It's very, very hard to get rich running a theater company, for example, to be able to see those profit numbers pile up on paper, as one could do if he or she were running, say, a Fortune 500 company. Or nearly any other type of company, for that matter.

So, why do it, then? Well, there's passion. Blind faith. Talent. Naiveté. Focus. A burning desire to say something important—and feel free to add your personal reasons to that list. The world is indeed better off, because there are those people who live to act, direct, write, stage manage, design for the stage, work tech crew for shows—and perhaps the most daunting prospect of all, found and build their own theater companies.

This book will examine the processes and practicalities involved in running a professional theater company. I was privileged to interview at length the key personnel who run fourteen of this country's most successful, free-spirited, and artistically vital theater companies, and I learned more from them than I ever thought possible (even though I've worked in professional theater for many years myself). These folks do not pull punches. They're realistic, from personal ideology, as well as from hard experience. They're also as excited about their companies today as the day they started working on them. Their artistic and business perspectives are fluid and fresh, no matter how many years (in some cases, decades) their companies have been operational.

I chose to let these fascinating subjects tell their stories themselves, in a series of directly quoted anecdotes that, to me, feel a lot like the type of discourse that might take place after a show, over a late, lingering dinner, when you—the hopeful, eager novice—are lucky enough to be seated next to a legendary elder who's in the mood to reminisce awhile. What will be discussed adds up to a full explanation of what factors make a solid theater company happen and persevere.

Diversity was a key component in my selection of the theater companies included within this book. Some of the companies are traditional repertory organizations—that is, in terms of definition, a resident company of actors performing a number of different shows throughout a set season. Other companies are more concerned with a very specific artistic concentration—producing plays that speak to multicultural issues, or women's issues, or classic theater, for instance. Some bust all myth, expectation, and convention, and that is their mission statement.

So, what makes a theater company successful? Primarily, the formula for success is a combination of a sharp artistic focus, a smart and objective business viewpoint, a fully operational venue, and a big-picture plan.

It's crucial to understand that art and commerce do indeed walk hand in hand. Successful theater company personnel know when to be creative and when to take their heads out of the clouds and get down to the nitty-gritty of making the money they need to keep going. They know how to translate abstract artistic visions into clear and concise sound bites that attract funders. They know the importance of applying for grants. They know the value of networking and thinking out of the box about marketing and strategic planning.

Another vital ingredient in the composition of these companies? Optimism—and pride. The people behind the most successful theater organizations are universally can-do in their attitudes. Although they are realistic, they balance that with the knowledge that pessimism is an energy drainer and, therefore a big potential nail in a company's coffin. So, they reject negative thinking. If these company heads want to do something, they figure out a way to do it, even if that takes a bit of time and brainstorming. They are not easily daunted.

Here now, in no particular order, is an overview of the theater companies whose stories we can learn from.

Steppenwolf Theater Company

Chicago, Illinois

Established: 1974, initial organization. 1975, incorporation. 1976, reorganization and ensemble established. Not-for-profit.

Founders: Jeff Perry, Terry Kinney, and Gary Sinise.

Key Current Personnel: Martha Lavey, Artistic Director; Michael Gennaro, Executive Director.

Distinguished Company Members: Scores of respected artists are members of the Steppenwolf ensemble. In addition to Jeff Perry, Terry Kinney, and Gary Sinise, these artists include John Malkovich, Joan Allen, Laurie Metcalf, John Mahoney, Tina Landau, Glenne Headley, Frank Galati, Martha Plimpton, Kevin Anderson, Austin Pendleton, Lois Smith, Jim True-Frost, Kathryn Erbe, Eric Simonson, Amy Morton, Gary Cole, Tom Irwin, Randall Arney, Robert Breuler, K. Todd Freeman, Mariann Mayberry, Francis Guiman, Rondi Reed, Moira Harris, Rick Snyder, Alan Wilder, Tim Hopper, Sally Murphy, and Molly Reagan, plus Artistic Director Martha Lavey.

Number of Plays Produced per Season: Mainstage: 5; Studio space: 4; Garage space: 3; plus additional programs' productions.

Casting and Employment Practices: Employs a mix of resident company actors with jobbed-in performers. Casting is done by general audition, by casting director, and by invitation for specific shows. Does hire outside technical employees.

First Season Offerings: *And Miss Reardon Drinks a Little, Grease, Rosencrantz and Guildenstern Are Dead, The Glass Menagerie.*

Recent Season Offerings: *David Copperfield, The Drawer Boy, Hedda Gabler.*

Awards, Citations, and a Few Notable Achievements: Steppenwolf has received numerous Tony Awards, Obie Awards, Drama Desk Awards, Theatre World Awards, Joseph Jefferson Awards for Chicago Theatre Excellence, and Clarence Derwent Awards, plus the National Medal of Arts presented by former President Bill Clinton and First Lady Hilary Rodham Clinton, the Illinois Arts Award, and the Gradiva Award from the National Association for the Advancement of Psychoanalysis (to John Malkovich for the play *Hysteria*). The company's sterling artistic achievements include its esteemed productions of plays such *The Grapes of Wrath, True West, Balm in Gilead, One Flew Over the Cuckoo's Nest, Burn This, Buried Child, The Libertine, The Glass Menagerie*, and numerous others. Many of the company's notable productions have played on Broadway, in the West End/internationally, and Off-Broadway.

The Company's Mission: Steppenwolf was started with a deep commitment to ensemble work and artistic risk. The company hopes to push forward the vitality and diversity of American theater work, while preserving the group's initial vision, in a collaborative, collective sense.

Speaking on Behalf of Steppenwolf: Michael Gennaro, who, prior to his tenure as Executive Director, worked as a performer both on Broadway and Off-Broadway and ran the Pennsylvania Ballet Company in Philadelphia.

The Pasadena Playhouse

Pasadena, California

Year established: 1917. Not-for-profit.

Founder: Gilmor Brown.

Key Current Personnel: Sheldon Epps, Artistic Director; Lyla White, Executive Director.

Distinguished Company Members: Countless luminaries have been associated with the Playhouse in the past and in the present, including Dustin Hoffman, Gene Hackman, Elaine May, Lee J. Cobb, William Holden, Frances Farmer, Agnes de Mille, Martha Graham, David Niven, Tyrone Power, Harry Dean Stanton, Robert Preston, Carol Lawrence, John Carradine, Rue McClanahan, and many, many more.

Number of Plays Produced per Season: Mainstage: 6.

Casting and Employment Practices: Employs performers, technicians, and creative staff from an in-house pool, plus jobbed-in talent. Casts show by show.

First Season Offerings: Twenty-eight plays were produced during the first official season, including works by Shakespeare, Dickens, Chekhov, and Molière.

Recent Season Offerings: *Side Man, Do I Hear A Waltz?, Les Liaisons Dangereuses.*

Awards, Citations, and a Few Notable Achievements: The Playhouse has been officially designated as the State Theatre of California, is listed on the National Register of Historic Places, was the first to present all of Shakespeare's plays, and has presented nearly five hundred world premieres.

The Company's Mission: To merge its peerless past with an exciting new theatrical future, to both attract new audiences and delight its loyal patrons.

Speaking on Behalf of the Pasadena Playhouse: Sheldon Epps, the company's current Artistic Director. Mr. Epps is a revered stage director whose work includes Broadway productions like the Roundabout Theatre's 2001 staging of *Blue.* He also directs television shows like *Friends* and *Frasier.* Also, Lyla White, the company's Executive Director, a well-respected member of the Pasadena community, and a formidable business and fund-raising force.

La Jolla Playhouse

La Jolla, California

Established: 1847. Not-for-profit.

Founders: Gregory Peck, Dorothy McGuire, and Mel Ferrer.

Key Current Personnel: Des McAnuff, Artistic Director; Terrence Dwyer, Managing Director.

Distinguished Company Members: Many film actors who wished to keep working on their stagecraft found the perfect sanctuary at the Playhouse in its early days—it was not uncommon to see Eartha Kitt, Jennifer Jones, Joseph Cotten, Tallulah Bankhead, and many other movie stars treading the boards. The tradition of the Playhouse attracting wonderful performers continues to this day, such as Matthew Broderick appearing in *How to Succeed in Business without Really Trying* before its hit Broadway run. The Playhouse is also associated with groundbreaking works by Tony Kushner, Randy Newman, Pete Townshend, and Lisa Kron, just to name a few. Respected director Michael Greif served previously as Artistic Director.

Number of Plays Produced per Season: Mainstage: 3; Second Stage: 3.

Employment and Casting Practices: Combines casting from its resident company with outside talent each season. Hires creative staff (directors, designers) plus tech staff from a mix of in-house and those jobbed in, dependent upon current season specifics.

First Season Offerings: A sample production from the 1947 season is *Night Must Fall.*

Recent Season Offerings: Recent years have seen lauded productions *The Who's Tommy*, *Big River*, *A Walk in the Woods*, *Slavs!*, *Faust*, *Jane Eyre*, and *Thoroughly Modern Millie* go on to acclaim on Broadway, Off-Broadway, and around the world. The Playhouse also staged the West Coast premiere of *Rent.*

Awards, Citations, and a Few Notable Achievements: The 1993 Tony Award for Outstanding Regional Theatre, plus over three hundred additional honors. The Playhouse has hosted approximately twenty-three world premieres, twenty-four West Coast premieres, and four American premieres.

The Company's Mission: Originally, to give film actors the opportunity to do good work in the theater at a quality venue that was geographically close to the film studios of Los Angeles. Currently, as well, to produce challenging, exciting, and innovative theater.

Chicago City Limits

New York, New York

Established: The company's members came to New York from Chicago in 1979. Commercial venue.

Founder: George Todisco.

Key Current Personnel: Paul Zuckerman, Artistic Director and original company member.

Distinguished Company Members: George Todisco passed away in 1982. Other members of the company from its early days, in addition to Paul Zuckerman, include Rick Crom, Carol Schindler, Linda Gelman, Chris Oyen, Bill McLaughlin, John Telfer, Denny Siegel, Carl Kissin, Andrew Daly, Frank Spitznagel, and many others.

Number of Plays Produced per Season: Year-round improvised comedy shows, 315 performances per year.

Employment and Casting Practices: CCL casts only from its resident company. Outside tech help is hired, although directors and designers are culled from in-house talent only.

Awards, Citations, and a Few Notable Achievements: The company has performed for United Nations delegates and at Lincoln Center. Its TV appearances include *The Today Show*, *Entertainment Tonight*, and many other programs, plus the troupe had its own series on the USA Network, *Reel News*.

The Company's Mission: Pioneering comedy improvisation excellence. Many of the most effective theater games, structures, and forms used widely today are CCL inventions.

Speaking on Behalf of Chicago City Limits: Paul Zuckerman, one of the company's most vital early voices and its enduring visionary.

Berkeley Repertory Theatre

Berkeley, California/San Francisco Bay area

Established: 1968. Not-for-profit.

Founder: Michael Leibert.

Key Current Personnel: Tony Taccone, Artistic Director; Susan Medak, Managing Director.

Distinguished Company Members: A huge number of fine, respected theater artists have flocked to Berkeley Rep. The company has also produced many notable and groundbreaking playwrights' works. At press time, the National Endowment for the Arts had just approved partial funding for a spring 2002 production of Tony Kushner's play *Homebody/Kabul*, which is set in Afghanistan.

Number of Plays Produced per Season: Seven plays in its two theaters, plus a touring production.

Employment and Casting Practices: Directors, designers, performers, and techies all selected from company associates, plus jobbed-in, depending upon current show/season requirements.

First Season Offerings: Early works had a very literary thrust, including plays by Arthur Miller.

Recent Season Offerings: *Dinner with Friends, The Oresteia.*

Awards, Citations, and a Few Notable Achievements: Numerous, including the 1997 Tony Award for Outstanding Regional Theater.

The Company's Mission: A commitment to do ambitious work through a strong commitment to its ensemble of talented artists, and its desire to stay connected to its community in order to satisfy and challenge the audience.

Speaking on Behalf of Berkeley Rep: Susan Medak, whose credentials and associations include the Board of Directors for Theatre Communications Group, LORT, the National Endowment for the Arts Theatre Program Panel, the Massachusetts State Arts Council, and respected theaters including the Milwaukee Repertory Theatre. Also, Mitzi Sales, who joined Berkeley Rep as Managing Director under Michael Leibert in the early 1970s and was responsible for much of its early genesis and major success.

Arena Stage's The Living Stage Theatre Company

Washington, D.C.

Year Established: 1966. Not-for-profit.

Founders: Bob Alexander, along with Arena Stage founders Zelda Fichandler, Thomas C. Fichandler, and Edward Mangum.

Key Current Personnel: Ralph Remington, Artistic Director; Molly Smith, Arena Stage Artistic Director.

Number of Plays Produced per Season: Numerous interactive performance workshops that utilize improvisation and are specially tailored toward each audience. Material is focused on social issues and incorporates music, poetry, and hip-hop culture.

Employment and Casting Practices: Resident company, cast per season.

Awards, Citations, and a Few Notable Achievements: The Living Stage is an artistic program under the esteemed auspices of Arena Stage, which, of course, has an international reputation for theatrical excellence and has been producing contemporary and classic works since 1950.

The Company's Mission: To reach out theatrically and interactively to kids, the disabled, the elderly, the incarcerated, those for whom theater is rarely geared, and to inspire the audience to express their own creativity.

Speaking on Behalf of Living Stage: Ralph Remington, an esteemed and established administrator, director, and longtime actor.

Mixed Blood Theatre Company

Minneapolis, Minnesota

Established: 1976. Not-for-profit.

Founder: Jack Reuler.

Key Current Personnel: Jack Reuler, Artistic Director.

Distinguished Company Members: Among the ranks of impressive, creative personnel who have acted, directed, and written for Mixed Blood is Don Cheadle, namesake of the company's Don Cheadle Apprentice Academy summer program for teenagers.

Number of Plays Produced per Season: Five, plus a number of educational touring productions, corporate touring/training (through the highly regarded EnterTraining program), and program events.

Employment and Casting Practices: Mixed Blood casts on a show-by-show basis, out of a resident/jobber pool. Directors and designers are jobbed in each season.

Previous Season Offerings: Among Mixed Blood's greatest hits: *Jackie Robinson, Eastern Parade, Daughters of Africa, Dr. King's Dream, Minnecanos, According to Coyote, Black Eagle,* and *Paul Robeson.* These productions have toured in educational venues for years and are presented on an ongoing basis to the Minneapolis community at large.

Recent Season Offerings: Spinning into Butter, A Jew on Ethiopia Street, Haroun and the Sea of Stories, Cut Flowers, Sola en la Oscuridad.

Awards, Citations, and a Few Notable Achievements: Three Twin Cities Drama Critics Awards, an Outstanding Achievement Award from the Minneapolis Commission on Civil Rights, the Actors' Equity Rosetta Le Noire Award, the Council on Black Minnesotans Dream Keeper Award, the Minneapolis Foundation's Diversity Award, the Martin Luther King Humanitarian Award, and a Best New Play Award nomination by the American Theater Critics Association.

The Company's Mission: To produce artistically risky work using culture-conscious casting, to provide a forum of expression for artists of color, to open up theater to a nontraditional audience, and to educate through its programs about issues of race and culture.

Speaking on Behalf of Mixed Blood: Jack Reuler, whose inspiration has always been the spirit of Dr. Martin Luther King's dream and philosophy.

Horizons Theatre

Arlington, Virginia/Washington, D.C. area

Established: 1976–77. Not-for-profit.

Founder: Leslie B. Jacobson.

Key Current Personnel: Leslie B. Jacobson, Artistic Director.

Number of Plays Produced per Season: Three plays, plus a Reading Series.

Employment and Casting Practices: Casts from actors in the Washington, D.C., area, show by show. Chooses directors, designers, and techies as positions become available from a combination of in-house/outside pool.

Previous Season Offerings: As Pro Femina Theatre, its original incarnation, Horizons built its quality reputation by presenting unscripted works about women and their experiences.

Recent Season Offerings: The Last Game Show.

Awards, Citations, and a Few Notable Achievements: Horizons was selected to perform for the United Nations and has a distinguished reputation abroad.

The Company's Mission: To produce work about women's roles and experiences, as well as men's, throughout the centuries.

Speaking on Behalf of Horizons: Leslie B. Jacobson, renowned feminist theater artist.

Wheelock Family Theatre

Boston, Massachusetts

Year Established: 1981. Not-for-profit.

Founders: Susan Kosoff, Jane Staab, and Tony Hancock.

Key Current Personnel: Susan Kosoff and Jane Staab, Artistic Directors.

Distinguished Company Members: A long list of Boston's elite acting talent return over and over to the Wheelock stage. Alumni include Oscar winner Matt Damon and Broadway actors Wang Luoyong, Jessica Walling, Angela Hall, CeeCee Harshaw, and Jamie McKenzie.

Number of Plays Produced per Season: Three plays, including one classical and one musical.

Employment and Casting Practices: Casts a mix of Equity and non-Equity actors per show. Hires outside management, artistic, and tech staff on an as-needed basis.

Previous Season Offerings: Antigone, Anne of Green Gables, The King and I, Romeo and Juliet, Little Women, The Jungle Book. All productions in the company's history have been concurrently interpreted in American Sign Language.

Recent Season Offerings: Hello, Dolly!, The Prince and the Pauper, Trumpet of the Swans.

Awards, Citations, and a Few Notable Achievements: The President's Coming Up Taller Award, The Actors' Equity Rosetta Le Noire Award, *Boston Parents' Paper* Family Favorite Award.

The Company's Mission: To serve the entertainment and lifestyle needs of children and families, to educate budding theater professionals in the dramatic arts, to cast people of color in lead roles, and to be a theater for all people.

Speaking on Behalf of Wheelock Family Theatre: Susan Kosoff, founder, Artistic Director, and distinguished Wheelock College professor.

L.A. Theatre Works

Los Angeles, California

Established: 1974. Not-for-profit.

Founder: Susan Albert Loewenberg.

Key Current Personnel: Susan Albert Loewenberg, Producing Director.

Distinguished Company Members: A virtual who's who of the best artists working in film, television, and theater, including Oscar winners Helen Hunt and Richard Dreyfuss, Edward Asner, Michael York, director Gordon Hunt, and many, many others.

Employment and Casting Practices: Jobs in additional directors and staff as the need arises. Performers are hired through agent submissions only.

Season Offerings: The company's work has spanned the gamut from its early cutting-edge workshop accomplishments in the California state prison system to groundbreaking incarnation as a theater producing radio plays. Now, its Audio Library collected works of over two hundred and fifty recorded plays is the largest in the country and is widely available to the public via bookstores, libraries, and satellite radio technology.

Awards, Citations, and a Few Notable Achievements: Almost too many to mention; of particular note has been the ARTS and Children outreach program, which is geared toward at-risk youth. Its educational programs are widely lauded as well.

The Company's Mission: To produce innovative theater and audio art, plus expand arts access to the community in part by using new technology.

Speaking for L.A. Theatre Works: Susan Albert Loewenberg, well-known for her work as an actor and artist, as well as a keen businesswoman who has built her company through savvy diversification.

A Traveling Jewish Theatre

San Francisco, California

Established: 1978. Not-for-profit.

Founders: Corey Fischer, Albert Greenberg, and Naomi Newman.

Key Current Personnel: Corey Fischer, Albert Greenberg, Naomi Newman, and Helen Stoltzfus, Co-Artistic Directors; Helene Sanghri York, Managing Director.

Employment and Casting Practices: Resident staff membership intact; no outside hiring.

Previous Season Offerings: Berlin, Jerusalem and the Moon, Snake Talk, Urgent Messages from the Mother, The Dybbuk, The Last Yiddish Poet, Sometimes We Need a Story More than Food, Trotsky and Frida.

Recent Season Offerings: Diamonds in the Dark.

Awards, Citations, and a Few Notable Achievements: The company has performed in over sixty cities nationally and internationally. Its following includes audiences in New York,

Berlin, Chicago, Oslo, Jerusalem, and Whitesburg, Kentucky. Public Radio International has distributed an acclaimed four-part radio series by the troupe entitled *Heart of Wisdom: Audio Explorations in Jewish Culture*. A Traveling Jewish Theatre's critical reputation is sterling and peerless: Corey Fischer's one-man show was voted one of the ten best productions of 1993 by the *Los Angeles Times*.

The Company's Mission: To create original theater projects as a group, plus in cooperation with outside theater artists from many diverse cultural and ethnic backgrounds, intending this work to encompass a wide look at humanity and the human condition. The company has a great respect for the Jewish and American traditions and their influences.

Speaking on Behalf of A Traveling Jewish Theatre: Corey Fischer, a longtime writer and performer, who is noted for his work and collaboration with film director Robert Altman and his stage work with Joseph Chaiken.

Jean Cocteau Repertory

New York, New York

Established: 1971. Not-for-profit.

Founder: Eve Adamson.

Key Current Personnel: David Fuller, Artistic Director; Dona Lee Kelly, Managing Director.

Number of Plays Produced Per Season: Six.

Employment and Casting Practices: Resident company of actors is cast for the entire season. Designers and directors are mostly chosen from among Cocteau associates. Tech staff and some designers are jobbed in by specific need.

Previous Season Offerings: Almost too numerous to mention—plays in the Cocteau's classical repertory include works by Beckett, Ibsen, Brecht, Chekhov, Euripides, Orton, Shaw, Pirandello, Shakespeare, and of course, Jean Cocteau.

Recent Season Offerings: *The Cradle Will Rock, The Merchant of Venice, Night and Day, The Subject Was Roses, The Misanthrope*.

Awards, Citations, and a Few Notable Achievements: The Obie Award, a Citation for Excellence in the Arts from the Manhattan Borough President, two Drama Desk nominations, an Outer Critics Circle Nomination, and six Villager Awards.

The Company's Mission: A devotion to classic theater selections of both the past and present day, produced as what Cocteau referred to as "poetry of the theater"—where all components of a live presentation create a whole experience for the audience and artists.

Speaking on Behalf of the Cocteau: David Fuller, an esteemed director, Broadway and Off-Broadway actor, and the former Co-Producing Artistic director of Theatre Ten; and Dona Lee Kelly, who began her career at the Cocteau as General Manager, and whose previous administrative positions were with Dodger Productions and Robert Cole Productions. She also taught acting with Stella Adler and was on the faculty of New York University's Tisch School of the Arts.

Bailiwick Repertory

Chicago, Illinois

Established: 1982. Not-for-profit.

Founders: An artistic enclave, which included David Zak.

Key Current Personnel: David Zak, Artistic Director.

Distinguished Company Members: Many trailblazing and fiercely brilliant theatrical visionaries have done great work under Bailiwick's auspices, including Larry Kramer, artistic associate Cecilie D. Keenan, Claudia Allen, and many more writers and directors. Talented stage actors Greg Louganis and Tim Miller have been among the many performers who have appeared in Bailiwick productions.

Number of Plays Produced per Season: Five.

Employment and Casting Practices: Casts Equity actors for mainstage shows, non-Equity for other productions. Open call each June. Directors are in-house, designers are jobbed in.

Past Season Offerings: *Present Laughter, Gypsy, The Christmas Schooner.*

Recent Season Offerings: *Corpus Christi, Something Cloudy, Something Clear, Being Beautiful Pride Series.*

Awards, Citations, and a Few Notable Achievements: Almost one hundred Joseph Jefferson Awards for Chicago Theatre Excellence, plus After Dark Awards Citations. Bailiwick's production of *Corpus Christi* garnered stellar reviews and awards, plus the enthusiastic support of its author, Terrence McNally.

The Company's Mission: A commitment to carrying out the vision of gifted directors. Bailiwick's well-regarded *Pride Series* program is additionally focused on the development of gay and lesbian theater works.

Speaking on Behalf of Bailiwick: David Zak, the company's enthusiastic and respected core leader since day one.

New Repertory Theatre

Newton, Massachusetts/Boston area

Established: 1984. Not-for-profit.

Founder: A small enclave of theater artists, including Larry Lane.

Key Current Personnel: Rick Lombardo, Artistic Director; Harriet Sheets, Managing Director.

Distinguished Company Members: Among New Repertory Theatre's accomplished associates is Austin Pendleton, who recently wowed Boston critics and audiences by codirecting an innovative production of *King Lear.* New Rep also works extensively with Brandeis University's professional theater training program to provide work to its acting and design graduates and to benefit from their talents.

Number of Plays Produced per Season: Five.

Employment and Casting Practices: Actors, directors, designers, and techies jobbed in, dependent upon current positions available each season.

Previous Season Offerings: Bus Stop, Blue Window, Spunk, Later Life, As You Like It, The Misanthrope, Sylvia, Skylight, and many others.

Recent Season Offerings: King Lear, Moby Dick, An American Opera, The Weir, Stonewall Jackson's House, One Flea.

Awards, Citations, and a Few Notable Achievements: Elliot Norton Awards, Best-Of citations by the *Boston Globe, Boston Herald, Tab,* and *Back Bay Currant* newspapers, plus awards from the Independent Reviewers of New England.

The Company's Mission: To foster the production of challenging, high-quality writing and acting onstage, where it otherwise might be lacking in the Boston area.

Speaking on Behalf of New Repertory Theatre: Rick Lombardo, Artistic Director, and the previously accomplished artistic head of both the Players Guild and the Stillwaters Theatre Company; and Harriet Sheets, the intensely focused business leader in New Rep's organization.

So, there's our illustrious list of experts. Whatever reason you have for reading this book—whether you're a theater student, a budding pro looking to found your own company, or a fan who loves reading about backstage blood, sweat, and tears—there's a lot of fascinating stuff to be learned from these individuals' hard-won experience, clear-cut perspectives, and concrete advice. This is how a theater company rises, solidifies, and consistently delivers, to its audiences and on its profit potential.

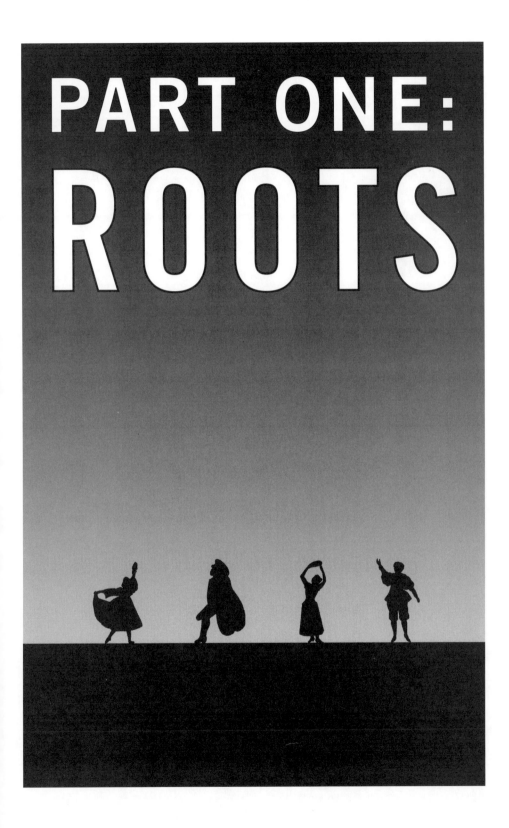

PART ONE:
ROOTS

CHAPTER 1

HOW WE CAME TOGETHER

That any theater company comes together at all, ever, is a miracle.

Usually, in the beginning, there is a burning need on the part of a founder to express a dramatic truth very specifically. Founders recognize that in order to do this with any measure of control, it's going to have to be done independently—they don't wait for someone to cast them in a dream project or write it and hand it to them.

An admirable goal, for sure. Once you decide that you are indeed going to start your own company, your next logical step would be to look around and try to find other people to participate in your vision. This, frankly, is where stuff can get weird. What if the people you choose are flaky and not dependable? Or have egos the size of Cleveland? Or things start off great, but pretty soon, everybody starts fighting over everything from material to who's got the most lines in your debut show to who broke into the petty cash box to buy pizza?

Or how about financial hurdles? Ignorance about money is the fastest way a theater company founder can run a dream into the ground. You need to think ahead to plan a feasible financial vision if you want to last longer than three seconds.

So, those are a few possible pitfalls. Now for the good news! You can beat the odds. How? You don't need to be independently wealthy with a huge staff to make your theater company work. You do need "the big picture": a plan toward building longevity. And you need information from those who have been there—experience is the world's greatest teacher, and if you don't have it yourself, you can still make like a sponge and soak it up from those who have been around the block.

In this chapter, our successful subjects give us an understanding of the origins of each of their companies, covering issues like artistic impetus for starting, how founders and staffers met up and determined their common goal, early business planning (or shockingly, lack thereof—but even mistakes can be lessons), compromises, soldiering through difficulty—you name it, they've been through it.

Take heart, and inspiration, starting with Berkeley Repertory's resolve to integrate fine literary properties with the San Francisco Bay area's 1960s sensibilities.

Commitment to Words and Community

According to Susan Medak, the Managing Director of Berkeley Repertory, "Michael Leibert started Berkeley Repertory in 1968. Michael's group began performing in small storefronts about six blocks away from the campus of the University of California at Berkeley.

"The decision Michael made to settle in Berkeley had to do with what the community stands for. This community loves itself. It loves its words, loves ideas, and prides itself on its tolerance. My sense has always been, a theater company's relationship with its surroundings is the key to its success. A friend of mine who's been very successful in the theater has always put it best: 'In this business, geography is destiny.' What's marking the companies that have been successful in a mainstream area, like Wichita, Kansas, is that they best know that small-town world. In Berkeley, the audience is and always has been completely driven by a love of the written word. And Michael's original commitment was to literature-based work. So in the beginning, the company was producing Arthur Miller, Alan Ayckbourn, very literary shows.

"After starting things up, Michael then worked with a small resident company on six to eight shows. The memory of that moment in time—the late sixties, the relatively new idea of political activism—for the actors, it was indelible.

"Berkeley, known for its activism and university sensibility, informed this company. The company moved to a new space on College Avenue, a 150-seat storefront, with a big peace sign on the front."

Mitzi Sales, former Managing Director at Berkeley Rep, came on the scene then: "I think the basic impetus, as lore would have it—and I was there three-and-a-half years after it got started—was, you know, Michael was looking for something to do, he'd gotten out of grad school, and he'd been in the theater department. He had some friends who were Equity actors, so I think the most important thing that Michael Leibert did was start the theater as an Equity company. He did this because the actors he knew and wanted to work with were already members of the union, at least a couple of members of his closest coterie.

"He had had a very successful production as a grad student of *Woyzeck* at the International House Space in Berkeley, and he thought, 'Wow, what a piece of cake! I'll just start a theater.' There was this little space on College Avenue, which is not particularly far from the campus—straight down the street. And all of the people that he would be working with were already living in the neighborhood. He thought, 'We'll put on *Woyzeck*, it'll be a big hit, we'll sell all these tickets, we'll build the theater, and people will come.' Well, of course, this was very, very difficult.

"But the thing that Michael had that other people didn't have was a wife with money. So, he had a patron, and one of the ways to start a theater company is to find a patron.

"Michael originally named the group The Theater. When they went for their articles of incorporation, Michael was told, "No, no, no, you have to have some distinguishing name.

"And so, the Pomegranate Players was picked. But that was a joke—they were never really advertised as the Pomegranate Players; nobody thought they were the Pomegranate Players."

Rebels Embracing Risk

For Steppenwolf, the desire to make an artistic statement was fueled by confidence and fearlessness. The founding members convened in 1974, in Deerfield, Illinois, to put on their first show at a Unitarian church. This original meeting of the minds was facilitated by the fact that each founding member recognized that they had in common an intense love of the theatrical art form, a need to express themselves through it, and the smarts and self-assurance to feel that if they were true to their love, they couldn't fail.

Michael Gennaro, current Executive Director of Steppenwolf, relates the tale of the company's inception: "Keep in mind that the founders, Jeff Perry, Gary Sinise, and Terry Kinney, all kind of knew each other—I think Gary and Jeff knew each other the longest, and then Jeff knew Terry. Their first production was *Rosencrantz and Guildenstern Are Dead*. After they did that, they said, we gotta keep this going. Kind of their impetus, within that first group of about nine people—some of them are still around, like Al Walter, John Malkovich, Laurie Metcalf—I think if you ask them, their impetus was, 'We couldn't get work anywhere else. We can do things with a certain visceral style—that's what we're all about. We're as good as anybody, and we can work like that.' And I think underlying all of that, all of the time, was to never settle for anything less than as far as they could go. I mean, in some ways, you could say it's just a striving for excellence, but beyond that, it was like, no performance is ever set. It's like, we keep improving upon it every single time we do it.

"I think, then, the insularity of the group kind of drove them all the time. What was the financial vision? They didn't have one. How many staff members? This is a group of people who just got together to do everything, and the whole point was just to get onstage and work together. The trust that developed over time, and the way of working together as an ensemble, that was the driving force.

"The group had people they admired, like John Cassavetes. They would tackle any play, regardless of the age requirements. If someone wasn't right, too bad. If they wanted to do it, then they would do it. They saw themselves as rebels and did what they wanted to do. So, everybody had their day jobs, which included John driving a bus and Gary working in a hat store. But their whole day was made up in getting together and working as a theater. Strangely enough, that's still the driving force of this theater. This theater has never really been driven by . . . there have been, kind of, plans—but that's not really the way it's worked."

Socially Conscious Vision

For Jack Reuler, a desire to keep a social leader's dream alive compelled him to start a theater. Utilizing its status within a community service organization also allowed him a feasible financial vision from the very start. Jack, founder and Artistic Director of Mixed Blood, says: "I started the organization right out of college. I'd gone to college intending to be a veterinarian, and somehow [Mixed Blood] helped me to take a left turn—a great left turn.

"A childhood icon of mine was always Martin Luther King, and seven years after his death was when I decided to start the theater, at a point when the civil rights movement was at its lowest. When I was at school, I had a job with a social service organization called the Center for Community Action [in Minneapolis], which was to seek out needs in the community and set up programs to meet those needs. There was this community theater, Theater in the Round, it's called, which is still the primary community theater in the Twin Cities. They did a production of *The Great White Hope*, and Ernie Hudson [*Ghostbusters*] played the lead. The show was quite successful, but then there was a financial issue. Ernie said, 'If I'm going to keep doing the show, and I'm going to keep playing the lead, then I need to be compensated for my efforts.' The media took up on it, interpreted it to be a racial issue, and the public actually started sending Ernie money.

"In retrospect, I really do think it was about money, but the point that was certainly revealed, to our area, through the media, was that there was an absence of opportunity for the professional theater artist of color to make a living. As I was thinking about who I was politically, and as a twenty-two-year-old, this showed me an impetus. I said, Here's what we need to do: try to find a home for Martin Luther King's vision onstage, where we can create a world not necessarily as it is, or was, but how we want it to be, as viewed through that lens. That was the impetus for the organization, and why I come to work every day.

"I was actually a senior in college when all this happened, then I sat down and laid out what the theater was going to be. Really, for the first four years, it was a program at the Center for Community Action. From the time I decided to start the theater until we did the first show, it was just me. No staff. By being part of the Center, which was pretty much a fledgling organization, I had what little support there was from there—a typewriter and a bookkeeper, who handled the whole organization, including our program.

"In terms of finances, it was 1976, and the $30,000 budget that we had came from three primary sources: CETA, a public employment program; Bicentennial money; and the Jerome Foundation. I think those three sources made up 100 percent of the budget. We did six or seven shows, and everybody got paid, right from the beginning. Other than board membership, we've had very little volunteer effort.

"That first summer, we had a company of twenty-three, which as I remember was ten African Americans, six Native Americans, seven white. We worked three shifts, nine to twelve, one to five, seven to ten, every day. Working the show, rehearsing the show, working tech."

Exploring Your Identity through Artistic Experimentation

Corey Fischer's desire to learn more about his own ethnic culture actually begat one of the country's most exciting alternative theater companies, A Traveling Jewish Theater. Mr. Fischer says of the company's early days, "When we started, for me, it was a natural evolution based on a number of experiences I had had in the two or three years prior— experiences with other experimental, or you might say, alternative theater companies. Working in New York with Joe Chaikin and, at the same time, being increasingly curious about and interested in all the aspects of Jewish culture that I had not grown up with—out of that mix came a desire to do some work in theater from a Jewish perspective, not really knowing what that meant. Theater for me has always been a tool to explore and discover rather than a place to simply plug in ready-made assumptions.

"Naomi, Albert, and I had known each other for a number of years in various contexts. Naomi and I had done a lot of theater together. Albert, at that time, was mainly a musician. I had seen his work and admired it. So, I asked the two of them to join me in creating a piece. I didn't realize we were starting a company.

"We were working on a particular piece based on a series of legends that I had found. Albert and I performed, and the three of us co-wrote. I also made masks and puppets. We spent about nine months working on that and opened it in March 1979, at a church in Santa Monica called the Church in Ocean Park. It was very progressive, and somewhere along the way, it became clear there was a whole world that we wanted to continue exploring.

"On our first trip to New York later that year, we got an incredible review from the *Village Voice*. We were performing at Theatre for the New City in their old space, when they used to be on Second Avenue, and had a wonderful response from both audiences and critics alike. That kind of launched us. There was no initial financial vision. If we had thought about that, we probably would never have gotten started."

Using the Repertory Format to Its Best Creative Advantage

In 1971, Eve Adamson, who had directed much innovative work Off-Broadway, decided to maximize the possibilities of the repertory format. Adamson believed that presenting work in the rotating format that is true repertory could best expose audiences to a variety of creative statements made by classic dramatic literature. She also believed that the repertory format would be a positive artistic challenge to actors. Thus, Jean Cocteau Repertory was born.

During those early years, Adamson did most of the administrative and behind-the-scenes work by herself. She directed most of the company's productions, utilizing a loyal and fiercely talented troupe of actors to voice her vision. By 1989, Adamson had decided it was time to move on. Robert Hupp, who had come to the Cocteau originally in 1984 as Managing Director, succeeded her as Artistic Director.

Carrying forth Eve Adamson's original vision for the company is paramount for the Cocteau. Robert Hupp worked closely with Adamson for five years prior to taking on the company's top position, and Adamson kept her hand in, directing productions for seasons subsequent to stepping down as Artistic Director, work that included plays like *Hamlet* and *The Cherry Orchard*.

Hupp eventually left the Artistic Director's chair as well. A search was mounted to find a new company head. The person chosen was David Fuller, whose professional history was closely linked with the Cocteau. Fuller's strong personal friendship with Adamson, plus their fruitful creative collaborations in prior years, was a major plus.

David Fuller is not only respectful of, but also deeply aware of the history of the Cocteau, which continually informs the work he does with the company. He believes his experience and knowledge is a key factor in its continued success.

David remembers his introduction to the company: "I was in college. There was a book published by Theatre Communications Group that had a page on different theaters all across the country. I remember Jean Cocteau listed in it, the kind of work they did, and I was always interested in classic theater. That sort of put it in my head.

"I came to New York in the late seventies as an actor. I auditioned for the Cocteau and was admitted into the company; I worked in the company from 1980 to 1982 as an actor. I started a friendship with the people in the company at that time, including Eve Adamson.

When I was acting during the next decade, I also kept up my friendships with the people at the Cocteau and kept an eye on what was going on here, even though I was doing a lot of regional theater. I assisted Eve with a show or two here at the theater, when I was back in New York. I also directed a reading of a play for her, but I was out of town a lot.

"I finally came back to New York in the early nineties, based myself here, and became a director and producer. I continued my relationship with the Cocteau. I found out the company was looking for an artistic director. The members approached me, and I said I'd like to be considered. In 1999, they selected me to run the theater. I think I was selected because I am a link to Eve. I have a good sense of her artistic sensibility. The reason I think she started the company was to work with an ensemble of actors over a long period of time on a number of different projects. I have a background in repertory theater, and I was interested in working in a company of actors.

"You have to look at the Cocteau's vision in terms of the broad range of work we do; all the plays have something to say about the human condition. More often than not, they need to be produced because they need to be seen again, or in the case of new plays, the Cocteau has a history of doing plays that people can't see anywhere else. I don't think there's a production of *Oedipus the King* anywhere else in New York, and I know there's no production of Tennessee Williams' *Small Craft Warnings* right now [the Cocteau's then-current productions]."

Great Minds That Think Alike

In the 1970s, Chicago was exploding with the creative energy of improvisational comedy. There was no lack of enthusiastic performers who wanted to express themselves this way; the trick was finding your comedic kindred spirits.

Founder and Artistic Director Paul Zuckerman has been with Chicago City Limits since those early days: "Chicago City Limits, as a company, did its first show on Labor Day 1977. These were all actors participating in the workshop program at the Second City in Chicago. It's probably fairly similar today, although there's probably more opportunities in terms of improvisational theater than there were then, but basically, Second City was the carrot for most of the people in those workshops. Chicago had a kind of unique atmosphere—lots of improvisation going on. Each city seems to have its specialty. Chicago—you think of blues and improvisational comedy.

"In addition to the Second City workshops, there were lots of bars and clubs around town where groups were encouraged to perform. Out of those workshops in Second City, very similar to our workshop program today, people got together, a couple of people formed a group, the group worked at a club for a little while. They usually had artistic differences, which I think pulls groups apart the most. If you notice some basic artistic differences at the top, it's almost like a relationship—they're going to get worse as time goes on.

"Chicago City Limits is really an evolution of a bunch of these groups that formed, performed in a club for a week, two weeks, or a month, then something splits them apart, a couple of people at the core go on to find some others, and this goes on and on. Most groups fall apart at some point; once in a while, though, a snowball gets bigger as it rolls down the hill. Two people from one group find three other people, one of those people turns out to be in sync artistically with the others, and the group evolves.

"So by 1977, we had a core of people who shared an artistic vision. At the Second City, they had moved almost entirely away from performing improvisation to mostly a sketch comedy show. There was this real need amongst ourselves to perform what we were doing in workshops. That stuff was fun to do—the audiences enjoyed it, we enjoyed doing it. So, Chicago City Limits, out of this evolution, started performing a combination of improvisation and sketch comedy in clubs.

"We were five actors and a stage manager. A small group, but doing everything. Performing one or two nights a week, rehearsing six or seven days a week. You can't get enough of it. You talk it, you sleep it, you eat it, you breathe it. I still had a job working at an ad agency at this time. We'd work the clubs, then go to somebody's house, 12:30, 1:00 in the morning. And we're talking about it, we're drinking, and it's late, 2:30, 3:00 in the morning, we're talking about, 'Hey, you gotta be real in the scene, and you've gotta emotionally connect'—it just becomes your religion.

"You've gotta have that fire in your belly, because there's great adversity every step of the way. We didn't have any financial vision—our vision was totally artistic at the time."

Compromise or Else

David Zak started Bailiwick Repertory with six friends. They shared a common artistic vision that was very strong. The problem was, everyone seemed to want to pursue that first and foremost—the administrative nitty-gritty was not quite as appealing to take on.

The great weapon Bailiwick had in its arsenal was, and continues to be, David Zak. He stuck with the founders' original vision and has carried it through to today. And he's done it essentially by himself, being the remaining member of that founding group. "Bailiwick was founded in 1982 by a group of seven artists and was always envisioned as a directors' company as opposed to an actors' ensemble," David recalls. "Several of those founding members went to Webster University in St. Louis; several of us subsequently met doing theater in Chicago.

"Developing a common goal was very difficult. Everybody wanted to work on the artistic stuff—the administrative plan was more complex. Over the first twenty-four months, six of the seven original members left for various reasons—some went Equity, etc."

Old School Determination

Of course, sticking to your guns artistically is hardly a new concept. Consider the case of Gilmor Brown. You may know him better by his nickname, "The Great God Brown," as immortalized in the title of a well-known play.

Indeed, legendary is a great adjective to describe Brown. So is determined; so is industrious. The Pasadena Playhouse was the eventual end result of his efforts. The following information was culled from archival materials provided by Peggy Ebright, Board Member and Director of Community Relations, and Ellen Bailey, librarian, The Pasadena Playhouse.

Gilmor Brown was an ambitious thirty-year-old who had persevered against very daunting theatrical odds by the time he arrived to live in Pasadena in 1917. Brown had started his first troupe, the Tuxedo Stock Company, as a mere child. As a young man, he acted with a group of sophisticated and seasoned British stage actors. After a failed stab at breaking into the New York City theater community, Brown founded a family-and-friends-staffed company called the Comedy Players, which garnered good reviews, but folded due to cash problems. He joined the Crown Stock Players, where his reputation began to solidify further. When that troupe toured a production that made a stop in Pasadena, Brown made a mental note to return.

Pasadena was filled with well-to-do, educated, culture-hungry residents, and upon his permanent move to town, Brown started cultivating every townsperson in sight. He shared his vast knowledge of theater with impressed potential audience members, ingratiated himself with the local civic organizations, and soon found the Savoy Theatre, a former burlesque house, very run-down but, indeed, an empty venue, a place Brown could launch his theater company. He named his players the Savoy Stock Company.

An actress named Lillian Buck, who had worked on an earlier production with Brown, won the coveted spot of company leading lady by donating $500 to the company's coffers—a novel way Brown could realize a first feasible financial vision. Brown cast himself and early film actor John Allard as the male company leads. Wendall Wilson was an additional company actor, as was Marjorie Sinclair, a popular local debutante whose social connections led to large audience turnout and whose friendships with those in the local media secured positive newspaper coverage.

Brown further positioned his company for success by performing *Crucifixion*, a pro-peace production that comforted and reassured its audience, as America was poised on the eve of war at the time. The cast was huge, so Brown offered roles to many local townspeople. This was savvy, because many of these folks were conservatives who hadn't exactly warmed to the newfangled and "racy" concept of drama being performed in their own backyard. Becoming part of the excitement changed many of their minds.

Brown enjoyed a successful production with *Crucifixion*, but as a whole, his season at the Savoy lost money. Regrouping, Brown convinced the community to back a new non-profit troupe called the Community Players. This incarnation performed four one-acts at another local venue, the Shakespeare Club; the performances featured a young Martha Graham. The one-acts were a smash, giving Brown the confidence and the cash to head back to the Savoy to stay.

Quick Study

Susan Albert Loewenberg didn't set out intentionally to turn the traditional theater paradigm on its head, but she achieved just that in record time. Her company, L.A. Theatre Works, began life as an arts program for the incarcerated. She's since developed it into an innovative stage and audio publishing business.

"I think the thing that's unusual about L.A. Theatre Works (which has officially been in existence—that is to say, incorporated as a nonprofit—since 1974, but which actually started around 1972 in an informal way) is that where we started is very, very different from where we've ended up. In fact, our name was even different—we were called Artists in Prison.

"The impulse was that we were a group of young theater artists—actors, writers, directors, designers—coming out of the social action of the sixties—mostly from the East Coast—who found ourselves in Los Angeles at a time when theater was very, very dead. Basically, L.A. was a place for fourth-rate touring companies. I was born in New Jersey; I went to Sarah Lawrence, and grew up in the New York theater. I was going to New York by myself on the train from the age of twelve to the American Academy of Dramatic Arts— I was a child actor. I was used to a certain standard.

"[But] we found ourselves, these transplanted New York theater people, working [in Los Angeles]. I was an actor, I had nothing to do with production, I was working in film and television and doing an occasional theater thing. I'd met up with a number of people working at the [Mark] Taper [Forum] in various capacities, and we began meeting and talking. One of them was very interested in doing workshops in prisons. We decided to see if we could go into a county jail and do theater games and improvisational workshop, and we did. We found it fascinating.

"I remember observing what was going on in these workshops was a lot more interesting than what was going on in the theater scene in Los Angeles. It was just more authentic and more organic. It was more like what we were used to.

"At that time, I didn't even know what a nonprofit organization was. I didn't know what a grant was. I didn't know what matching funds were. I mean, nothing. I was, I think, myself, at a crossroads. I had decided to give up being in the theater, and I had gone to graduate school at UCLA in history. But I was still doing some jobs, involved with this informal group. Somebody said, 'Well, if you incorporate as a nonprofit organization, you can actually get some money— you can get what's called grant money.' I said, 'I'll take it on.'

"I connected with a young woman, Linda Lichter, a young lawyer. She's still on our board today and is one of the top entertainment lawyers in Hollywood. She incorporated us as a nonprofit. She's still looking over the contracts!

"By that time, we'd begun to branch out in a number of situations where people were incarcerated, and it was beginning to get kind of interesting. I remember finding out about grants and applying for our first grant with the California Arts Commission, which was the predecessor to the current California Arts Council, under Governor Ronald Reagan. It was relatively informal—I remember there was a three-person commission. I put in my application, somebody helped me with it, and I began to understand what a match was and all of that. I pleaded my case, and we got our first grant, which I think was $2,400. We were off and running.

"As Artists in Prison, we made a reputation, a pretty fast one, between 1974 and 1980. We actually started doing full productions with inmates that were based on the old theater games acting exercises model. We would bring in a writer, do improv. We'd have a workshop leader, begin to construct a script out of the improv, all of the stuff that kids are still doing today. We began expanding to work with the Federal Bureau of Prisons and the state prisons. We'd actually get people on the federal level furloughed to perform these plays at the Mark Taper Forum lab and at UCLA and USC. We'd also do them inside the prison walls. People would actually come down to the prison, be checked in, and be able to go into the auditorium to watch these things. We got a national reputation in a short period of time.

"We got our first funding from the NEA in 1976, under a program which no longer exists called Expansion Arts. Then, we began expanding, not just working in prisons, but actually creating plays within the community, very much in the way the Cornerstone Theater Company does now in Los Angeles.

"We created plays with various segments of the community—I remember liaising with the Women's Building and doing a fabulous play based on a workshop we did with women ages twenty to eighty. We did work with Japanese men, we did all kinds of interesting stuff, and began to get funding from other parts of the Endowment and the Arts Council.

"We began getting a little bit of corporate funding. We had a group of seven people, a kind of seven-person co-op, with me at the head. A lot of those people ultimately fell away—one of them went on to become a very, very successful radio and television producer; one of them is now one of the top production designers in film; another is now one of the top costume designers in film and theater; another is a major playwright; two of them were directors, one of those becoming a magazine editor; and one is a theologian. So, it was a very diverse group. It was very interesting."

Creating Our Perfect Theatrical World

Susan Kosoff, Jane Staab, and Tony Hancock didn't just dream about making a living in the theater—they made that sometimes-illusive fantasy a reality. This trio succeeded by pinpointing exactly how they could make enough money to make having their own theater company viable. Through trial and error, they developed a plan that worked.

Says Susan Kosoff, cofounder and Co-Artistic Director of the Wheelock Family Theatre: "Tony Hancock, Jane Staab, and I had been working together at the Harwich Community Theatre on Cape Cod for many years. In 1971, we started our own theater on the Cape, the Harwich Winter Theatre. We got all set up and got approved by the board of directors at the Harwich Community Theatre, who knew us very well, for the use of the facility to start a winter company. The Cape, in the 1970s, was very different than what it is now, in that there was a lot of community theater, but nothing professional. So, the board graciously gave us the use of their facility and paid for the insurance, which was a big deal. They also gave us all of their lighting equipment, you know, everything that was in the building to use. We had a credit line, things like that. We also were given use of a house from people who were away, so we could live rent-free for our first year. Major!

"The first season we did a bunch of plays—I think five. We would job in actors from New York, and we would also use community people. The reason I tell this is because we did this for five years—eventually, we didn't have free rent anymore, but we continued to have the use of the theater, and so, we could build an audience. It gave us the adrenaline to do theater—what we really wanted was to do original work, to write our own, and give actors from New York, our friends, opportunities, roles that maybe they weren't going to get a chance to do otherwise. They'd come, and for that, we'd give them room and board and transportation.

"For us, there was that incentive to write, to try things out, and we did it for five years. But we never made a living. We always had to have part-time jobs in order to support the theater. The three of us stayed for the full five years, while other people came and went as staff members. We tried different things—sometimes we'd have a big staff, sometimes we kept it very small. We'd always pay the bills first, and then, if there was any money left over, we would split it evenly among whoever was there. That was the only way we ever made any money. People often ask me why I never got a doctorate degree. I say, 'That was my doctorate.'

"We learned a lot, not only in terms of theater, about how to run a theater and what it would take, but also about the kind of theater that interested us. I think that many of the things that we learned, we then took with us to Wheelock. After five years, we realized that if we sold out every single night, every single performance, we still weren't going to be able to make a living. It dawned on us that we shouldn't go on like this forever.

"So, we stopped and all kind of went our own ways—Jane went to New York to act, Tony traveled, and I went to Wheelock College, where I had been teaching part-time at the graduate school. They had been after me for a while to come on full-time, so I did that. For about five years, we all did different kinds of things, all did some theater, Jane doing the most, as she was making it as an actor. I was there in academia, doing some directing, but I would say that my primary work during that time was not in theater. And I missed it.

"We knew that we couldn't do what we'd done before. We had to support ourselves with it. We couldn't work full-time jobs, plus handle how demanding theater can be. But whenever we would get together, we would talk about theater and how we would like it to be if we did it again. As much as I loved doing theater, I loved the idea of creating a theater, because part of what I liked best about the Winter Theatre was the community that we had created, the opportunities to do creative work and to work collaboratively. All those things are so much a part of theater!

"While I was teaching at Wheelock College, they had, at one time, had a very good and active theater department. There was quite a wonderful facility there, but it became under-utilized and neglected, falling by the wayside. After talking with Tony and Jane, I went on sabbatical, and I wrote a proposal to the administration of Wheelock, in which I outlined a three-year start-up plan. It was also very much a concept paper about the kind of theater we wanted to create. Wheelock is committed to working with children and families, so what we proposed was that we would create a theater that would serve children and families—that would be our target audience. We would use their facility and create a professional company.

"There were different kinds of things that we took into consideration. One of the things that we really knew was, not only did we want to make a living, but we wanted to pay actors. On the Cape, people would come up from New York to work, but they wouldn't use their real names, because the theater wasn't Equity. So, we wanted to work with Actors' Equity.

"Then, there was a sense of our former experience that really informed how we thought about the theater. For example, we had really loved working with young people and adults together—we'd gotten a lot of high school and young college kids involved, and also younger kids, on the Cape. What happened when professional actors from New York worked with community people was, it raised the bar for the community people, and their acting really came up, which obviously affected the quality of the production. In addition to that, the professional actors liked it, because they got to be mentors. So, that was something else that we built in.

"I think also that it had been a long-standing feeling of mine that theater had increasingly become for just a few. It's become expensive, it's often pretty white, upper middle-class, etc. So, from the very beginning of Wheelock, we built in certain kinds of goals—a multicultural, nontraditional casting policy. We also really wanted to think about the broadest audience possible, so we wanted our shows interpreted in American Sign Language, for example. Some things like that have become much more common, but at the time, were unusual.

"This was around 1980. We started officially in 1981. It took a good year—it was lots of meetings, to get the staff that I wanted assembled, have conversations with administrators, make everything happen. We didn't have a mission plan—I came up with that three-year start-up so that we started small and slowly, then the idea was to grow, so we wouldn't blow out right away. The college administration gave us the go-ahead."

A Feminist Perspective

The 1970s were a politically vital period, specifically in terms of social issues. Leslie B. Jacobson's feminist values informed her work as a theater artist.

"Horizons began in 1977. I was a freelance director who'd moved to Washington, D.C., in the mid-1970s. There was a women's theater in Washington at that time, and in 1974, I had written and directed a play about Zelda and F. Scott Fitzgerald for that company, the Washington Area Feminist Theatre (WAFT).

"Theater is always on the brink of extinction, and WAFT lost its space in '76. That, coupled with some internal problems within that organization—which I was not running, I was just a participant—that theater sort of fell apart. But there were a number of people I had met there while directing both my production and other new women's plays that I was interested in. Theater people always sort of collect those individuals they would like to work with at some other time. So, I started to work together with four other women to develop a theater piece for performance using improvisation. Out of the work of that, we decided to form a new theater, since WAFT no longer existed, and we did feel the need for a theater that was really looking at life from a woman's perspective.

"We first called ourselves Pro Femina Theatre. The idea was, there's a chamber music group called Pro Musica—and actually, a critic who was very supportive of our work put this idea beautifully: that we were writing to the *femina*, the female spirit that's in all of us. We created a series of shows exploring relationships. We looked at mother-daughter relationships, at the meaning of success for contemporary women, at relationships between women and women and men and women in contemporary society. Those were some of the topics we took on, all original material.

"We would usually develop a show over a three-month period. Pretty intensive rehearsals—we'd spend three months rehearsing five and six days a week. The first month would be spent defining the topic and the viewpoint; the second month, exploring through improvisation; and the third month, really refining, setting, and creating a script. One of the shows we developed was about women and aging. One was about the meaning of adulthood to modern women.

"That remained the kind of constant throughout this period. There was a corps of actress-playwrights who I liked to work with, who liked to work in this way, but that was somewhat fluid; some people moved, to California or New York, and then new people would come in. These shows were developed with three to five actors, but it wasn't always the same three to five actors; there was overlap. But there was still a core of a few people who made up the theater.

"We didn't have a permanent space at that time. We did tour a lot. We were invited to perform in Copenhagen, Denmark, in 1980 as part of the United Nations meetings on the status of women. We performed in New York City a couple of times, [but] mostly in the Washington area.

"We didn't have a business plan, and we should have."

Filling a Quality Void

New Repertory Theatre came to be because its founders felt there was a lack of a specific type of quality Boston theater in the 1980s. There was no serious, midsize local company doing works that made its audience think, discuss, and challenge assumptions. Entertainment value, however, would never be neglected for dry, boring substance at New Rep.

Larry Lane served as New Repertory's first Artistic Director. In setting the course for the small professional theater, his goal was to select and produce works that were quite challenging artistically and intellectually. Additionally, top acting talent was a key component in Mr. Lane's ultimate and ongoing plans for the company.

New Repertory's first season included Chekhov's *The Brute*, Lanford Wilson's *The Mound Builders*, *Desperate Love: Three One-Act Plays*, *The Loveliest Afternoon of the Year* by John Guare, *Canadian Gothic* by Joanna Glass, and *Misalliance* by G. B. Shaw.

Busting Theatrical Stereotypes

Since day one, a performance of Arena Stage's The Living Stage has never been a prim and proper affair. This company doesn't do tradition, stuffiness, or boring exposition. In the sixties, it was a haven for hippie artists who wanted to work within that Woodstock cultural framework. In the seventies, the laid-back, although politically extreme times influenced what was happening onstage. Today, hip-hop, throwing down rhymes, and as always, letting the audience in on the action is what keeps The Living Stage's message fresh.

The Living Stage Company was founded in 1966 as an outreach program. Its goal was to introduce participatory improv to those who might have little experience with theater: kids, the elderly, the disabled, and the incarcerated, for instance. This professional company is led by Artistic Director Ralph Remington and is inspired by the fiercely innovative vision of Arena Stage's Artistic Director, Molly Smith. Ralph Remington says: "We've worked basically to try to get audiences—whether they're kids or adults with some kind of difficulty or challenge—to tap into the creative spirit inside themselves, so anything they create is in a fashion that hasn't been in their lives. The form comes out of poetry, improv, or music. The shows we've done are tailored to individual audiences, whether it's about racism or conflict resolution or homophobia or violence. We go to schools, get to know their populations, meet with the administrators or teachers about particular issues that are affecting the population. It's a lot of fun. I worked with Living Stage first in the early eighties, when I was at a sister company. I trained with [Living Stage pioneer] Bob Alexander, and that's when I learned our method. It's pretty powerful."

Staying True to Your Roots

It's kind of stunning to think of today's La Jolla Playhouse, with its cutting-edge productions and hip reputation, as the home base for many of the more traditional-minded film stars of the 1940s and 1950s. Traditional-minded? Think again. La Jolla Playhouse's famed founders were quite ahead of their time in mapping out a marriage of multimedia.

La Jolla Playhouse was established in 1947 by the distinguished performers Gregory Peck, Dorothy McGuire, and Mel Ferrer.

The goal for the company, as explained by its three founders in a statement accompanying its first program, was that of bridging the separation between film acting and stage acting. Mr. Peck, Miss McGuire, and Mr. Ferrer believed that once a film star became involved with the moviemaking world, he or she became more inclined to put off a return to the common roots of theater that so many performers shared.

Many film actors who started onstage did so in New York. Once they moved to California to start working in cinema, they found that there were very few theaters there to work in. So, La Jolla's Southern California location, in close proximity to Hollywood soundstages, was intended to allow such movie actors the geographic ease to split their time going from play to screen project. The reason its founders found this allocation of actors' work time so important was artistic: Stardom was valuable, but growth as an actor, through work in challenging and quality stage roles, was also vital to the stature of any performer.

And there you have it. A more wildly divergent assortment of starts you could hardly imagine. Where they went next is even more interesting.

CHAPTER 2

CLAIMING SPACE

Obviously, if you want to start a theater company, you'll need to find a space where your company can present its work.

This might seem to be a very daunting task. There's a lot to consider, especially if you've never had experience with the specifics of theater spaces to begin with. You might worry that you'll have to find a perfectly outfitted space, with a huge stage, pristine, with top-of-the-line tech equipment, in order to attract an audience. You may not be certain about what space dimensions, elements, or tech requirements will be right for your productions. You may have so little money to work with, it seems totally impossible to be able to afford even the tiniest space or to buy or rent any equipment whatsoever.

Don't worry! Our experts have encountered all of these space dilemmas and more—and each company figured out a way to make things work. In this chapter, we'll travel back to the first venues used by each of our theater groups, reviewing the challenges that needed to be met in terms of staging those initial shows.

Comedy Isn't Pretty

A house doesn't have to be particularly attractive to the eye in order to be filled every night. The audience in a space doesn't necessarily have to be so gorgeous, either.

When an unconventional audience does, in fact, applaud what you're doing, it can be incredibly fulfilling and can build your confidence regardless of what space you're in. Says Paul Zuckerman of Chicago City Limits: "Tough bars on Chicago's West Side are good training grounds for anybody. If you can work those clubs, you can work any club. The place we used to perform in Chicago, Kolbart's Komedy Kove, was owned by a former cop, and the bouncer was a three-hundred-pound guy with a shaved head. It had been a strip club converted into a comedy club, and I think most of the patrons were never informed of the change. It was a rough crowd. If they didn't like us, they threw things at us.

"In retrospect, it was kind of cool, in a way. Behind the bar, they had the stage, where the strippers used to be, where we performed. In that milieu, the artistic goal, if you will, started to form. It became a challenge not to perform least-common-denominator theater, but to win these audiences that were not traditional theater audiences. You go into that club where the truckers are—last time they drove here from El Paso, it was a strip joint, and now it's a comedy club—and you're doing Shakespearean improvisation, and they're enjoying it, you go, 'All right!'

"There's an old saying in show business: If you buy the premise, you buy the bit. If I invite you to a slaughterhouse, and I put down chairs and I do a show, and I don't say I'm in a smelly slaughterhouse, if I create a reality and I don't break that reality, you will accept that reality. People come out of college, and they've been working with state-of-the art lights and state-of-the-art boards and sound. You come to a city like New York, and you're happy to find a shabby black box. It doesn't matter! If it's good theater, it's good theater. And by the same token, you can't dress up a piece of crap on Broadway.

"In a very big way, that was the lesson we learned [at the Komedy Kove]. It was all about the show. It was all about connecting with the other actors onstage and with the audience. It's nicer to be in a nicer space; I've worked some beautiful spaces, but I'm not sure the most beautiful spaces have been the greatest shows either.

"In New York, the first space we moved to was the Jan Hus Playhouse on East 74th Street around the beginning of 1982, and we stayed there through the nineties. We sort of outgrew that space. It was still in a church, even though it was one of the oldest Off-Broadway spaces in New York. It's no longer an Off-Broadway house, but the space is still there. But there was too much sharing of that space. We needed a space seven days a week.

"We had our eyes open for ten years, and I always felt we had one shot to five in terms of making a move—it's very expensive. We looked at lots of spaces that were sort of okay and might have been okay, but unless it was perfect . . . we really took our time with it."

Chicago City Limits ultimately moved to its current space, on First Avenue in the sixties in Manhattan. It provided much more visibility. "We felt this one was as perfect as any one we were going to find. The location, on the avenue, we felt was very important; it gave us instant visibility. The size of the theater was good; it held two hundred.

"Another element of our business that had grown over time was our corporate entertainment, and at the Jan Hus, you'd get your clients all juiced up about your show, and they'd come, but they're still in the basement of a church. The new space had more of a legitimacy, if you will.

"Know when to hold 'em, and know when to fold 'em."

Street Credibility

Paul Zuckerman makes a key point when he speaks about perceived legitimacy. As we've discussed, beggars can't be choosers when it comes to securing a space. Chicago City Limits proved to its early audiences that if your work is good, you can do it anywhere and get a positive response. But are there situations where right off the bat, it might really pay off to set up at the "right" address, in, say, an established theater you rent on a per-show basis, so you can trade on its name value?

Yes—if your fledgling company is ready for reviewers to come, and if you're polished enough in terms of your first production offerings that you feel confident you're going to gain good critical response. Critics—certainly not well-known ones—often will not check out a new company's production, no matter how much you call and fax and e-mail and sweet-talk them. This is snobbery, for sure, but that doesn't change the fact that it happens all the time in major cities. This rude practice is rampant in New York.

However, if you are able to afford renting a weekend's worth of time at a very respected venue, say, an Off-Broadway space, even though that venue will no doubt require you to advertise as "The Young Whippersnapper Theater Company at _____ Space," critics may fixate on the Off-Broadway name and not so much on yours. Then, they may indeed show up to review you. The fact that an Off-Broadway house is willing to take your money may appear to critics, and audiences, as an endorsement. David Zak talks about the early performance venues of the Bailiwick Repertory: "Our first shows were in rental spaces around the city. Instead of paying rent, we worked on the spaces. I think it helped that we made our debut in a legitimate theater space—it got the critics in early. I think it also helped that our first show was *The Country Wife*. You would have to be insane to produce that show, and so everybody came to see if we were indeed crazy."

David Zak is crazy like a fox; he employed a very good attention-getting strategy. Keep in mind that if you follow his lead, you'll have to deal with a number of practical considerations when you're renting a space, considerations that you must have cash to handle. These considerations include insurance, equipment rental, and additional hidden costs. (See chapter 3 for more in-depth coverage of these and other business and financial points.)

Again, too, you need to make sure the show or shows you intend to present in a noteworthy space are as flawless as they can be. Until you can honestly say that this is the case, there is absolutely no shame in putting up your work in a school auditorium, a church basement space, even a vacant lot if you have to! It's far better to build your name in baby steps successfully than it is to blow all of your money on a big-name splashy debut that isn't well received.

Tools of the Trade

No matter what space you're working in, you want to make sure you've got a good amount of strength in terms of technical aesthetics. This is not to say that you need the best lighting board known to mankind—you'll soon read how dimmers that do the job can be found (and have been) in the unlikeliest shape, in the unlikeliest of places.

What you do need to be able to count on is that whatever equipment you can get works. You don't want spotlights that quit on you mid-performance. So, when you're evaluating a space to see whether it will work for you, one of the very first things you ought to do is carefully evaluate its equipment, to make sure it's functional. Equipment function is much more important than the depth of a stage or the size of a room—because those things can be adjusted to and dealt with. A broken soundboard is a broken soundboard, and you probably don't have the money or inclination to have it fixed at this stage.

It can pay off to try to put aside a bit of money to rent a piece of equipment that you know will be reliable. Make it the one that is most important to your work technically— that's a good investment. Also, cultivate others who can compensate for technical shortcomings with clever design sleight-of-hand. Rick Lombardo, of New Repertory Theatre, says, "One thing I noticed, when I became this company's Artistic Director in 1996, was that historically, the Theatre had focused on plays and actors, not physical production. Good plays need strong visual components as tools, so I began finding the financial resources for getting those tools and dedicating resources toward getting designers."

How to Improve Any Space

So, let's go through the actual process of evaluating a space for your company. Whether you are leaning toward a name space or a more low-key spot, there are several key steps in figuring out what space is right for you and what you can do to make it even better.

Look through the phone book and local newspaper for any and every possibility in your area, first of all. You should know, of course, how much you can realistically spend on a space before you make an appointment to see it. Perhaps some negotiating on rent might be possible, certainly. But keep within a smart ballpark price range—don't let your eyes get bigger than your stomach, so to speak, and waste your time, not to mention the space owner's time, haggling over a space you're never going to be able to afford. Publications like *Back Stage* are good resources for advertised rentals, as are lists your local arts councils may be able to supply.

It might seem elementary, but never agree to rent a space you haven't visited in the flesh! Space dimensions recited over the telephone don't tell you everything; they practically don't tell you anything. You want to be able to inspect everything up close and personal, strut around on the stage, get your hands on the equipment, and eyeball every square inch of the place.

The space you end up in won't be perfect; almost no theater space is. The good news, though, is that a theater space is just a room. It's a room filled with a stage and curtains and boards and seats, sure, but basically, still a room, and you can do a lot to change and improve upon its dynamics with a little know-how. You can, in fact, make virtually any space work to your particular advantage. Corey Fischer, of A Traveling Jewish Theatre, relates how the company transformed its initial performance space: "We initially performed at a church in Santa Monica, called The Church in Ocean Park. It was very progressive—you know, Santa Monica's a bit like SoHo or the East Village in New York, but it's got the ocean! That church was very much a cultural center, and they did a lot of performance.

"It was interesting—a year later, when we went back to that space, we put a lot of time and effort into putting some acoustical panels on the ceiling, because it was a very echoey space. We had learned a bit. Our then-technical director figured out a pretty simple way to cut a lot of the echo by putting these baffles up.

"It was just a big, open space. We brought in all of our own lights, and Albert and I, during the first performances, were doing everything, including running the lights from onstage. It was very cumbersome. We only did that, I think, for one performance! Then, we recruited Naomi's daughter to run lights offstage for the next couple performances. Then, a technical director appeared and stayed with us for the next two or three years.

"In terms of choosing a first space, my advice would be this: There are a lot more important earlier questions to ask, meaning that nothing's going to make sense unless one is starting out from a place of very deep commitment. Theater is so hard to do. There's no reason in the world to take it on unless you are burning with passion and commitment and love for what you're doing, for what you want to say and create. Once you get to that—there's a wonderful quote about commitment—I am paraphrasing, but, 'once one is committed, the universe provides.'

"In terms of space, the two most important things to look for, or to try and create, are sight lines and acoustics. You can always bring in lights, you can rig stuff, but there's not much you can do without sight lines and acoustics. You can do what we did, putting panels on the ceiling, but that's almost like starting to build a theater. Things that help with sight lines, of course, are having the audience on risers. For the kind of theater we do, we really try to avoid places where there's a high stage and the audience is flat—in other words, a standard auditorium or multipurpose room. Those things are not good, and if we're faced with a space like that, or when we were kind of not able to be so choosy, we would at least try to get the people in charge of the space to bring in some risers. Sometimes, we would do things in reverse—have the audience sitting on a high stage, put some rented bleachers on the stage, and play on the flat floor ourselves.

"Acoustics . . . again, there's not a whole lot you can do. Sometimes, if the space is very echoey, you can hang drapery, blacks, to absorb some of that. It's always deceptive going into a space without people in it. Every space changes tremendously when you get bodies, which absorb sound. They often soften it.

"It's easier to deal with a space that's very live, in the sense of being very echoey, than it is dealing with a space that's dead, that already feels muffled when no one's in there. It's going to be even worse when people are in there, and there's really nothing you can do about that except hope your actors have good vocal training."

Don't Get Too Comfortable

Once you've found a space in your community that you can afford, work with, and improve, if necessary, whatever you do—don't fall in love with it.

Wait a minute, you're probably thinking. We have just found this little treasure—we haven't even had our first rehearsal in it yet! Ah, but you give yourself away. Visions of permanency are dancing in your head already. You picture your company becoming a mainstay in this, your safe, secure little room, integrated in and popular with your land-lord and your community environment, as long as you want to be. Maybe that will happen, but maybe it shouldn't, for one good reason—permanency may feel all warm and squishy and safe and secure, but it doesn't promote growth for your organization. You always want to keep growing. Growing beyond your initial space should always be viewed as a very positive possibility, even from the day you first inhabit it.

Consider this cautionary tale from Leslie Jacobson of Horizons Theatre: "In 1983, we got a parish hall space in Georgetown. That helped us build a more stable audience base and to really present a season, because we weren't constantly moving from space to space.

"It was a historic building, so that was kind of nice—it had a wood floor, very high ceilings. Since it was a historic building, which predated the Civil War, we couldn't do any-thing permanent to it. But we really learned how to use that space. Sometimes, we'd do shows in the round, or three-quarter round. We'd set it up differently. We had an extremely good relationship with the minister of the church, and he was enormously supportive of our work. He never asked to see a script. I mean, I used to go and meet with him in the spring of the preceding year, and we'd go through dates and when we could be in there and when we couldn't, and we'd talk philosophy— it was just a very, very pleasant relationship.

"But as we became more and more successful, we just took up more space and became more present. Some of the parishioners . . . it wasn't that they disliked us, but they disliked the fact that there was this other organization in the church's space. It seemed like whenever they wanted to use the parish hall, the theater was in there. It did create a kind of conflict.

"As we continued to grow and develop, it seemed like we were outgrowing our space. And this is a time in the late eighties when there was a lot of real estate development going on. It looked as if we were going to move into space on 14th Street, near where the Woolly Mammoth Theatre Company used to be, and where the Studio Theatre is now. We started a capital campaign that was very successful, and we were supposed to move into this new space in '91. But in '90, all of a sudden, there was this kind of recession. What happened was, the developers suddenly got cold feet—because they were supposed to do certain things to the space, and we were supposed to do certain things, so we were both raising money. They were supposed to bring the space up to code, have the sprinklers, and we were raising the money for the seats and the lighting equipment and all that stuff. Well, the city started to demand more stringent sprinkler systems and other things to bring it up to code, and the developers suddenly decided that this was costing them more money than they actually were interested in spending. So basically, they said to us, 'Instead of the space being ready next year, maybe it will be ready in three years.'

"For a tiny organization, that's like telling you the restaurant you thought you were going to open next month is really going to open three years from now. So, this was really very difficult for us. We had done a really fabulous newsletter and subscription brochure for our new season and our new space, and we didn't have a new season and a new space.

"We didn't have any space, because the minister that we'd had this fabulous relationship with at the church left. He took another parish in another state. The people who were temporarily running things at the church . . . it looked like we were going to have a new space, the minister was leaving, so this was an opportunity for them to reclaim their parish hall. That's what they did.

"We went through a period in the early nineties where we really were nomadic and weren't sure what was going to happen. But somehow, we kept finding places to produce in. We didn't do three shows a year, but maybe we did one or two or one show and a series of staged readings. But we did keep our doors open. We never completely closed our doors."

Pragmatic Planning

So, you can see that things occasionally do just rise up and hit you in the face out of nowhere, and there's no way you can foresee them.

But let's go back to that concept of growth. It's never too early to start planning how you'll get bigger—and the earlier you start thinking about that very thing, the better. Your initial production could prove so popular, so quickly, perhaps, you'll have to add performances and eventually bigger capacity.

What is the foolproof way to gauge how fast your company is growing from day one? Simple. It's the seats. How many are you filling? That number is your best indicator of success. Better than audience surveys, better than media response, better even than how much revenue you're actually taking in per any given performance.

Anybody can count bodies in seats. If you're filling bigger and bigger numbers of chairs in your early days, that's proof you're doing things right. So, when that happens, how do you grab the ball and run with it? To paraphrase the Clash, should you stay or should you go now? You should stay. At least in the immediate future. Don't get ahead of yourself. But respect the signs of audience growth, and start pragmatically planning your future space needs well in advance of actually making them.

Steppenwolf grasped this concept of spatial growth planning very, very well from its earliest days. Michael Gennaro says: "The company's first performance space was a church basement, up in Highland Park—Immaculate Conception Church. Someone kind of said to them, Hey, you can make use of this space—I think it was a sixty-seat space. That's why [the original company members] started working there.

"There were, literally, tops, three or four rows of seats. So, you were on top of them. That was when the buzz started happening down in Chicago about, 'You gotta go see these kids up in Highland Park.' They were just experimenting and taking everything as far as they could take it.

"Some of the original things done within that space were *The Indian Wants the Bronx*, *The Lesson*, *The Dumbwaiter*, and *The Seahorse*. One of the things that makes this organization unique—and I've run a number of nonprofits now—is that the normal structure is, you have an artistic director, an executive director, and a board. That's the structure. In this place, in between those, amongst those three constituencies, is the ensemble. Their influence factors into every single decision that's made in this place, and that's the way it's been for twenty-five years—whether it's buying real estate or whether we're going to change the board structure, they are always consulted. What that does is continually bring you back to the original artistic vision of the company. Some people go, 'Well, I think this is the kind of work we're going to do, so let's find a space that works.' No! What you're trying to do is say, 'This is what our mission is, this is what our work is—any space can fit that, as long as we remain true to that work.'

"You have to be kind of entrepreneurial, as well as lucky. The space kind of just doesn't really matter at one point. Because every move Steppenwolf's members made thereafter was driven by the fact that the audience couldn't get into the place, there were not enough seats. Every move worked from that point.

"After the church basement, the company went down to the Hull House, which was a little bigger space, in 1980, 134 seats. Basically, you're judging the capacity. That was a moment where everybody kind of looked at each other and said, 'Wait a minute—now we're moving down into the Loop. We're not as protected as we were up in Highland Park.' Because up there, you know, they could kind of do whatever they wanted—what were people going to say? That was a move that caused some people to leave, and then bonded even further the people that were together.

"They went down there, and obviously, the place went crazy. They did all the same things and upped the ante again—brought on new ensemble members. The next move was in '82— the company moved onto Halstead Street, into a place that had 211 seats. So, they upped the ante again.

"At some point in time, things came to the same crossroads—you can't get in to the theater, too many people. So, that's when probably the biggest step they had made in some time came. They had a board made up of friends and some business people, with one person in particular, the chair at the time, Bruce Sagan, who is quite a visionary. They said, 'You know what? It's time to build our own theater.' A lot of the board was like, 'You're crazy—that's too big of a step!' They ended up building the space we're in now, which is a 511-seat theater, and took a real gamble in doing that.

"The first year—I think they had had 1,200 subscribers, something like that, up on Halstead—they went up to, I think, 14,000."

Anything Is Possible, and Here's Proof

The space you have to work with may not seem ideal to you. Maybe it's tiny, or maybe it smells like someone squished rancid tuna sandwiches under the radiator. Maybe it's freezing cold in the winter and is sure to be boiling hot in the summer. Maybe you don't like it; you feel like you've had to settle for it, either because finding space in your area is nightmarishly hard to do or because it was all you could afford.

Still, anything is possible for you to do within its walls. Adversity can sharpen your thinking and make you see ways to clear up a problem better than you think. Your desire to do great work is the barometer of how well you can suck it up and handle space adversity.

Absolutely nobody was doing more unconventional work in a more unconventional space than Susan Albert Loewenberg in the mid-seventies. No matter what disasters you might think could befall you, she had it worse and made it work.

"Within the prison, they had an auditorium, so you could present things. We would work in classrooms, actually do the workshops. You can't imagine what it was like. In theater, everything is possible—it's an everything-is-possible environment. In prison, nothing is possible. Everything's a problem.

"You had to work with lockdowns and people getting into all kinds of trouble and people not showing up. But you were also working with a lot of fabulous, raw talent, bottled-up creativity that just needed to be released. It was a very interesting challenge."

The Value of Intimacy

Intimacy is also key within any space setup. No matter how large or small your space is, setting it up so the audience is as physically and emotionally intimate with your actors as possible makes the room, and the work, electric. If you have a flexible space, you can try rearranging seating in the round or three-quarter configuration around your stage. That forges an instant bond, pulls the audience into the action of the play physically, and gives them the illusion that they are part of the show, if they're close enough. Lighting the front rows subtly works even better to foster that sense of inclusion.

If your actors are in literal spitting distance to the audience, it's actually a good thing! Mitzi Sales remembers arriving from Texas in Berkeley and seeing the audience-friendly theater she'd be working in vividly and positively. Mitzi says: "It was very small—153 seats. It had started, actually, as, I think, an 80-seat theater in this storefront, and after a couple of years, they had managed to break out one of the walls that surrounded it. So, it became three-sided; the audience was on three sides of the stage.

"It was an old, brown-shingled building that had been raised. It had originally been a home in Berkeley. In the really beautiful neighborhoods around the University of California, as you drive through or walk through the neighborhoods, there are these lovely, old, brown-shingled homes. It's sort of the quintessential Berkeley look.

"What happened on College Avenue was, it became a little neighborhood/ commercial site area. There had been this home, and whoever bought the property had raised the brown shingle up and put a building with two storefronts underneath it. So, what you had was this odd little building on this little commercial strip. When I say 'little' commercial strip, we are talking two, maybe three blocks long. The theater was in the area of College and Ashby, a neighborhood/commercial district surrounded by neighborhoods. Which was charming! It was so homey.

"You had this very comfortable, very intimate theater space. You were practically on top of the actors; you could feel their heartbeat. Everything about this was appealing."

The Devil Is in the Details

Intimacy is a good thing to pay attention to. In fact, you should be paying attention to absolutely everything. It's remarkable what people don't notice. Shocking, in fact.

I've seen productions performed completely on the wrong set in repertory, because one company was too lazy and careless to strike the other's stuff. Didn't it occur to them how tacky that made their show look? That is a pretty extreme example of poor taste, granted, but ignoring details can be just as telling and just as obnoxious. Don't leave old drops, left by the space's previous owners, hanging just because you don't want to take them down. The audience is, of course, going to notice, be insulted at your lack of sophistication, and hold it against your show. It's arrogant and disrespectful.

Go over your space with a fine-tooth comb, and change whatever's hanging loose, sticking out, peeling, or exposed. If there's the front bumper of an old Dodge in your wing space (I've seen that as well), remove it, won't you, please? Your actors don't need to be stepping around old garbage any more than your audience needs to see it. A clean space makes everybody happy.

Be very vigilant in terms of period details as well, especially if your space has been around for a long time. When Ralph Remington assumed the reins at The Living Stage in 2001, he made sure the space was brought up to date visually. Mr. Remington says: "The space is kind of a black box, built in a way for audiences to come in—the company wasn't doing a lot of going out. Now, there is more going out [with productions], as opposed to, you know, people coming in [to see shows].

"It was painted white. White walls, with mounted photos of images reminiscent of the times—Che Guevara, very seventies images! It had to be updated. The photos that were there had to leave, the posters had to leave. You're doing rehearsals, you're doing performances, you need to be surrounded by modern stuff.

"So, the space was updated, with a new backdrop, new technical stuff."

A Conventional Success Story

Susan Kosoff, Jane Staab, and Tony Hancock of Wheelock Family Theater could be seen as tremendously fortunate in the quality and workability of the space they were blessed with.

Here's a good illustration of the pluses of a traditional space setup—and how to deal smartly with its few minuses. Susan Kosoff has this to say about the space provided for the company by Wheelock College: "The house was quite handsome. We were grateful. There are no obstructed views, the seats were good. So, the view that the public saw from the very beginning was a good one, in that it was inviting and it was attractive.

"The lighting equipment was old, but it was adequate. Over time, of course, we started to make changes, and it was completely overhauled. The lighting system needed to be new, all of that, which is a huge expense. The college actually absorbed that.

"There was no intercom system. There was a lighting booth, and there was a sound booth, but you couldn't talk backstage—and there's a big distance there! We would, in the beginning years, rent equipment to do that.

"The stage dimensions are strange. It's about twenty-seven feet deep, and it's about forty feet wide. I think that because the proscenium opening is large, it gives you a sense of expanse. There were pipes for hanging things.

"All of this, we've upgraded over time, slowly. In addition to the lighting pipes, there wasn't much in terms of drops. The actual equipment was minimal, and we really had to build a stock up. There were no tools for building, no power tools.

"It's six hundred fifty seats. That was one of the reasons we knew we could do this. The theater on Cape Cod had two hundred seats, and what we'd realized was that you had to have volume in order to make the kind of money that we needed to support a theater. Either that, or charge very high prices, which we weren't interested in doing.

"It helps to think about what productions you want to do. The space on the Cape was a twenty-by-twenty-foot platform, essentially, but we made it work. But we knew what we were getting into. The advantage to Wheelock was that we had a big house and a big space, but it also meant that our sets cost three times as much as they had on the Cape. But for us, it was okay, because we wanted to do very cool sets, and young people in particular like the visuals. We wanted to be able to have some technicals, because I think that's become such a part of the culture now. I'm not so crazy about it, to tell you the truth.

"The space was old, and in many ways, it was a blessing, and in many ways, it was a challenge. We had to work with it. It took us a while to figure out what kinds of sets worked the best, which ones were possible and which were too big for us. The wing space is small, but you can fly things.

"Tony really got to know the space really well, so he could also work with guest designers, and we could make the most of our sets. We really weren't interested in renting sets or anything like that. We really wanted to do it all ourselves, so we did!"

An Unconventional Success Story

Jack Reuler made his space work just as well by doing it all himself. In his case, however, his theater space didn't start out as a theater space. It didn't start out as a church basement, or an empty meeting room, or any of the other logical possibilities that come to mind. Instead, it had a much more unexpected, and historic, past life. Here's how Jack Reuler made an unlikely place into a dramatic oasis—for nearly no cost:

"In those months between when I decided to do theater and when I started doing theater," Jack says, regarding the beginnings of Mixed Blood, "I actually went out looking for a space. The offices of the Center for Community Action were upstairs from this 1887 firehouse. After a day or two of running around, looking at spaces, they just said to me, 'Well, why don't you just go downstairs?'

"That's what I did, and we've been here since the very beginning. It was a war story only in that our building had been a fire station from 1887 to 1963, and our lab, to this day, is where they used to keep the horses, and my office was used as a bathroom.

"It was literally just a big, open sixty-by-forty-five room. Beautiful wooden floors. It wasn't a theater, and I think what I was hoping to go out and find was something that was ready to have plays in it. So, where the war story comes is, how do we do that—turn it into a theater?

"They were building a bridge across the Mississippi River, about three blocks away. At night, we would run over to the construction site and take the plywood they were throwing away. We had to jump our van every time we tried to start it, so it wasn't a very good getaway van. So, we built seating platforms, and we built stages.

"We found a guy whose store had this really antique lighting system—God brought up light for the first time with these lights. He stored them under the merry-go-round at the state fair, and in the spring of '76, as the snow was melting, we went under the merry-go-round and got probably twenty-eight lights and six dimmers. That was our first lighting system.

"I yearn for those days. As a matter of fact, somebody just starting an organization now came by here, looking for things we wanted to get rid of. I was, like, 'You have hit the bottom of the barrel.'

"The University of Minnesota was remodeling the student union, and they gave us two hundred folding chairs. The same guy who rented us those lights for almost nothing was an electrician and sort of did the wiring out of our service entrance to give us the juice to run the lights with.

"It is a classic black box, in the sense that we probably have six or seven configurations of where seats and stage are. We had three or four last year alone, and the first year, of the six shows we did, I'll bet we had three or four configurations.

"I've gone and done shows in many different kinds of spaces. I think I'm completely free to assume the possibility of a space by never having had a conventional space. We've got a garage that we rent that has an entire rig of lifts and trusses and lights and curtains, and we get hired out all the time to go into a million types of spaces to do those shows. I guess if I had to give a piece of advice, in Minneapolis right now, there's a huge number of nomadic, homeless organizations that I used to think had a great benefit. They didn't have the headaches of a facility and whatever it takes to run a facility. But now, there's become such a shortage of space for the number of groups; it's not about money, it's just about the space. If I had to make a recommendation, I'd say, get a space, rather than remain mobile.

"I like site-specific stuff, but that is a change of pace from what we do normally."

Slow and Steady Has Always Won the Race

In terms of vast improvements, like the ones Jack Reuler had to make literally from the ground up, it pays to start moving on changes quickly, since they take time. For upgrade work, however, it can be a smarter idea to try to live with the conditions you have for a short while, then upgrade your equipment or cosmetics gradually. This, of course, applies as long as you have adequate, working equipment with which to run your rehearsals and shows, and as long as the premises are safe for actors, staffers, and audience members. That's essential.

Here's a tip to remember, though: Don't depress your company members. They may lose morale if they have to stare at peeling paint on the dressing room walls for too long. Paint isn't all that pricey, so buy a bucket and a brush and freshen things up. You'll be surprised how much good will a simple act like this will buy you!

Upgrading slowly, but steadily has worked well for many companies for many years. Here's how Gilmor Brown handled space renovations at Pasadena Playhouse circa 1917.

Brown's stage was only thirty feet deep, so to give an illusion of more depth, set pieces were erected in front of the back wall. If an actor had to make a cross-stage entrance, he or she had to dash outside the theater and through an alley.

There was no stage apron, limited fly space, and only one bathroom for the company members to share. The ceiling leaked. The dressing space was stuck in a most unappealing basement area. Tech equipment was very spare, in terms of lighting, storage, and rigging. All twenty-eight shows of the theater's first season were done under these difficult conditions.

Brown began to improve these conditions slowly, but steadily by the company's second season. His plan of action included incorporation and pulling a board together. The board consisted of prominent Pasadena residents, one of whom actually donated the entire budget for the theater's next season, a whopping $2,000.

Brown encouraged wealthy locals to get involved with the theater's set and costume needs, thereby improving physical conditions at the Playhouse. Donations like antique furniture became set pieces, and many a local lady constructed costumes by hand out of opulent, charitably provided fabrics.

Eventually, a warehouse space was added (a nearby rental) to house set pieces and costumes.

If It Ain't Broke, Don't Fix It

Jean Cocteau Repertory started off small, and even though it has indeed expanded its facilities with a 1974 move to the space it resides in today, many of its original space issues remain. Storage, for instance. Yet, the Cocteau has worked out a reliable way of dealing with its limitations over time, quite expertly. Tried-and-true solutions should not be discarded easily: if it ain't broke, don't fix it, and if you have to improve it, be creative. For the Cocteau's initial season, Eve Adamson rented a vacant store space on Bond Street in Lower Manhattan. Adamson then worked out her seating plan by obtaining fifty chairs from the Brooklyn Fox Theater, for the bargain price of $1 each.

That was pretty much the entire space. Adamson kept her day job as a teacher in order to pay rent on the store space, simply taking from her own paycheck to take care of the expense.

Eventually, though, Adamson's growing success required a move to a bigger space. The theater's only move was to the Bouwerie Lane Theater, a landmark space on New York's Bowery, where, of course, it still resides today. Historically, David Fuller explains, "The theater was an Off-Broadway presenting house for most of the sixties. The most famous show to have its start there was *Dames at Sea,* starring the very young Bernadette Peters." The stage itself is on the small side, and there isn't a lot of storage space. Since Adamson moved the company into this space in 1974, there's been lots of creative making-do in terms of storage, tucking set pieces wherever there's room—in the lobby, the stairwell, the hallways, wherever a slice of space is available.

Although some of the facility's elements were installed long ago, like its electrical wiring and plumbing systems, there are many fabulous advantages to the space. Though small, the stage is raked, allowing for infinite blocking possibilities without fear of messing up the sight lines. With a little ingenuity, a director can create stage pictures that make the space look much larger. The acoustics are quite good as well.

Tips to Remember When Choosing an Initial Space

o **Ask Questions**. No question is stupid. When you're physically within a space and looking it over, don't be shy about asking the person you're potentially renting from every question that comes to mind about your surroundings, from whether the roof leaks to where the light switches are.

o **Safety Is Vital.** Is your space up to code in terms of public safety requirements, such as fire code? Has there ever been a major fire in your space or in the building it's located in? If so, is your electrical wiring going to be safe? Such a fact is important knowledge to have. Research your space well before you make a final decision. Go to your local city hall and look up information on the building that's available by public record. Ask around. Arm yourself with any and all bits of knowledge that can have an impact on your decision whether to move in or pass.

o **Don't Decide Alone.** Of course, any cofounder or company members you've already assembled have an important say in where they're going to work. Bring everybody into the space, and let them see how they feel within it, if possible. Another bonus: You have new and objective sets of eyes to go over any details you might have missed, plus ask additional questions. After your group has looked at the space (preferably, everybody can get together and field trip to several spaces, not just one), get together in an objective space, and discuss everyone's feelings and opinions. Don't be a dictator and think it's your way or the highway in terms of a final decision. Listen to your people. Making the decision as a democracy will actually strengthen your bond as a creative unit as well—this will be your first decision as a cohesive team, but not your last.

o **You're the Tie Breaker, Though.** Democracy is good, but there are factors your company members may not know as much about as you do. Such as financial considerations. If everyone is urging you to take a space you don't think you can swing financially, feel okay about telling them that. They need to understand that sort of thing. Same goes for any other major reasons you alone are aware of that would require you to decline, such as safety considerations or any other important reasons.

o **Beware of Hidden Costs.** Will signing on the dotted line for your space require a security deposit? First and last month's rent up front? Insurance paid up front? Maybe questionable little fees could be snuck into your deal, like a stake in electric or water bills. Make sure you fully understand any and all hidden fees before putting any deal for any space in writing. Consulting an attorney is always a good idea; if you think you can't afford one, an organization like Volunteer Lawyers for the Arts might be a helpful resource.

Don't agree to any terms that make you uncomfortable, financial or otherwise.

CHAPTER 3

OUR FIRST BUSINESS PLAN

One of the toughest lessons any theater professional has to learn is that art and commerce walk hand in hand. Focusing your attention solely on the fun and fascinating creative aspects of your company will mean you don't survive. Period.

I have always felt that one of the biggest problems with most college and university theater arts curriculums is that they rarely even broach the subject of finances. In order to succeed in the business of theater, you have to have a good grasp of the fact that it is a business in the first place. Whether your goal is to make it as a thriving troupe or solo, you are guaranteed to waste tons of time, money, and earning potential learning the hard, cold realities of the business once you've entered it.

If you've already dipped your toe into the professional world, you know how intimidating the theater business can feel. For the most part, it's based on first impressions of you and of your work. If you make the wrong first impression on someone, you don't get another shot—goodbye, here's the door, see ya later. It's a career in itself just trying to figure out what the "right" impression is, too; it's different to nearly every mover and shaker you meet in the business. This is true for actors, directors, writers, designers, and yes, budding company heads who are instantly judged on the business and artistic value of their choices, their business acumen, their planning skills, and their understanding and articulate expression of their own mission.

Say you need to present your vision for your theater company to potential funders or write it up in a grant proposal. Do you really know what it is you want to do now, a year down the line, five years down the line? Money folks aren't going to give up the green to an unfocused pipe dreamer.

Don't feel too bad, though, if you feel you're at a disadvantage in terms of business know-how and experience. The most established theater companies, like those we're consulting, have been in that exact same position. They've overcome their initial shortcomings in this area. You, too, can learn what you need to know and do just fine.

In this chapter, our subjects will speak their minds on a variety of issues regarding business matters, reflecting upon their initial plans (or lack thereof) and related points. We'll give you food for financial thought and key business facts you should know.

Let's start off with a basic reality check.

Says Paul Zuckerman of Chicago City Limits: "In the beginning, we didn't have any kind of a financial vision. Our vision was totally artistic at the time.

"Talk about clichés about show business and business, but it's a harsh reality you have to face. It becomes more and more of the evil twin as times goes on, and as you do reach success. All of a sudden, you go from a band of people working together to the need to pay rent, to the need to pay auxiliary people, the need to generate income because you can't do this for free your whole life. So, all those financial needs start to spring up, and you start to develop . . . I'm not sure it's a business like you would develop if you went to Wharton, but it's a good idea to start thinking how you're going to do it. How are you going to get the money? What are you going to do with the money? How can you sustain it?

"A lot of it is trial and error, but a lot of it is learning and not making the same mistakes twice. For instance, advertising is expensive. You need to do it, but you've also got to learn who's drawing the audience for you and who's not. Even though something might be a great deal, maybe something four times as expensive really gives you the income. Whereas something else, it might be nice for you to read your name in the paper, but you're not getting any bang for your buck.

"[In New York], we started to try to find a space. We wanted to be able to flourish as a theater company. We found a space on West 42nd Street, for what we felt was expensive, but affordable rent for at least the short term. One of the first things we did was hire a public relations company. Talk about money well spent! My ABC in the New York Times this weekend will cost about $300–400. [The ABC listings spotlight current Broadway and Off-Broadway listings in a directory format.] For about the same price as that each week, you could hire a public relations firm. If I get the lead article in a Friday New York Times theater section, I've bought myself, what, $20,000 worth of publicity. I couldn't pay for it if wanted to pay for it. So, we immediately threw everything into rent and public relations.

"We're a theater company—no show is all that important compared to the ensemble within the show. But let's say I've written a play, and I've gotten it up in Duluth and somewhere else, and now it's kind of gaining momentum. I want to hit the big city, let's say go Off-Broadway. Well, you get your backers and stuff, there's a budget, you do a kind of traditional theater model. Ninety-nine point nine percent of the time, you lose money. Once in a while, you have a hit.

"You can't look at any one show, you can't look at any one defeat or victory as the be-all and end-all."

That's good, basic strategic thinking and presents some of the financial choices you will have to make as your company both starts and matures. Before we go any further, let's go over some financial basics you need to be aware of from the word go.

Budget and Initial Expenses

You can never have enough money for your company's operations. Never. But you probably don't have much at all at this point, right? A proper budget plan will maximize what you do have and allow you to generate more income. Consider the following: Low over-head is the best guarantee of success and survival. Think before you spend as much as a single dime. If you can put off an expense in your early days, put it off. Also, don't employ more people to work with you than you absolutely need in the beginning.

Here are the initial steps you can take to get your financial strategy off the ground:

1. Add up all of the absolute expenses you must pay out per week. You must pay monthly rent on your space—break that figure down to a per-week figure (it can be easier to really see your expenditures clearly if you look at them in a smaller time increment). You should pay your actors something (and you may have to if you're using Equity people—more on that later), so figure that amount in. You should pay your crew (a must if you have a professional stage manager who belongs to Equity). Best case scenario: You should have money, even just a little, to do some form of advertising—add that to your total. You must factor in rental fees, faxes, phone calls, insurance (we're getting to that), everything else you can think of. That's step one of making a workable budget.

2. Now, add up all of the capital you have to work with, including any income your company has already generated—say, if your first show has already gone up (but you really should make up a budget before that ever occurs). Hopefully, you've got enough to cover your initial expenses. If not, call your dad and beg tearfully. Just this one time.

3. Dad may be able to provide one get-out-of-jail-free card, but next time, it's going to be all up to you. Determine how much money you're going to need to stay solvent, and make a profit, by calculating the number of seats you're going to have to fill per performance to cover your expenses (plus make a little cash over that, hopefully). Are you intending to sell concession items? You can project that potential profit into the mix if so. But please, be brutally realistic about what you can make.

4. No matter how little money you have, plan for the unexpected catastrophe expense. Even a little money can help cushion emergency financial blows. Try to put a little cash aside from your profits each week, just in case. Try, at least.

5. It's never too early to start projecting into the future, budget wise. Surround yourself with other people who can take some of the load off your shoulders by keeping a clear head where planning is concerned.

Rick Lombardo of New Repertory Theatre has this to say about business planning: "Keep three things in mind short-term. First, mission—why do we do what we do? Next, work out a realistic budget document. Then, manage on a day-to-day basis.

"A long-range plan means you ask where is the institution now, then ask, what do you see yourself becoming? To get there, you need a constant dialogue with your staff. Plus, you've got to keep your eyes open in terms of survival—you must know the answer to, why does it matter?

"I look for employees who can multitask. I like a three-year planning process, from soup to nuts in terms of budget to production."

Insurance Considerations

Most rental spaces, not to mention unions, will require you to arrange for insurance. It's hard to paint an exact picture of what you'll need to take care of here, since every space will be different. Every production, depending on the number of personnel you're using per show, may have different insurance requirements as well.

It's a safe bet, though, to plan for adequate coverage in the event of a tornado inside the building during show time. You will probably need to provide workmen's comp for your actors and your tech people. Consult Actors' Equity for specifics ASAP. Equity can penalize you financially and/or shut you down totally.

Even if you're not working with Equity, it's a good idea to take a look at insurance for your actors' welfare. How can you get the best deal on sufficient coverage? Pull out the phone book, and call around to every insurance company listed—some actually specialize in theatrical insurance, especially in large cities. Be totally honest about your situation, so you can get adequate coverage for a good price, sure. But don't scrimp and pass on buying enough insurance—especially if you find you need specific coverage for audience members. The last thing you need is a patron falling down your stairs, suing you, and ruining your company's reputation and finances before you've barely gotten started.

If you're lucky enough to be covered by an overseer, such as your landlord making it his or her policy to take care of insurance needs, you're lucky. It does happen—if you have educational sponsorship like our trio did at Wheelock Family Theatre, for instance. Their main concern was just working out a standard budget, with no complex extras. Susan Kosoff says: "My initial budgets for Wheelock Family Theatre were based on previous experience mounting shows. All insurance concerns were addressed by Wheelock College."

If that's not the fortunate position you find yourself in, what's a ballpark picture for how to go about covering your insurance needs sufficiently and economically? Here's how it's been done in the past. During the Mixed Blood Theatre's earliest days, says Jack Reuler, "We got liability insurance for ten cents per patron. We paid worker's comp with payroll taxes. There was no health insurance at the very beginning, but we hooked up with Equity after about fifteen years. Quite honestly, not all that much has changed since then, except for health insurance for staff."

A good point: Unless you are paying full-time staffers full-time salaries, it's very probable you will not be held responsible for health insurance coverage. Again, Equity requires health insurance for its members for some productions—check this out if you think such a situation could possibly pertain to you.

Unions and Union Costs: Actors' Equity Association (AEA)

Actors' Equity Association, as we've mentioned, is the professional actors' and stage managers' union, based in New York City, but governing nationwide and with related union presence abroad. Equity exerts a great deal of control over the productions it sanctions for its members to appear in. The organization is very protective of its members' interests, but will certainly be fair to a company acting in good faith as well.

Although every case is different, depending on the kind of agreement a producer or theater company reaches with Equity, the production entity may post a bond with the union. This bond insures salary coverage for the cast in case a show runs into trouble. The amount of the bond is evaluated and set by the union.

There are also a large assortment of contract categories Equity negotiates with different types of theater companies. Here's a primer:

- **BAT (Bay Area Theatres)**—This contract is specific to San Francisco–area theaters with a seating capacity of 399 seats or fewer. A company's box office revenue determines a minimum salary guarantee for Equity members. Performances are limited.

This contract is used primarily for specific productions, rather long term for everything a theater company might do.

- **CAT (Chicago Area Theatres)**—Similar to BAT. This contract has a tier system for salary minimums based on the employers' operating budgets.
- **COLT (Chicago Off-Loop Theatre)**—This contract is somewhat antiquated now. Chicago companies use a CAT arrangement instead.
- **DT (Dinner Theatre)**—This contract is dependent upon the size of a venue's seating in term of salary amounts.
- **FNPTC (Funded Non-Profit Theatre Code)**—An arrangement for small New York–based companies, which takes a piece of the company's income pie, about 15–20 percent of profits, for the purpose of Equity member reimbursements.
- **GAA (Guest Artist Agreement)**—This contract allows for a company or school to employ one Equity member temporarily.
- **HAT (Hollywood Area Agreement)**—Similar to BAT and CAT arrangements.
- **LOA (Letter of Agreement)**—Very helpful to a beginning company, this arrangement can allow a company to use Equity talent without paying steep salary fees, as long as the company demonstrates the intention to move toward a more profitable Equity deal in the future.
- **LORT (League of Resident Theatres)**—The regional theaters' contract.
- **Ninety-Nine-Seat Contract**— Allows certain companies to pay Equity members on a per-show basis in a small (99 seats or under) house.
- **Showcase Code**—Allows for Equity members' salaries to be waved for a short-term production. Minimum compensation may be required. A show has to close up permanently following its run under this agreement. The Showcase Code is tiered; different levels of compensation are required and different performance stipulations enforced, depending upon which tier the company is operating on. Contact Equity for specifics.
- **SPT (Small Professional Theatres)**—Individually tailored arrangements for companies with house capacities of 349 seats or less.
- **Stock Contracts**—For summer stock companies, mainly.
- **TYA (Theatre for Young Audiences)**—Arrangements for companies producing children's theater.
- **U/RTA (University/Resident Theater Association)**—For educational venues.

You don't have to work with union actors, especially in the very beginning. Yet eventually, most good professional companies do so. Jack Reuler of Mixed Blood continues:

"I approached Equity when I was twenty-four, because I had no idea how to manage a staff and loved the idea of a set of common rules by which we all had to abide. That naiveté proved to be a great move. Chicago had the COLT contract, and we just mimicked it, years before LORT." The combination of working with Equity and using COLT as a business model paid off for Jack.

If you should choose to approach Equity, it can be helpful for one member of your organization to build a relationship with the union, which can lead to fruitful negotiation for years to come. Your company negotiator should show him or herself to be a trustworthy individual who plays fair and respects actors' rights (always important—more to come on that shortly in this chapter). Susan Kosoff says: "The only union we've worked with is Actors' Equity. We have a point person on staff who has worked with the Equity staff since the beginning and negotiates with them on a regular basis. In the beginning years, we did a lot of our negotiating with AEA in person—it seemed more persuasive. But as time went on, we've done more via electronic communication."

Some of the other unions you may encounter are:

- **Society of Stage Directors and Choreographers (SSDC)**. The professional directors' and choreographers' union. SSDC acts for its members in contract disputes, sets salary minimums, and monitors relations between members and producers
- **The Dramatist Guild**. The national playwrights' union, which governs contracts for the production of its members' original work.
- **United Scenic Artists Union (USA) and the International Alliance of Theatrical Stage Employees (IATSE)**. The recognized unions for behind-the-scenes theatrical personnel.

A Key Point in Salary Planning

An actor's life is tough, filled with rejection, disappointment, and underappreciation. Actors work very, very hard for little pay.

So, even though you may be struggling financially yourself, show love for your actors by paying them what you can. Even if Equity doesn't require it, a stipend, no matter how small, expresses appreciation for an actor's value. So, budget accordingly. Leslie Jacobson of Horizons Theatre says: "The one thing we did start with was the commitment to pay artists. Artists very often will do whatever it is we all do for nothing, because our passion is so great. We felt that just as women don't get paid what they're worth in the work force, artists, whether male or female, don't get paid. So actually, we started paying our artists before some of the other theaters more financially solvent than we are did.

"We were one of the first small professional companies in the city to pay its actors on a regular basis. It was a profit-sharing model. I would say that historically, although we've had some very good managers, the organization's focus and energy has gone more into the artistic product than into the nurturing of the organization itself—and that's a problem.

"I don't think that's because we made a conscious decision to do that or that we voted on it. I think the kind of people who over the twenty-five years have collected around us have tended to be more the artistic type than the business type."

Your theater will get a reputation among actors as a good place to work. That, in turn, will attract wonderful performers to you and raise the bar in terms of your artistic output. Jack Reuler advises: "Get good talent and pay them—it'll come back. When talent is compromised for budgetary reasons, the mission and quality of programming are compromised."

Connect with Your Community

From the get-go, it's very important for your company's financial health for you to fully integrate with and cultivate the good will of your community at large. But of course, you can't do this cynically. Nothing is sleazier than apple-polishing. You have to genuinely like the people in your town in order to win their patronage and big-picture support.

Michael Gennaro addresses the Steppenwolf organization's genuine love for its roots and community and how that informs its business sense. Says Gennaro, "The thing that's passed on down [here], through the administrative side—this ensemble approach, and approach to teamwork, flows through everything that goes on here. I think it's one of the things somebody said early on about this place: The idea is to go as far out on the limb as you can, and the worst that can happen is, you fall off.

"That's the kind of the thinking that goes on, whether it's marketing or development or whatever, which is: Don't look at the old models. Create new ones.

"We're fortunate that we're financially viable enough that we can take risk. But at the same time, it rarely doesn't pay off. You look at these things where boards say, 'Don't try this— nobody else is doing it.' But I've rarely found a time where it doesn't work.

"You see [our people] on the stage, all they're trying to do is be better than they were the night before, and it influences the staff. They look at it and say, 'I gotta do a better job.'

"Any of those books you read about core missions of companies, you know, Hewlett-Packard, Apple, whatever—they're all the same.

"All of these people [the company members] would say, this could not have happened, perhaps, in any other city except Chicago. It's clearly their roots and their commitment to Chicago. I think it's because, A, we've got a mayor who believes in the arts and the theater. B, it was kind of a working-class, we're-gonna-do-this-no-matter-what [attitude]. If you look at the Chicago Cubs, this city supports homegrown. They're loyal to the death to their people. You watch Gary Sinise go on the *Tonight Show*, every third word out of his mouth is either 'Steppenwolf' or 'Chicago.' They're true to their word. When they come back here, they go to the Cubs games or the Bulls games, or they work with the mayor. It's not just lip service.

"I think that is a key that every company trying to get going has to remember. They can't let go of their community."

So, how exactly do you go about maximizing and utilizing the support of your community? There are easy and effective ways to do it.

Fundraising

Capital campaigns may seem like a pretty faraway option when you're first starting your theater company. After all, who's going to pledge money to your company when they have no idea who you are and when you've yet to establish a track record?

That seems like a logical assumption, but it's actually a misconception. You can successfully solicit capital right out of the box. How? One tried-and true method is to hold a fundraiser to establish your company in people's minds as early as possible.

David Zak says: "The only really effective business decision that was made [at Bailiwick Rep] was to hold a fundraiser at a downtown hotel prior to our first performance. That venue—a downtown hotel—was donated and also gave the event some prestige.

"Real planning only came later when we had a permanent home, and therefore, ongoing rent payments to make."

Talk about making lemons out of lemonade. Bailiwick Rep had yet to so much as move into a space, but still found a way to assert itself in its community and raise capital without any performances under its belt to trade on. If Bailiwick can do it, you can do it.

If you know of any business or organization that has a beautiful space, ask to borrow it, by all means. It's great if you're friendly with someone in a position to do the lending, of course, but if you are not, it's worth trading a season's worth of comp tickets to secure the privilege.

Use the media—newspapers, TV, the Web, whatever sources you can find—to give you names and contact information for wealthy arts patrons in your community at large.

Contact businesses and large corporations in your area by phone and ask who at their organization is the proper representative to invite to a community fund-raising event. Expand your search outside of your town, too, especially if you live in a small place without a lot of viable contacts—try combing through a large city nearby.

Print up a simple, classy invitation to your event, one that's very professional, yet very warm. Include, of course, all pertinent information such as date, time, etc. Send out any promotional material about your company you have already, such as a season brochure, with your invitations. Don't forget to invite your local media to cover the event—TV coverage is terrific, and at the least, some newspaper photos are needed to help herald your arrival and spread the word about your company even further. Offer yourself up for interviews, too—this is not the time to be a blushing wallflower.

The event itself doesn't have to be elaborate—serve good wine and cheese, cocktail party–style. Plan a performance to showcase your company's talent. Mingle and talk to as many folks as you can—deploy other company members to do this as well. Needless to say, when you're chatting up the fourth cousin twice removed from Howard Hughes, don't ask directly when he's going to write you a check. Just be very accommodating about answering questions, find something you truly like about each person you're talking to, and focus on that to make your interaction with that person most pleasant. Do that, and money will come your way.

Board Relations

It's never too early to start thinking about a board of directors. You first need to put up a great production or two to get people excited about being involved with your organization. Still, your preperformance fundraiser will help you get to know which people might be most enthusiastic about serving on your board early on.

It's good, indeed, to put together a board as soon as you can. The reason for this is community cohesion. A board that is tightly meshed within the community fabric will work hard on your behalf to bring new folks into your company's fold. Berkeley Repertory's leaders realized this early on. "Michael hired Mitzi [Sales] as Business Manager and Managing Director, and the two of them together were a strong team," says Susan Medak. "Because of the kind of growth the company needed, it needed to not be only artistic, but also institutional. You can't not have a sense of what you're building businesswise. A board of directors came together, as a base of support to build community support. You can't do without fund-raising. But also, it was so important that the community was saying, this is an organization that is going to be held in trust by the community.

"Helen Barber was our first board president. She was very strongly responsible for helping and keeping this institution viable. The board was deeply devoted to the theater, and the artists and board members grew tighter all the time. Caring for and feeding actors was a priority.

"In terms of a business plan, in terms of finding how to effectively start the growth of the organization, Michael and Mitzi found that help by building that board."

Grants

If you have a crystal-clear vision of where you see your company going, both artistically and commercially, and you can express this well on paper, then there very well might be grant money out there waiting for you.

Grants can come from a variety of sources—the government, private institutions, public institutions, foundations, and more. Locating grant sources is easier than you think—you can search them out on the Internet or in your public library. You can make a call to your local government and see what opportunities might be available. You can network within your civic community to find out what local grant money you might qualify for. The Foundation Center, headquartered in New York City, is a wonderful overall resource for nonprofit grant seekers. This organization offers detailed orientation to the entire process, plus a database, library, and much more. (See appendix B for more specifics.)

Almost all grants require that the applicant parties be incorporated as nonprofit organizations, so you will probably have to go through the process of incorporation before you begin sending in those proposals. To apply for a grant, you will have to go through an application process, prove financial need, and write a proposal clearly outlining your company's goals and philosophy, as stated above. You will in all probability be competing with other arts organizations for each grant you apply for. This is why it's so important to know your mission and be able to express it clearly, to convince the powers that be of its worth.

The National Endowment for the Arts is a very well-known source of funding, which, in the past, has provided much-needed support for small theaters. Susan Albert Loewenberg recalls her early experiences with the Endowment:

"We'd started getting money from the theater program of the National Endowment for the Arts. We then applied for the first institutional advancement grant. That was the first round of grants that the Endowment did to take small organizations and raise them to another level.

"It was a big deal. Fifteen organizations were selected across the United States. They weren't just theater, they were a mix of visual and performing arts organizations.

"We developed a business plan—changed our name to L.A. Theatre Works. By that time, we had begun to get out of the prison business, because a lot of the funding had dried up. The Endowment was no longer funding work in adult prisons."

It should be noted, however, that government funding for the arts has suffered in recent years, and at this time, the NEA is not a source upon which a small, start-up company should depend.

Expect to Make Financial Mistakes

Whether you get grants for your company or not, no matter how much you plan and fundraise, and know, you're bound to make financial mistakes in the beginning. This is nothing to be ashamed of. It's to be expected, as a matter of fact.

The thing to remember is to see your financial mistakes as learning experiences, so you won't repeat them. If you feel naive about money matters, weirdly, at times, that can actually work in your favor. You might unknowingly make bolder moves that actually pay off, moves you wouldn't make if you knew more and you were acting too cautiously (although that is not an endorsement of making crazy financial moves in any way, shape, or form).

Remember, too, that even if you're green and stumble around a bit at the beginning, determination to succeed can carry you past all that—if you're willing to persevere past financial hardships. Mitzi Sales tells us what happened to Berkeley Rep when a personal falling out had financial repercussions: "By the time I came, Michael and his wife were divorced—there was no patron. As a matter of fact, we had a loan of a somewhat modest size that we were repaying [his wife]. It was very much hand-to mouth. I do not think there was much of a long-range plan.

"Had I been a more experienced manager, I probably would have run in the other direction as quickly as I could, because I would have been able to look at the books and see— 'Oh, my gosh, we can't meet payroll! We can't pay rent!' Although it was practically nothing, we couldn't pay payroll taxes, even more important. But somehow, by that time, there was at least a core audience, and there was a small, small subscription base.

"There was really no fund-raising to speak of—very, very, very little. So, we sort of learned as we went, that first couple of years. Michael and I didn't take a salary for a couple of years. I was married, and my wonderful husband just supported me during that time.

"Michael lived upstairs, off the dressing room, in a little sleeping porch. The house that was raised up that became the offices and dressing rooms had a kitchen, had a couple of bathrooms, you know. So, he managed in that way.

"We just clung on."

A Novel Way to Make Big Bucks

Here's another inspirational tale of survival, dating all the way back to 1933. Things were going wonderfully in terms of audience response for Gilmor Brown's company—he had more audience than what he knew what to do with and not enough space in his theater to seat everyone who wanted to see his productions.

Around the same time this explosion of growth popularity was occurring, the fire department condemned the building. Many new companies, even though they were demonstrating signs of success, would have been financially daunted at the prospect of finding a new place.

Gilmor Brown, however, saw the move he was being forced into as an opportunity for wildly expansive growth. He declared his company would move into spectacular new multistage headquarters.

A fund drive was begun. A space was chosen for purchase, with a 195-foot stage, and three of the company's board members put up $1,500 for a down payment on it. Only another $23,000 to go, and the place was theirs!

Fired up, Brown's company incorporated a holding company to sell stock—and raised $20,000. The theater's loyal supporters began knocking on doors in Pasadena to raise cash. The academic faction in Pasadena contributed as well. And most astonishing of all, the largest percentage of cash raised to fund Brown's seemingly impossible dream came from small contributions of 50¢ or $1, which goes to show how many people believed in the work Gilmor Brown's company was doing.

Specialized Training Can Pay Off, Too

In today's professional theater, sometimes you need specialized training. We know that everyone working in the field doesn't have a degree from Harvard Business School. One of the beautiful things about drama, as an art form and as a business, is that talent, enthusiasm, hard work, and dedication of one's time can indeed get your foot in the door. It is essential for certain positions, however, that you have a firm grasp of what your work will entail before you start doing it.

Naturally, attending a solid, respected college program is a highly recommended background. Theater management programs are growing by leaps and bounds—if you really want to produce your own company, such business training might serve you better than an M.F.A. in directing. If you don't happen to have that background, even while you're starting to work on your company, squeezing a business-oriented night school course into what minuscule free time you have can help a lot. You could also gain work experience, say, if you still need to keep a day job, by taking a position in the administrative offices of an established theater company. This can be invaluable in helping you totally understand, one, the workings of an administrative office setup, and two, specifically, how finances flow correctly in a professional setting. Three, it's always great to learn from a supportive mentor.

Lyla White of the Pasadena Playhouse suggests, "I think, definitely, [there's a strong need] for business training. It's a real drawback if you have an executive director who does not understand fund-raising, who does not understand board development, who does not want to mentor a young staff . . . you need to mentor a young staff.

"I say a young staff, because what people are paid to do in the administrative part of a theater is not the same as they would make somewhere else. They come with a love for it. What you have to do is to find opportunities for them to grow, and to support them, and teach them. Celebrate their successes, and build a staff that's a team, where everyone feels heard and everybody feels that there's an opportunity not only to do their job, but to try new things and have great experiences.

"It all comes together when that curtain goes up. When that curtain goes up, we all feel a part of what happens. That is the exciting moment for us—it happens here 302 times a year and six openings. We get a chance to just say, 'We did that, and we did it together.'

"Just as on the stage, [the actors] are all playing different roles, we all play different roles in the administration. I hope my staff, and believe my staff, all feel as though they play an important part in getting that play on the stage."

Sheldon Epps (Pasadena Playhouse) seconds that opinion. "I think it's a huge problem, in the American regional theater, that there is no learning curve. You can graduate from the best graduate school as a directing student and come out having no idea how to be an artistic director. It's an entirely different skill.

"I was very, very fortunate that a grant that I got from Theatre Communications Group provided me with a residency at the Old Globe Theatre. For four years, under that grant, I had my real master's program training in what it means to work in, and to run, a large-scale institutional theater. I would have been completely lost about what the job actually is if I had not had that experience.

"I would encourage anyone who has an aspiration—and I hope there are people out there who have aspirations to do it—to try to find a way to have that kind of education. You don't get it in school. You only get it by going to work at a theater company and finding out how to keep that balance, how you keep your head, when you're thinking about not only the play on the stage, but the marketing of the play, the selling of subscriptions, the care and feeding of the board. Learn to be a good ambassador to the community, who you are depending on to provide a large part of the resources for producing that play that you want you do."

Ralph Remington (Living Stage) began his theatrical business education training with a most novel enterprise that novices could be well-served to try out themselves. Ralph advises, "Look at the business angle of theater as a means to an end. I had to learn to do that well to get where I wanted to be artistically. But doing that, then you're more marketable, which actually helps your career. It's a good thing!

"I went to college in Berkeley. One of the good things that they did was offer a production seminar, a yearlong thing where you, the student, had to create a theater from scratch on paper. You put a theater anywhere in the United States in an actual community, on an actual street, get a space, name the theater, create logos for the theater, create everything from the ground up. Budget every production, every play. Everything had to be drawn up and written out, your personnel, everything.

"It was great. For me, once the idea was on paper, I knew I could do it in life. I'm surprised colleges don't do more of that—it would help students a lot."

Keep Your Marketing Focus: The Best Basic Strategy

At this early stage, you probably don't have a lot of money available for marketing. You may, in fact, be relying on free public service announcements on TV and radio, free ads in free newspaper circulars, and a grassroots poster-hanging campaign in your community. Believe it or not, that's okay. (More on the details of marketing in chapter 6.)

You need to learn your most important marketing lesson, one that will serve you throughout your company's lifespan, before you take on any marketing ploys that are more complex: Keep focused on the main purpose of your company.

If you keep track of that main purpose, you can communicate it to your potential audience clearly and continuously, and people will come to see your work. It's important not to get too distracted by other details, like newfangled programming schemes and sticking your finger into a multitude of other pies. Concentrate on your company's main reason for existing in the first place.

Dona Lee Kelly talks about how she and the Jean Cocteau Repertory Company are making sure that their diverse programming practices do not detract from their core mission: "You have a lot of specific priorities. When I came into the company, they were doing so many different things that really moved the focus of this administration away from the core activity. The core activity is producing great theater. That's what it is. Getting people into the seats—that's another thing. Then, we also had the Student Matinee Program, which is secondary, but another important aspect, and that really took specific focus.

"Also, with David [Fuller], I've been pushing to really articulate the artistic vision. We have what's called the New Classic Readings Series, and it's part of our program, but again, I wanted form. It has to be focused—I have to tell funders, 'These are the reasons we are doing this.' Not only to tell funders, but that the whole organization is focused on it—that we're not just doing a reading, but we're doing it for a number of things that are going to serve the organization.

"They also had an evening of bringing new people into the theater, but again, that takes away from your core activity. It's really getting back to articulating artistic growth, changes, and initiatives."

First Season Financial Goals

Of course, your main goal is to make it to a second season. But what are some of the other goals you should shoot for financially for your first season?

To Turn a Profit

This is pretty obvious. Yet, it doesn't always happen so easily. Sometimes, it takes a while for a theater company to make a little money, perhaps beyond season one.

If that seems to be what you're facing, don't freak out. Try not to rack up too much debt. To avoid debt, a little extra capital, raised however you can raise it, sometimes makes that small difference you need. Susan Kosoff (Wheelock Family Theatre) says, "The first few years, we did all right. We were in the black, and the college continued to support us; they have remained very loyal to us. They give us a stipend; it's not huge, but it certainly has helped. Many times, it's made the difference between what we've been able to make and what we've needed.

"We were lucky. We got a couple of grants early on. That was kind of good, in the beginning."

To Be Able to Pay for Marketing

It's a great sign if you can find the cash to upgrade your quality of marketing. Cash well spent on a judiciously selected newspaper ad that will reach a lot of people really does bring in patrons.

To Be Able to Pay Yourself a Salary of Some Kind

During your first season, maintenance is your goal. This means that even though you may be making a little money, you need to put it back into the company. Pay your expenses, pay your actors, and pay your crew. Then, pay yourself last. If at all.

You will make more money eventually if you stick to your focus and make your art the best that you can make it, so be patient. It will be tempting to treat yourself to a little of those box office profits—but keep your hand out of the cookie jar.

So, set yourself a goal of a $1 salary by season's end. This money you can take without guilt and with a great feeling of accomplishment. That $1 is literally the sign that your hard work is paying off! Just don't spend it all in one place.

Maybe you'll find you can pay yourself a salary of more than $1. Wouldn't that be great? It just might happen.

To Be Able to Make Sense of Your Taxes

I have just one thing to say—save your receipts.

Oh, sure, you need to find a good tax preparer or accountant to help you out in the end, but before that occurs, save every scrap of paper that comes with everything you buy. Put it in a clearly marked file folder or box, and don't lose that file folder or box.

Also, save all your payroll and expenditure information. Save all paperwork pertaining to fees you pay a union, if applicable.

Save receipts for major purchases. Save the receipt you got when you bought that light bulb during your first tech weekend. You would be amazed at how many theater folks tend to flake out when it comes to the drudgery of organizing financial information. Just do it as you go along throughout the year, and you'll be amazed at how much time and tax money it could save you in the future. Use your computer, loaded with a financial record-keeping software, to help you keep track of income and expenses and project budgets and to organize your numbers for tax time.

Future Shock

It may seem rather ridiculous now, at this time of your humble beginnings, to dream about where you'll be financially in five years. Go there, though. You need an idea of where you're going in order to get there.

Terrence Dwyer (La Jolla Playhouse) believes in the power of positive planning. Here, he discusses some of his hopes for the next five years of his phenomenally successful company.

"We continue to grow and expand, simultaneously in an artistic and business direction. I'd like to enhance our presence in the field nationally. I'd like to work on building an endowment to fund our new building.

"We have a certain set of responsibilities artistically: Integrity. Unpredictability. More visibility sometimes broadens your scope, and your cash flow."

La Jolla Playhouse takes the impression it's making on its audiences very seriously. It aims to grow, but very smartly pays attention to what its patrons expect and enjoy as well. This brings up another important point in long-term financial planning—proper product evaluation, which you must always keep in mind.

What are your products, the shows you offer the public? Your artistic output is what you're selling, plain and simple. So, to make money, to some extent, pay attention to feedback and give the people what they want.

Some foolish theater folks dismiss audience reactions as the impressions of lowbrows who don't really understand the intellectual genius that's been so generously parked in front of them. Theater is for everybody; don't be an elitist. The audience is smarter than many artists give them credit for, and if the audience gets wind of the fact that you think they're a pack of morons, they'll stop coming to your theater, and you won't make any money.

Ask a few experienced theater personnel, maybe a director, actor, or writer you respect, to come see your company's work and give you an unvarnished opinion. Invite as many of these people that you can, in fact. Better yet, from a financial point of view, ask a producer with a good track record or an administrator from a successful theater company to attend and to give you an honest evaluation of your show's commercial potential.

If you hear negative comments, push past emotion, and think of them as an opportunity for information. This doesn't mean you should take nasty, jealous, or empty, mean-spirited "advice" seriously—blow off comments you know are just catty.

But do ask questions of those people you trust and respect. You don't have to use every suggestion. Still, any kind of feedback will help you determine whether you should jettison something you're doing that, in the end, will cost you money. If tons of people tell you the same comment over and over, by the way—it's a safe move to believe them and make an objective change.

Proceed with Caution

Go slowly when it comes to money matters in your first season. Jack Reuler (Mixed Blood) suggests not overplaying your hand, either in terms of planning or trying to do too much, too soon: "Don't overproject box office. Remember, the more you do, the more you lose—that's nonprofit producing."

Work on making your first production the best it can be. This will help get your name out there, which will bring in an audience, which will, over the longer haul, help your company to become a financially viable organization.

CHAPTER 4

FINDING OUR CORE ACTING TROUPE

A truth accepted by many theater people is, casting is everything; once you assemble the appropriate people for the appropriate roles, much of your work is already done. I think it is true that an actor's persona can bring a lot to the table, yet I also believe you must carefully evaluate a performer's talent, technical abilities, and team-player tendencies before making a final casting decision.

When you are putting together an acting company, it's vital you consider your overall priorities first, whether they be fitting players to specific shows or roles, qualities you prize in a person you'd like to work with, or whatever else matters crucially. Then, you should take care to be sure actors mesh well with you, your director, fellow cast members, and your ultimate goals and vision for the work. Even if you intend to job actors in, you must use the same evaluative method.

The only time you really have to do this is during the audition process. A well-planned tryout schedule is the ideal way to screen. There are tricks that never fail to reveal the best, and worst, of your potential cast members. They are fully covered within this chapter.

Every company profiled is surprisingly different in how it has handled the task of casting and what its casting philosophy has evolved into. Casting can be done by a certain practical theory to some extent, but it also happens by feel, as when you know someone is right—or wrong.

To be good at casting, and to do the best by your company, approach it like a psychologist might approach a patient. Evaluate technique, but use your intuition, your people-reading skills as well.

Most importantly, trust your instincts. You already know inside what it is you really want, and your gut feelings are the way you reaffirm that knowledge to yourself.

Good Vibrations

First off, go into auditions with the best intentions yourself. Don't expect trouble. Don't get off on the power trip of having people reveal themselves to you through their work just so you can blow them off. Actors are a vulnerable lot. Their art comes from a deep, emotional place. They suffer almost constant rejection from idiots who do not understand the finer points of the acting craft, who only understand they need to cast someone taller, thinner, shorter, or fatter. Make it your business to understand where actors are coming from. Run your auditions humanely from the start, and you'll give actors hope regarding the quality of the production you might all end up working on.

If you are not an actor yourself, it would be a wonderful thing if you'd pick up a good book on acting method before you even start the audition ball rolling. Of course you're busy, but try to make the time to do even a little bit of reading on the complexities of what your actors do on a daily basis. I guarantee, you'll be impressed with the effort that goes into good performance. A classic primer to check out would be *Respect for Acting* by the legendary Uta Hagen.

The beauty of an actor's dedication is very well illustrated in the following reminiscence of Paul Zuckerman, who talks about the communal determination of the Chicago City Limits acting company: "I would say laziness wasn't there. This was a group, when we moved to New York—seven of us stayed in two hotel rooms for a year. We had no money, really, so all of our time was spent rehearsing, talking. The religion is loud and clear here—our series of adversities and successes really binds people together strongly. You become a family.

"I think there was a stubbornness we had in common, an up-against-the-wall mentality. Maybe it was that we were children of the sixties and had that glimmers-of-the-revolution sort of orientation. The adversity, in some sense, forged strength, and the difficulties became challenges, and small victories became major victories. And you know what, we didn't come out of a sort of traditional theater background, and I feel that we might not have taken chances if we'd known more. It was a riskier theater. I remember a reviewer early on saying the thing he liked about us the most was that we weren't so stage-smart.

"You had to learn how to do things that maybe you would have been taught somewhere else—like, how do you end a scene? Well, you had to figure out how to end a scene—does it come full circle, yeah, that works sometimes, or do you resolve a conflict, yeah, that works sometimes, or does the relationship evolve, yeah, that works sometimes—but you don't know that till you've done a bunch of those things, unless people teach you that someplace."

Giving Notice

Whether you're placing your casting notice in the newspaper or posting it on a callboard, you want to make sure it's specific. If the roles you're casting call for precise physical requirements, say so. If it' s musical talent you seek and you need singers who act or actors who move well, say so. If age requirements come into play, do tell. If you require that your cast give up large amounts of their time to rehearsal, be up front about this.

You also have to come clean about money. If you intend to pay your company a stipend only, say so. If the positions you're casting are salaried, make sure this is clear. If participating in your production is sanctioned to earn performers points toward membership in Equity, state this fact. If you can only use union actors, or can only use non-union actors, explain this in your casting notice.

Don't be concerned that such honesty will limit the number of actors who will be auditioning for you. You can always hold more extensive auditions beyond your initial try-out date. You can't, however, lie to people about what your production can offer them and not expect them to bail on you once they discover the truth. At the same time, be flexible regarding your casting needs. Don't write out role descriptions so rigidly that you aren't open to that happy accident—a great actor showing up who maybe doesn't look exactly as you visualized, but who can certainly slap on a fake mustache.

Also, it is really recommended that you try to budget for some form of payment for your performers. If you are working with Equity, as you know, varied forms of compensation will be required. If not, even a small financial token of appreciation is the fair way to go. It will also foster good feelings, as will paying each of your actors exactly the same amount. You want camaraderie, not hierarchy. The only exception to this rule is, again, Equity specifications you are required to fulfill.

Jack Reuler (Mixed Blood) was completely honest with his initial company members at the time he hired them, especially about the upstart nature of his enterprise. He remembers back to the circumstances of his early hires: "It was really a company. We were offering ten weeks of employment at, I think, $110 a week. We were looking for people who could work those kind of shifts.

"I'd picked the plays, so I sort of had this little grid. The first season we did *Status Quo Vadis*, a play called *Brother Champ*, an original play, then a play, perhaps the first and only production, where all the Native characters in the play were played by Native actors. Then, we did a tour of *Dutchman*—Lou Bellamy, who was the Artistic Director of Penumbra, directed that. Then, another play called *Black Cycle*—sort of a forgettable piece. That was our first season; we did ten weeks, five shows. They ran from two to three weeks each.

"I've always valued human chemistry over talent. If I had to make a trade, it was, who could sacrifice a summer to be in a hundred-year-old fire station with twenty other people? I was still so thankful people wanted to participate. It was really, 'Are you sure you know what you're getting into?' Because I certainly didn't know.

"A lot of those people from that first company stayed for a long time. Don Cheadle—I think he was twenty-two—did his first show, an original play called *Liquid Skin*, in which he played a man going through a sex change. It was really more about the people around him and their reactions, a really interesting piece of art. He was young and new, and he was great then, and he knew he was going to be a star. He stayed and did three or four shows between '88 and about '93, and then he directed a couple of shows.

"I think the greatest of the people who have worked here are the ones who have stayed working here. A lot of people come back. I think in the earlier years, Mixed Blood was a stepping stone to get somewhere else, and now it's a place to aspire to."

Material Concerns

Prior to the first day of your auditions, you need to sit down with your director and musical director (if you're working with one) and decide as a team what, if any, specifics you're looking for in terms of casting. Make a general casting blueprint that you can refer back to when you need it. Susan Kosoff, of Wheelock Family Theatre, says: "We started with *Alice's Adventures in Wonderland,* and that's a show that is so dependent on Alice. We knew who we wanted for that when we chose the play. We wanted to do the play because we knew it was enough of a children's classic to be appealing, but we also knew who we wanted to play that role, and we got her.

"We cast some other people that we had worked with in the past, and we had open auditions. We talked to everybody we knew. Over time, we've gotten better and better people at auditions. Our first show was a musical, so we needed people who could sing. For example, the woman that we got to play Alice had gone back to school at Emerson College, so she had a couple of friends who we used in the show. We sort of called on past people that we knew.

"We just did a variety of things. We had an open call, people came, and we tried to put together the best cast we could put together. We now have people who have been in eighteen, twenty shows with us.

"We did [in 2001] *Rebecca of Sunnybrook Farm,* and there's a woman in Boston, an African American woman considered one of the best in Boston [who was in it]. She's said to me, 'I will be in any show you ask me to do once a year, because I believe in what you do.' Then, there are other people who want to work, like the quality of our work, and audition for us. As we're choosing the plays, we think, frankly, in terms of, this person could play this, or this person could play that.

"We do try always to have a mix in our casts. Our casts are large; that's another thing that's different about us from other theaters. We don't limit cast size. Because we also want to get a lot of young people involved, one of the things we've had to do in recent years, because we've had so many student matinees, is that some of the smaller parts for younger people will be double- or triple-cast. We always try to have a mix in our casts of people we've worked with before and new people. We want to bring on new professionals, and we also want to bring on new young people to develop their talent."

That Obscure Object of Desire

If you're putting together a permanent company, in addition to being concerned with fitting material needs, you're going to want to work with people you like. Also, you're human, so you're going to be attracted to those individuals who satisfy your desire for certain tangible, or intangible, personal qualities.

The qualities that are supremely coveted in actors are as far-ranging as the companies these performers may be judged by. Still, there are a few things a good leadership might keep an eye out for. Says David Zak, of Bailiwick Repertory, "Many people in Chicago are great at a very naturalistic style. We were looking for people with excellent classical training, especially vocally. And of course, if you look hard enough, you can find them!"

From Rick Lombardo, of New Repertory Theatre: "I look for people whose first goal, overall, is to commit to the artistic product to their fullest extent. The people I know here, I think, share the same human and artistic values. For example, the quality of our last season [2000–2001] was extraordinary. So, the question becomes, can we do really challenging work this year, artistically developing from last year? I lean on the artists really hard and want them to have team values."

David Fuller, of Jean Cocteau Repertory, opines, "Everybody must have kindness. When I went to drama school as an actor in the seventies, Alec Guinness came and talked to us. He had just finished shooting *Star Wars*, and he was starting to become so famous worldwide.

"We were talking about method versus a technical way of acting, which all young actors have trouble with: Which is the best, if you have to choose? I don't believe there's a choice, I believe it's a compilation of all of it, but anyway, someone said to Alec Guinness, 'What do you think about the actor who lives their part between takes, sustains their character, takes their character home with them?'

"He said, 'I should think they're insane, wouldn't you?' I thought, that's true. He went on to say that his biggest advice to give a young actor was, 'It's most important to be a good human being.'

"That's kind of how we run this organization. We may become an internationally famous repertory theater, or we may not, but at least we're going to be good people as we run it. I naturally gravitate away from 'show business people,' which is probably why I'm in nonprofit theater. There is a type that I see often that I just want to take to the side and say, 'Could you just stop it?' I don't want to get too existential, but take a look at the sky, take a deep breath.

"It comes with age, probably, but you have to assemble people with whom you like to work, first of all. People with whom you can laugh—that's very important. People who have innate kindness. You just have to be nice—otherwise, what's the point?"

Be Ready for Anything

Right before your tryout date, go through one of the scripts you'll be doing, and pull out two meaty monologues—one for men and one for women. Or if you'd prefer, choose a classic piece or any other piece you feel will be challenging and evocative of the work you intend actors to do within your company.

Actors will probably be bringing in a prepared monologue of their own. Even if you want them to do that, a cold reading of your choice can be a great indicator of how well a performer can think on his or her feet. Don't be cruel, though—there's nothing clever or cool about throwing a completely foreign bunch of sides at a performer and saying, "Wow me."

Be considerate—give a little information to your auditioners, even though they'll be reading cold. Once you've chosen your material, don't just rip a page out of the script and photocopy it—retype it onto a clean sheet, and add a little general paragraph at the top of the page regarding who the character is, an overview of the scene, and a brief description of the play's plot. This is a really great courtesy to the actors.

The audition can also consist of a dialogue scene between two characters. Your stage manager customarily reads the scene with the actor, so you, the producer, and the director can concentrate on watching the actor's work.

You also want to put together a brief bio sheet for your auditioners to fill out. This is how to gather names, phone numbers, union affiliations, if any, even notations of any special skills a performer might want to mention (sword swallowing can really perk up an intermission). Have your auditioners note their availability, so that you can be aware of potential schedule conflicts.

Seriously, though, leave room for those happy surprises. Oftentimes, a performer's unexpected skills can be a real boon to your company. Here's how Leslie Jacobson (Horizons) approached her company's first spate of tryouts—with a completely open mind. "We did have formal auditions initially. There were some people that I sort of invited, based on some work we'd done together in other places. The auditions would be pretty rigorous. Because of the way we were working in those early days, we were looking for people who were talented performers, but also had an interest in creating material for themselves and for others. Who were able to write as well as that.

"You know, not everybody's interested in that, and that's totally fine. But there are people who are, and we got some extremely talented people who had very interesting skills that we wove into the shows. One person was a professional puppeteer, as well as an actress and a writer. Some people were singers or dancers as well. The shows used a lot of highly theatrical devices to keep them interesting and entertaining, as well as thought-provoking.

The Audition Process

Plant your stage manager or assistant stage manager in the waiting area to meet and greet, man a sign-in sheet, and escort each auditioner into your inner sanctum.

Each actor should have filled in his or her bio sheet and been given the opportunity to study sides ("sides" is the term used to refer to the scene, or copy, that an auditioner provides, which the actors will use when they audition) give an actor to before being seen. When an actor is ushered in to read for you, take a moment to read over the résumé. Pull out an interesting fact and use it as an icebreaker. It will make the actor feel comfortable and more in control of things. Understand how nervous this person must be. Treat an auditioner as you would wish to be treated if you were in his shoes.

As an actor is reading for you, keep a poker face. Never sneer or laugh or look bored. Don't let your eyes glaze over, even if you're bored out of your mind. It's nice to smile after a performer has finished reading, whether you like his work or not. If you don't think you're going to be able to use this actor, thank him graciously for his time, and tell him you'll be in touch. This is very important. Actors tend to check their messages obsessively—it stinks when you're waiting to hear about a job, and you never get any form of reply.

Even if you don't cast an actor, call and say thanks anyway. Keep it brief, thank him for his time and talent, and simply state you'll be going in another direction. Don't criticize, get personal, or be rude. But definitely say something. If you do like an actor's work and can see he would be perfect in the lead, play it cool; you don't want to get an actor's hopes up, then end up casting someone who shows up later and seems even more perfect.

Is it acceptable to take the recommendation of collaborators and friends during the casting process? Of course—the opinion of an artist you really respect can lead you to finding really amazing people. Steppenwolf, needless to say, only works with artists of the highest caliber. Yet, a lot of the company's inclusions have been as a direct result of a good word being put in. Says Michael Gennaro, "The company is up to thirty-three members; there is no formal rhyme or reason as to why people are brought in or not.

"Over the years, it had kind of been, [company members] would work with someone and go, 'Yeah, this person works like us. They have the same sensibility.' The artistic directors were always members of the company. Gary was for a while; Jeff was. And the managing executive directors were always people who had been, not so much ensemble members, but the kind of people who were around or had been in productions and kind of had a business sense to them.

"In '95, the company and the board decided to make a change, because they had to step up, I think, the business end of the company. That's when Martha Lavey, who was in the company and still is, came on as Artistic Director, and me, the first person from the outside, who's run other companies. Over the past couple of years, I think there's been maybe a little more strategic thinking involved in inviting people into the company. But it's still kind of a very informal process, one that probably will never be formalized, nor should it ever be formalized.

"Some have left over the years. Some have left and come back. Glenne Headley left, but then came back when we won the Medal of Arts. We invited her and she came, and everybody started crying, and she said, 'I'm back.' It's kind of like the Supreme Court—once you're in, you're in. It's a lifer thing.

"What's key now is, we're also at a point in time where these people have all matured to an age and a point in their lives where we have to start looking toward the future, and youth. Not only youth—I think the two important things are, youth and diversity. They gotta be organic to what the place is about, or it's not worth doing."

Putting Together a Company That Will Go the Distance

Personality is a crucial aspect to the casting process. Actors go into auditions with their best face forward, and who could blame them? They want to get the job they're up for. Unfortunately, if an actor's true personality is less than accommodating and you cast him, this could be big trouble. An actor with a monster ego is an evil snowball that rolls downhill, picking up speed, until it finally smashes your production into smithereens. Often, other actors get infected with swelled-head syndrome, and soon, you've got mutiny on your hands. If you truly strive to put together a company that will last, you need to detect these issues before you settle on your actors (after which it will be a total hassle to make changes).

How to detect trouble before it rears its head? Listen carefully to the way an actor relates to you. Do you feel it's fake or genuine? Does he or she sound like a real team player, who wants to work for the good of the show, who understands that if the show works, it benefits everyone? Does the actor frown even slightly regarding issues of money or billing, if you so happen to drop these topics into the chatter? (A closer look here: Why not state flatly that your cast will be billed in alphabetical order? An ego-stoked actor will almost always register some level of dismay about that.) Most importantly, what is your gut telling you about this actor? Do you like this individual? Do you like this individual's work? If so, cast away, my friend. If not, keep looking. It's your call.

Mitzi Sales (Berkeley Rep) is of the opinion that an actor's willingness to play parts of any size is a good indication he or she will benefit a company. "We had a small core, and those actors did every role. That was very good for the theater," says Ms. Sales.

"I think that the only thing they had in common was the desire to perhaps work in a company together. So, there was a certain willingness to play small roles, to not always be in a featured or leading role. They recognized the importance of supporting each other. They're actors, so there was a certain amount of ego and all of that. But I do think there was a remarkable amount of loyalty from a great many individuals.

"Eventually, people drift off to Los Angeles or come to New York, of course. But a great many people stayed for a rather long time. Fortunately, the San Francisco Bay area is a very appealing place, and it does attract artists. We were fortunate to be in a place where there were a certain number of people. ACT was graduating people, and so on."

Be Professional

If you want to attract good people to your company, present yourself in a professional light. Actors want to work for good leadership, just as you want to work with good actors.

Keep your demeanor smooth. You will catch more flies with honey than you will with vinegar, so said the wise man. Show your auditioning actors right away that you're a cool, organized, fair, reasonable boss. State flatly that you intend to handle conflict or problems in this company with negotiation, honesty, and common sense. Make sure you stress communication above all—tell your potential cast members that you'll be up front with them at all times and that all you ask in return is that they will be similarly clear with you.

Ralph Remington makes it very clear what his reign at The Living Stage is going to be like—and has a very strong idea of the impression a company's leader should be giving. "The company is comprised of myself, an artistic director, and four actors, and then there's a production staff of about three people and an education staff. So, that is a way for everything to be aligned—we are aligned, the community is aligned, everything that's going into Arena is properly aligned. The right hand always knows what the left is doing."

Winding Things Up

Huddle with your director and musical director, if you've got one, post-audition to choose actors for callbacks. Decide which actors might fit which roles, and call them back in to read more material for you, especially if you are torn between two or more actors for one role or one space to be filled within the company. Callbacks are also a great chance to test how quickly actors can learn music or pick up dance steps.

At callbacks, feel free to bring in pairs of actors to read together, in varying combinations, to help you decide final casting. Some actors are so competitive, they don't even want to sit in the same room during callbacks. Petty behavior? Sure, and possibly an indicator that this person might be difficult to work with. Keep in mind that callbacks exist for you to exhaust all casting possibilities. A really professional actor will always understand your true purpose and won't be sensitive.

A quick aside: Don't discount amateurs completely, either. Sound weird? It's not. I've had good experiences directing actors with very little previous experience, who just kind of show up at auditions and blow you away with their raw talent. I wouldn't recommend you use such a person for a permanent resident position, but for a job-in, a greener performer can be very malleable in the right role. Use the callback process to determine how directable such a person might be.

Many moons ago, Pasadena Playhouse proved this casting theory can work. Gilmor Brown regularly used Pasadena residents as extras, and sometimes in major roles as well. A lawyer named Sam Hinds, for instance, actually went on to a film acting career from his initial experiences doing shows with Brown.

Once you've seen all the auditioning actors and held callbacks, it's the moment of truth: selecting your final cast. Don't stress out. Go with your instincts, mellowed with your intelligence. Your director is the production team member with the most valuable insight here. Who does he or she feel will be easiest to work with, give the best performance, have the right quality for the right role, have the most talent and versatility in order to handle a demanding company spot? Let your director be free to make the primary choices. As producer, you can suggest or veto, but this is properly the director's turf.

You've just foolproofed your casting process the best you possibly can.

Finding Your Artistic Soul Mates

Some companies are formed strictly out of ideology, rather than out of formal auditions. This fits certain specific company needs, say those where its founders' mission includes performing its original work as well as writing, directing, and producing it. Essentially, this means that once you've found your artistic soul mates, your obvious predilection is to cast yourselves.

A Traveling Jewish Theater is a great example. ATJT's three original members were, of course, drawn together by their collective need to explore the same cultural and ethnic issues on stage. Helen Stolzus, a fourth ensemble member who joined in 1987, was the perfect addition, in that she came into the company interested in the same forms of exploratory expression.

Finding people who feel the same passion for the same type of work you do is essential if you want such a casting arranging to work out as well as ATJT's has.

A Casting Coup

This is the tale of how a small, but highly regarded experimental company became graced with fabulous star power in very little time. This infusion of talent took the company in a new and lucrative direction as well. "We became one of the major, important, smaller experimental theater companies in the United States. We had quite a reputation," says Susan Albert Loewenberg, of L.A. Theatre Works.

"Around 1985, someone brought an idea to me that I resisted at first. I had certainly never worked with any name actors—it didn't interest me. I wasn't interested in conventional theater at all. Neil Simon and Wendy Wasserstein were the last things on my mind! However, the idea was that there was a significant resource in Los Angeles—famous actors. They were theater-trained, but they were famous because of film and television. They had no way to ply their craft in any significant way.

"One of the things that I had felt keenly for a long time was that I could never figure out why most theater was so terrible. I realized it was because we didn't have great, world-class directors working on things. We didn't have the great international directors coming to Los Angeles—the Peter Halls—we didn't have these people for a variety of reasons. Probably because the centers of power weren't really interested. The Taper never invited these people; it just didn't happen.

"So slowly, I became convinced that we should do something. We formed a group of thirty-four very famous actors, including Stacy Keach, Richard Dreyfuss, Julie Harris, Helen Hunt, Marsha Mason, Ted Danson, Ed Asner. I mean, it was a pretty historic group. We told everybody they had to kick in $6,000 each, because I didn't want it to be something they were doing as a part-time hobby. They had to make a commitment.

"The group was very energetic. We were going to do plays as a LORT theater, six-week runs, bring in world-class directors. We called ourselves A Project of L.A. Theatre Works. It was a very exciting and interesting time.

"We did our first benefit. Oddly enough, we had this idea to do a radio show. We got KCRW involved, our local public radio station. We recorded a play, which they aired live in performance as it was being recorded, onstage. Grant Tinker was running the Culver Studios at the time and gave us a huge soundstage.

"We had eight hundred people there; we charged $250 a ticket. We sold, I think, six hundred tickets at that price and $50 tickets for the other two hundred. We had Steven Spielberg there, we had Barry Diller there, we had Mo Ostin there, we had everybody there. It was fabulous! We did *Once in a Lifetime* starring John Lithgow, who's part of our group, and Marsha Mason. I think, of the thirty-four actors, twenty-five were in it. Helen [Hunt] was in it. Of course, she wasn't famous then, she was a young actress. She was getting there, but she certainly wasn't where she is today.

"It was a fabulous performance, but it was a lousy recording! I don't even know how it was broadcast, it was so bad. It's a shame, because it's not salable. Nobody knew what they were doing. People loved the radio show, they weren't that critical, but when I look at it today, I couldn't even use it. But the live show was great!"

Here's to all of the casting triumphs in your future.

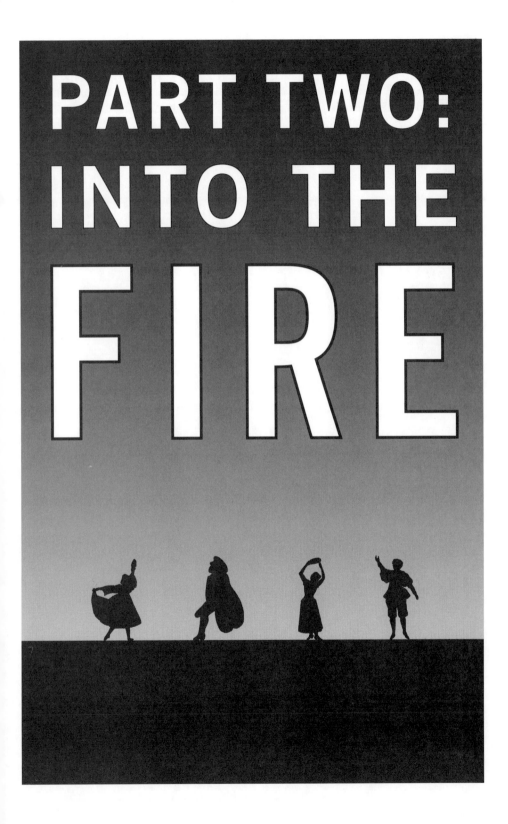

CHAPTER 5

MOUNTING THAT FIRST PRODUCTION

Preparation, production, and rehearsal is not rocket science, but for sure, it's key to whether your show—and your company as a whole—develops a decent reputation in your community. Your first show sets the tone. Your goal is to do a fantastic job, yes, but also not to raise the bar so colossally high that you can't get over it.

Should you need to make changes, jump in with enthusiasm, and without fear. Even the best theater organizations have needed to regroup at certain points. It helps, too, to remember that the best time to implement changes is when you're first starting out. No intelligent person—be it a funder, an audience member, or even a critic—could possibly think less of a company attempting to enact positive adjustments at the beginning of its life span. It's when you don't make the changes you really ought to make that people tend to look at you funny.

Get Your House in Order

Not to waste your time or insult your intelligence with elementary stuff you already know, but scheduling rules, my friend. When you're running a company, you've got to be scrupulous about keeping track of audition dates, leaving adequate time for a rehearsal period, and locking in show times. Don't leave everything to your director and stage manager; stay on top of things, and double-check their work by putting together your own planning system. Here are a few useful tips to get you organized.

How much time will you need for a fully scheduled production period? Give yourself, ideally, three months for preproduction (which includes making a budget, choosing a venue, interviewing directors, and preparing auditions). Then, six weeks, from auditions to opening night, could serve as your production period (although you could do it in four weeks if you had to). If you are developing original material or a new play, you will probably need a longer rehearsal period.

What You Don't Know about Rehearsals Can Hurt You

Your director bears the direct responsibility for a production's rehearsal period, it's true. It behooves you, needless to say, to stay very involved and informed in what specifically goes on during rehearsals.

Keep abreast of how things are progressing. Drop into rehearsal often, and be a positive presence. Ask questions, in a friendly way. Stay in the loop.

This doesn't give you license to be an annoying pest or a ruler with an iron fist, horning in on the director's turf. Give him the space and peace of mind to make the production great. If there's a problem, assert your self and help fix it. Don't offer too much advice if it's not really necessary, or bend the director's ear with insignificant chitchat, or discuss the state of theater in today's postmodern world. There isn't tons of time to waste, especially for the rehearsal of a first show.

Susan Kosoff (Wheelock) discovered the time-crunch factor firsthand. She's made it work, though, from the first production to the present day. "The planning time had been great, as you might imagine, for the two productions that first season," says Ms. Kosoff. "But the actual rehearsal time was dictated by our contract with Equity—three weeks, five days. Actually, sometimes, we've done a week more, especially with musicals. But pretty much, we stick to about a month for rehearsal. I will say, there are times when I wish we had more, but almost always, it's okay."

When You Want to Make It Better

The more you watch your show, the more you'll want to improve it.

You can't help wanting to. This is not to say you were tremendously dissatisfied with the staging, writing, or casting; you wouldn't have put the show up in the first place if you felt it had major flaws. It's simply that the audience, any audience, no matter how large or how small it may be, starts to shift your perspective. The audience becomes a teacher, and if you're smart, you'll become its student. If you are "only" producing the show, not directing it, you will probably want to feed any suggestions you have for improvement back through the director. He is at the helm of the creative end of the production, after all.

Once the show is in front of an audience, you start to see where the biggest laughs come. You start to fixate on that pacing problem toward the end of act one. You subtly study faces in your crowd—are they smiling? Scowling? Are eyeballs glazing? Certain scenes seem to drag on for a century; others feel like they need a little something more.

Maybe you need to do some reworking.

Go to your next performance armed with a pad and paper. Note the audience's reactions. Note your own responses to what does and doesn't work. Nobody else has to see what you're writing, so let it rip uncensored. You'll quickly see, when you read over the notes you've made post-performance, which points matter, and you can then take action to correct problems.

Let's look at a few typical rework scenarios you might have to deal with.

Restaging a Scene or Two

This is the easiest fix to achieve.

As soon as you recognize a staging problem within performance, you should alert your director, cast, and crew. Call a rehearsal to make your adjustments as soon as possible. Your director should tell your actors prior to this rehearsal that a change will be made, so that no one is thrown off adversely. Actors are habitual creatures. Their sense of security comes from routine and the aspects of a production they feel they can count on, and therefore have some sense of control within. To redo a scene, an actor may have to adjust his or her character motivation slightly and, for sure, will have to adapt visually and spatially, often very quickly before doing an actual performance and making the audience think what's new feels natural.

So, expect at least one cast member to protest or have a mini–nervous breakdown at news of a staging change. Reassure this sensitive soul. More importantly, make sure the director takes care to make this actor comfortable with the adjustment. Allow extra rehearsal time when you're restaging. The director should reblock clearly, and then drill, drill, drill. Changes must be repeated ad nauseum, so cast members can get them into their bones. This will result in not only better staging in performance, but actors' confidence in carrying them out.

If you've only got one pickup, or maintenance, rehearsal scheduled per week, and there's absolutely no other time to thoroughly cover your restaging, then it's okay to use all of that pickup time—just this once—to get the adjustment down cold. It's ideal to hold one restaging rehearsal, though, then hold a second maintenance run-through rehearsal of the entire play incorporating the restaging, so actors and crew can get a complete sense of fusion before they embark on a full-fledged performance.

Restaging a Larger Portion of the Production

A bigger fish to fry, obviously. First of all, you're going to have to suspend your performance schedule, hopefully just briefly. The truth is, if large sections of your show really need to be restaged, your show will never make it.

Work out a rehearsal schedule with your director that accomplishes all of your restaging goals in as timely a fashion as possible. Be real when it comes to the amount of time you'll need to allot for this. Next, hammer out an arrangement with your venue, if need be. You may be required to pay for stage space even though your show will be dark. That's actually not a bad deal, because you can probably use the space to rehearse during what would have been performance times, and your cast will feel somewhat reassured that things will be back to normal soon.

Now, here's a more difficult situation: Your venue wants you to give back your performance reservations, so it can make money on another show that's ready to go up. Initially, the venue may promise you can reserve more time when you're ready to perform again, but in reality, unless you can reserve the time that very second and put that reservation in writing, it probably won't work out. If another show is indeed put into your performance slot and it turns out to be a long-term moneymaker, the venue isn't going to pull it so you can remount when you're ready. This is just common sense in terms of business.

If you can't get a firm commitment from your venue, I say, find a new venue and start fresh. You need to present your show in a place that's got positive energy. You want a supportive, welcoming environment. It's out there—just find it.

Replacing Key Personnel

Sadly, if you discover that your director isn't capable of staging—or restaging—the production to your satisfaction, he or she is going to have to be replaced.

If your director isn't getting the job done, first sit down and try to talk through the problems. Give your director a chance to explain. If your experience with this person tells you to believe it when you're told he knows what's up, and he outlines step-by-step to you how he plans to fix the production, takes your comments and feelings into consideration, and displays a willingness to collaborate with you until the show is shipshape, then maybe you can give your director another chance.

If you know that your director is incapable of doing the job, though, you've got to make a change. Tell your director that you do admire his initial creative vision, but that in practice, it's not feasible. Don't insult this person. Be supportive, in terms of explaining your issues with your director's performance, because the director probably will ask you quite directly what your specific criticisms are. Most directors will be professional enough not to overreact—this is probably not an unexpected turn of events. A halfway competent director will already know inside that he is not delivering the goods.

Replacing an Actor

Of course, you need to do this in the same calm, kind, rational manner as you would replacing your director. Once again, be supportive of this person's general talent, and never be abusive. State your case, and let the actor know it's just not working out and you wish him the best. (When you think about it, replacing an actor sounds a lot like breaking up with a boyfriend or girlfriend, doesn't it? You've got to get free, but you've got to be humane, too.)

There's one important factor besides feelings you must consider whenever you replace an actor, however. That factor: mutiny.

I once directed a show featuring an actress so outrageous, so in love with her own talent and fab reviews, that she started stealing scenes and verbally trashing her fellow actors—onstage. In front of the audience. It was outrageous. I fired this insubordinate individual—and guess what happened.

All three of the other actors who she'd been treating so terribly quit in solidarity.

This would appear irrational. It was, indeed, irrational. But I wasn't looking at the situation from my cast members' perspectives. I later found out that the actors who quit felt I would never fire anyone. I'd built up a strong sense of family and common support within our company, and they all counted on that. What no one had counted on was a diva exploding among us. So, when I did what I had to do, what was best for the show and was in everyone's best interest, the actors I was in fact defending were shocked, felt threatened, and attempted to reject me before I could reject them.

You can't control the actions of other people, but you can avoid unexpected mutiny by calling a cast meeting immediately after you fire an actor. Do this before you bring in a replacement. Tell your group the reasons you did it, clearly outlining the fired party's transgressions as they affected the rest of the cast. People listen to you when their own welfare is involved, when they understand you're playing on their team. Express your support of your remaining cast members. Ask them to share their feelings about what has happened. Get any misconceptions or complaints out in the open before the entire group. Clear up problems together.

Rewriting Text

Hopefully, if you're working with the writer of an original show, he or she will have a gung-ho, collaborative attitude. If not, though, you've got to expect a fight (maybe just a little squabble, maybe World War III) when you call for rewrites. Always remember this: Without the writer, you wouldn't have a show. Convey your respect. Also, don't think you know how to rewrite yourself. Feel free to express your opinions in a nice, intelligent way, but give the writer lots of credit and slack. The writer is your primary source. A good relationship with your writer is your best guarantee of production success.

You Can't Always Call Audience Reaction

When thinking about your first performances, in advance of actually doing your first show, you probably figure that there will be a certain demographic that's going to love the production. Say you're doing *The Leonard Nimoy Story* for a room full of Trekkies—it'll be a smash, right? Talk about a no-brainer.

Not so fast. A room full of Trekkies might just be your harshest critics, because they are going to have the highest expectations of any audience your company could possibly host. If a specialized audience's reaction is tepid, it doesn't necessarily mean you need to change the show, though. Sometimes, such a group will be focused on minutiae that a mainstream crowd will simply not give a hoot about.

Corey Fischer (A Traveling Jewish Theatre) found that his group's unconventional approach worked wonderfully with audiences who appreciated a fresh sensibility. Even though in a more conventional setting, initial reaction wasn't as fabulous, it was just a matter of finding an audience niche. "The very first couple of performances [we did] in Santa Monica—immediately, it was pretty clear we had something people wanted to see," Mr. Fischer recalls. "After that initial euphoria, we had some less-satisfying engagements, where we were in a more conventional setting, like a Jewish community center. Then, we did this tour, where we went to Baltimore for a theater festival.

"It was very validating, because there we were, in with our peers and colleagues, as well as general audience members. So, that was very encouraging. From there, we went to Vancouver, British Columbia, and Santa Cruz, California. Those stops were very exciting to us—all three of those engagements were not specifically for Jewish audiences. We were getting a really mixed audience, and people were responding very generously and enthusiastically. That was great confirmation.

"We then went back to Los Angeles and ran a production in a tiny theater in the West Hollywood area, a four-week run, and got a lot of reviews from the Los Angeles papers that were almost all positive. It was maybe a fifty-seat theater, and we ended up turning a lot of people away. We had a very good run."

Give the People What They Want?

Pleasing a crowd is not as hard as it seems. Here's a novel idea: Please yourself first. People respond strongly to a genuine passion displayed onstage. There will always be an element of viewership that clearly does not dig your point of view. But it's really the same in any aspect of life, isn't it? Not everybody wants to be your friend or wants to buy your old car. So what? You might not want to be their friend or buy their old car either.

I guarantee you that there will be more people responding to your work than not responding to it, as long as you're true to what you want to say theatrically and you say it boldly. Even if they don't like what you're doing 100 percent, they'll appreciate your audacity.

Worst case scenario, you put something up, and people absolutely revolt and throw psychic tomatoes at your actors—well, you can always change gears. It's wise to measure reaction very carefully before you do anything, however. Leslie Jacobson (Horizons) learned this in her early experiences putting on shows for large houses. "Definitely, we knew we were giving people things they hadn't seen on stage before. People were very excited— we were doing a lot of plays dealing with mother-daughter relationships in the late seventies. In fact, the book *My Mother, Myself* came out around that time. We were doing our first plays about mothers and daughter before it came out, and then it came out, and that obviously was something people were interested in. And we were interested in it—we didn't pick a topic because it was trendy, we picked a topic because it was on our minds.

"There didn't seem to be any good plays out there at that time dealing with the mother-daughter relationship, so we actually did several plays on that. That generated incredible discussion, because people felt they were getting to look at something that they weren't able to look at—there weren't any plays being written on that. Sometimes, they would make interesting comments that we would think about incorporating into the productions. Again, since we were the playwrights, we could use the early performances like previews and make adjustments. Sometimes, we waited to do that.

"I'll never forget—we performed at a facility around that time for about eight hundred people. We did a show that ran ninety minutes without an intermission. We felt that was important, because we didn't want to break the flow of the evening, but somebody brought up [in an after-show discussion] that they wished there had been an intermission, so they could have thought about some of the things [in the play] during the break and then come back.

"I looked out at the audience and said, 'How many of you would have preferred an intermission?' A sea of hands went up, a huge number of hands. So, I'm thinking, 'Hmm, maybe we should put an intermission in this.'

"But then I said, 'Okay, how many of you preferred it without an intermission?' Another sea of hands went up. Probably four hundred people wanted the intermission, but the other four hundred didn't! So, that actually taught me something important, which is, it's extremely valuable to get feedback from an audience, but you have to wait a while before you respond to it. If you responded immediately to everything this person and that person said, when it's all over, you might realize you changed this, but half the people really liked it, [so] why did you change it?

"The other thing about companies—the ones that don't still exist are the ones where some terrible thing happened at some point. It's sort of like, the people who are still married are the ones who didn't get divorced. I do think that we really liked working in this way. We did, actually, about nine shows in this way. We also had workshops on how to develop material using improvisation as a tool, not as an end to itself. It was very fulfilling. It's also exhausting and time-consuming."

How to Handle Your First Reviews

First reviews may seem monumental, but they're really not.

Sure, they make you beam when they're good, and they make you hurt when they're bad. Or they do neither, because you've decided you're not going to read them at all, ever.

Not reading reviews displays your immaturity. You ain't foolin' nobody, baby. If you knew for certain those reviews were amazing, you'd have them memorized in two seconds flat. By declaring you are above reviews, you reveal just how much they matter to you.

Also, refusing to read reviews doesn't do your company any good. You need to learn what the consensus is about your company, in order to use that information to make changes you agree are necessary. Or to be in touch with your community. Reviews also display perception of your company, at least according to the critics who author them. Any and all information, and opinion, both good and bad, that you can gather benefits your company's forward propulsion in one way or another.

Most companies' initial openings don't attract Ben Brantley or John Simon, by the way. So, if a hugely respected and powerful critic isn't sitting front row center, his or her dissenting opinion can't really affect your opening night. Small press or TV reviewers can't destroy you, no matter how much you worry about this. The power balance just isn't the same. Your show is also not so huge a positive or negative force yet that it's begging to be knocked down a peg by a reviewer, something that definitely can happen in a heavily promoted commercial situation, like Broadway.

If you get a bad review, take it with a grain of salt. Don't feel like you have to take the reviewer's suggestions about your production, if you don't agree with them. Don't feel this person hates you on a personal level. Just take it in, and file it away.

Many first shows get mixed reviews—in fact, that tends to be the norm. If it happens to you, see what you can learn from it, then move on.

Is there ever a case where a first production gets a phenomenal review from a major respected source, and it makes a big impact on a new company? Sure, it happens from time to time. David Zak (Bailiwick) recalls how his company made a big splash their first time out. "The first show was very intense and very gratifying. Lots of politics going on, as the 'pecking order was established.' The *Chicago Tribune* review was excellent, and so, audiences really came in, and things went well."

Fabulous! If something similar happens to you, savor it. If not—don't worry. There's always next time.

Let Everyone Have a Say

Needless to say, you must also pay attention to audience feedback, and when and if you've got one, your board's opinions, which are often a spot-on indicator of community reaction. Michael Gennaro, of Steppenwolf, explains: "One element that's been crucial to this place, and is the downfall of many places, is the integration and the embrace of the board. There's been evolution of the board over the various stages of this company. There've been very key decisions as to who the chairperson is and what that person brings to the table at that moment in time that the company needs. Whether it's a visionary, whether it's a fundraiser, whether it's a strategic person, whatever it is, there've been very clear choices made along those lines. That is something you have to stay in touch with.

"We're in a place where we have fifty-five board members, and I'd say thirty-plus of them are involved in a very hands-on manner. They are constantly being called upon for their expertise and their advice. That just makes things so much easier when you're going out and raising money.

"Let me tell you, the day after an opening, Martha [Lavey] and I will hear from a lot of people about what they thought of the play. It's very satisfying when they call you and say, 'I've got some criticism of the play, but acting—first-rate. Production values—first-rate. Now, here's my problem with the play.' That's okay.

"And/or, the amount of people who call passionately upset about a play—that's okay, too. I can't stress enough for anybody starting out how, as you're building a company, you've got to really pay attention to your board. They're an equal partner. Really important is the chair. You've got to have a leader. There are leaders in the ensemble, people who bring up important issues when they're important, there are people who sit back. There are people who constantly drive the company, Gary Sinise being a perfect example. You're not always going to agree with those people, but you've got to have them.

"We don't have one member who's come onto the board who wasn't a multiyear subscriber prior to that. You can sit down with them and say, 'What have you seen lately?' and they'll rattle off five or six productions over the last couple of years."

Listening to Your Community

Lyla White (Pasadena Playhouse) sees to it that her company's community at large has a voice, and actually considers that one of her major responsibilities. "With the audience, the subscribers, publications, you have to answer phone calls when people are unhappy. You have to really want to do that. You could say it's communication, you could say it's teaching.

"Before I became the Executive Director, I began to see victory in the increase in donations. When people come to a play and buy a ticket, they feel like they're supporting the theater. They also feel like, they've bought a ticket and have expectations of what they're going to receive in return. When they donate, make a donation at whatever level, they feel invested in you and in your future. They become part of the theater. Not that the ticket buyer isn't, but the donor reaches a new level of involvement.

"The donor volunteer is another level of involvement. It's hard to steer a ship with fifteen thousand subscribers, to keep moving them up in their involvement with the theater, but that's my job, and I started that before I became Executive Director. As the Executive Director, I've continued to feel like that's my focus and what I want to do.

"It's definitely not a community theater, but I want that community spirit and feeling of ownership. It's our theater. We're in this together. It happens at different levels—we've done a lot of special events and have a lot of community support there. The city has gotten behind us. We have a lot of support, not financial, from them, but emotional, other support. They're proud of us."

The Moment of Making It

Chicago City Limits had this epiphany, not simply within its circle of friends, but during its early performances. It became clear the group was onto something major. Paul Zuckerman recalls, "Success creates challenges. In this milieu of the clubs, all of a sudden, we were getting a little bit of an audience. People were coming to see us on a Thursday night. There's a magical time for any theater company, where you break from your friends and people you know coming to the general public hearing about you and coming.

"If you think of all of these groups, as Chicago City Limits did, which split, then form, then split, then form, there becomes a kind of critical mass of people who know, 'Oh, they're getting together with these people, and it should be an interesting show.' That's how our audience started to happen. We had a couple of regular nights, did some late-night radio, things just to get on the radar. And there was an audience! On Thursday night, you go into the club, and you're looking around, and you say, 'Gee, I don't know these people—it's cool that they came!' It sort of surprises you.

"That, to me, is a real leap, and that's the real obstacle that most theater companies run into. How do you get there? I was reading two interesting biographies last year, one on Elvis and one on Bob Dylan. Both of them had skyrocketing transitions. Elvis basically went from knowing two songs and performing one of them in public, and six months later, he's the biggest star in the country—unbelievable. I guess that fuse ignites faster and spreads wilder and quicker in some instances.

"Our theater didn't explode quite like that, but it was a pretty good firecracker. It's a funny thing. There's an old phrase I've heard—'If you're green, you're growing—if you're ripe, you rot.' They talk about that in terms of sports teams, too—the hungry team wins. I think there's something to that. In our period of acceleration, when people really started to come to see us, it was also a period of great artistic explosion for us. Here we are now, feeling pretty good about ourselves, feeling artistically very competent, able to really work a crowd. There is no substitute for stage time. Certainly in comedy, but I suspect in every form of live theater, the show you do after two thousand shows is better than the show you do after a hundred shows."

Seek a Few More Helping Hands

A point of success is also the best time to build up your human resources from the outside. An audience base, of course, is key to start working on in earnest. Assembling a board can be very shrewd as well. Plus, don't discount this as the ideal opportunity to attract some new and interesting talent with your newly minted reputation.

Mitzi Sales gives insight as to how Berkeley Rep mined similar resources once its first flush of success was evident: "It was like, 'You know something? We think we can really make this go,'" says Mitzi. "So what does that mean? What that means is, finding a board of trustees that is going to help us become a community institution, help us make money, help us make plans. I find it interesting that I stayed for eighteen years, and I often tell people that one of the reasons that it was possible to do that was, every four years, the theater went through a very big transition.

"From 1972, really to 1976, we were scrambling. The company was building. The artistic output was becoming more and more consistent. We attracted some really good actors, a wonderful associate director. People who came through, who were teaching at the university, but who also would direct a play at Berkeley Rep, who would act in a play, who would design a set, really gifted directors, designers, and actors. There was an interesting little talent pool that perhaps other theaters wouldn't have had at a critical point.

"We were certainly not paying competitive salaries at that point, so we were relying on that talent pool to help us grow, help us stabilize."

Use These Key Indicators to Plot Your Success

When all is said and done, there are three specific components that separate the men from the boys in terms of meeting your goals. If you can ace each of these requirements by claiming them as your own, you're doing great.

We owe these components, by definition, to Sheldon Epps, who has achieved all of them in record time in his current position at Pasadena Playhouse. Epps says: "Three things. One is box office success. Crass as that may be, you've got to pay attention to that. When we did very, very difficult, very challenging plays like *The Real Thing* and *Side Man*, they've been tremendously successful at the box office.

"Two: critical success. Not only writers saying, 'This is the kind of play that can make this theater exciting again,' but, 'They're doing this kind of play extremely well.'

"Three: recognition within the artistic community. That there are people—writers, agents, directors, actors—who come to us now and say, 'I've heard about what you're doing. It sounds very exciting. I'd like to come and do a play at your theater,' or 'I'd like my client's play to be done at your theater,' in a way that wouldn't have happened seven, eight years ago. It's a clear indicator that we're once again considered at the top of the heap.

"That's very gratifying, that people I've known and been associated with for a long time pay attention to the theater now, and respect the theater now, in a way I don't think they would have several years ago.

"What the effect of that is, because of that respect and recognition, we get the opportunity to produce plays here that we might not have gotten the rights to several years ago."

As can you—if you strive to keep building upon your success.

CHAPTER 6

BUILDING WORD OF MOUTH

Once your company has established itself, spreading the message about the great work you're presenting becomes one of your next objectives. It's an objective you've got to take pretty seriously, too, for a couple of reasons.

One that's pretty obvious is for the sake of expansion. The more people who know about you, the more people might come to see your show. Thus, your work will be viewed and appreciated by a larger audience base, you'll build a subscription base, and soon, you'll be rivaling the Super Bowl for attendance and media coverage. Okay, maybe that's stretching things a bit.

Second, for the sake of maintenance. If you start building effective word of mouth within the immediate vicinity of your community, you lend your company an air of stability, whether your company is completely stable yet or not. People tend to respect by osmosis. If your company is mentioned constantly in the local paper, on radio or television, or postered all over town, your friends, neighbors, and local residents you don't know will start to see your group as a new bedrock of the community. They'll sanction your integration by attending your productions, and perhaps one day donating money and taking a place on your board.

In this chapter, our experts will help us make sense of how to best get the word out. We'll cover the topic from a variety of angles. For example, how did esteemed companies gain momentum in terms of not simply audience attendance, but critical responses and interest from new theater artists in terms of collaboration? How did marketing strategies change once a company felt the first flush of success? How has networking played a role in that success?

Spread the Joy

The best advertising is really just spreading excitement.

Not a novel concept. But in the case of a fairly new theater company, an organization that doesn't have a lot of cash to blow on marketing itself does have a very valuable tool to use that costs absolutely nothing: enthusiasm.

If you really want to share the thrill of your company's work with others, say so! It's that simple. How do you do this without appearing insufferable and obnoxious? Smile—and remember what it was like to be ten years old and starring in your fifth-grade play. You were excited, and everybody thought you were adorable. I'm not saying you should regress to a childlike state of drooling wonder—believe me, that's not an effective marketing strategy any day of the week. Just recapture the purity of your excitement. When you are truly thrilled about something and express that honestly, your attitude is totally contagious. People want to check out what you're so whipped up about, because if it makes you happy, it could very possibly make them happy, too.

Always promote what you genuinely believe in. Don't try to pull the wool over anybody's eyes—you really can't. If you can successfully fake enthusiasm for a production that stinks, and you indeed do trick folks into coming to see it, they won't like what you dragged them into. Then, they'll either resent being suckered, or they'll doubt your artistic aptitude in the future. Neither of these scenarios would do your company much good.

If your enthusiasm for a project isn't genuine, better to keep your trap shut.

Make Your Own Publicity

So, you're awash in genuine enthusiasm about what your company has to offer and ready to shout this from the rooftops.

Well, shouting from the rooftops is pretty cheap publicity, but then again, using your phone, fax, and e-mail is more effective, and doesn't have to be all that expensive either. So, get organized, and make a master list of critics, media sources, and free advertising resources. Free stuff first, before you pay for any expensive advertising, because sometimes, a quality reviewer can make your name at this stage better than a giant billboard overlooking Times Square ever could. Paul Zuckerman says, "In Manhattan, Chicago City Limits built primarily on word of mouth. There were some struggles in the early days, but we'd get reviews—the credibility of a positive review in the *New York Times* or the *Daily News* greatly outweighs an ad. Your audience enjoying your show is the best form of advertising."

The Power of a Strong Review

In the previous chapter, we went over initial reviews and how they probably will not make or break you, even if they're truly heinous.

As your company progresses, though, the impact of reviews begins to weigh far more heavily. A negative review at the very beginning of your company's visibility is not the end of the world, but if you keep racking up piles of stinking notices, they will start to define you in terms of public opinion. People will ignore you at best and will ridicule you openly at worst. You don't need that.

Still, you do need to get reviewed to earn credibility, within your community and also artistically. So, it all goes back to putting your best foot forward, creatively. At this stage in your company's development, if you read a number of reviews that point out an identical fault, it might be a good idea to take a look at this sticking point in your work and fix it. This is not going back on your resolve to do what you feel is right creatively, above all other opinion. It's simply smart business practice to fix any product you are offering the public that you find might be defective.

The power of a strong review by a major reviewer is, of course, worth its weight in gold. How do you get a noted reviewer to check out your show? Be persistent. Now, persistent does not translate in any way, shape, or form into stalking, so no night-vision goggles or boiled bunnies, please. Persistent in this case refers to polite follow-up.

Send written correspondence to a reviewer first, briefly introducing your company and describing the production that you're inviting this person to in a fax or e-mail. Send that off, then wait a reasonable amount of time for a response. If you don't receive one after a week or so, a courteous follow-up by telephone is acceptable.

If you get a mixed review from a well-known critic, don't despair. You've still hit the jackpot, promotionally. If you're savvy, you'll choose the best, most complimentary sections of the review—usually it's best to pull out the strongest sentence or two—and put it on your poster and in the body of any and all ad copy you're running. Plaster it into your program. Send it out in all future promotional brochures and literature.

If you happen to get a glowing review from a famous critic, your life is about to change, and how! This is exactly what put Steppenwolf on the map. Michael Gennaro says: "I think the thing that kind of set them off was [when] Richard Christiansen, who's the main reviewer for the *Chicago Tribune* here, went up to see them. He said he was never so exhilarated and frightened at the same time in his life by a performance. They were literally just experimenting and taking everything as far as they could take it."

Build Your Base

Start compiling a permanent mailing list. Such a demographic tool is invaluable. You can send folks promotional material as frequently as you'd like, and hopefully spark their interest in your future productions. When your company is ready to start selling season subscriptions, you have a ready-made resource of people who might like to buy.

How do you compile the rudiments of such a base? At the performances of your very first production, insert a contact form in your program, asking for names, addresses, phone numbers, and e-mail addresses. In addition to the names you collect directly, round up all of the contact info for anyone with whom you've had positive contact thus far—this ranges from all of those community movers and shakers you may have invited to an initial fundraiser, your favorite local radio deejay who gave you a free plug on his top forty broadcast, the merchants you buy supplies from in your neighborhood, your family and friends. Everyone you can think of.

All of this information ends up in a master mailing list. Alphabetize it, and forward a copy to everyone within your organization. Let everyone know that you'd like them to add as many names to the list as they possibly can. Update the list again. Do this as many times as necessary to keep the number of names on your list as high as possible and, in addition, current. Leslie Jacobson, of Horizons Theatre, says: "We started to build a mailing list. Every now and then, we'd get thirty women's organizations or something to add to it, but basically, that mailing list was people, one at a time, getting their names added.

"Washington is a very transient area, so we have to keep cleaning it periodically. We have about four thousand names at the moment, and we just did a cleaning from last year. Those are not names that we bought from some mailing house or something. Those are four thousand names we collected over the years—people who'd seen things and asked to be put on our mailing list."

Good quality presentations are a wonderful way indeed to build your mailing list. So is good, quality face time. If people like you personally, they're more likely to want to become involved in your theatrical enterprises. David Zak (Bailiwick) explains: "Our mailing list started with all of our school chums, teachers, people we worked for. For a while, I was delivering plants and put everyone I delivered to on the mailing list. In fact, our donor base—probably at least a third of it—consists of people I met either at school or through that first job. Sometimes, people have never attended a show here, but liked me and keep making donations."

The Funder Factor

It's also a good idea, once you've got a few solid shows under your belt, some reviews to trumpet, and an emerging audience base, to up your efforts to attract funders.

Separate from applying for grants, you might want to consider organizing another fundraiser, if you've already held one prior to your first opening. If not, throw your first. Invite corporate representatives and local philanthropists to an evening at your space, complete with a full performance. (See chapter 3 for more on fundraiser specifics.)

No funder gets into the financial end of the business solely to champion great art. This doesn't mean a great many don't care to back good work—lots genuinely wish to associate themselves with quality, thank God. From a funder's perspective, though, quality needs to be commercial. Put yourself in the funder's shoes. What's the upside to pouring dollars into a show that six people are going to want to see? Funders such as investors are interested in material that smacks of wide appeal.

They also have a frequent aversion to controversy. After all, a local funder isn't going to want to risk his neck by getting behind a show that contains material sure to raise the ire of the community that supports his company. This is why funders often pass the spice and embrace the vanilla.

Figuring out your potential funders' sensibilities, then, can be a helpful step in building relationships with them, which in turn might build your company. Listening to funders' feedback is the smartest forward move that you could make. You don't have to agree and implement these changes, but if they make sense to you, why not give them a whirl? It also wouldn't hurt, if you do think the advice some big cheese is handing you might have merit, to ask this cheese whether he or she would be willing to come back and see the show again, once you've tried his suggestions.

Your mission needs to have significance. Why would anyone contribute to the growth of a company that stands for nothing much? If your goal is solely to entertain and bring joy to your community, believe it or not, that can be significant enough, as long as this intention is expressed clearly, eloquently, and passionately. Make sure you can describe your artistic hopes and intentions very succinctly, both in conversation and on paper, to attract the funders you want.

You also owe a funder your best creative efforts, at all times. You owe a funder courtesy—take this person's calls. You also never want to waste a funder's time or the money this person is donating to your cause. You want always to respect the reputation of any business or corporation that puts its resources behind you.

The Next Level

Hard work and good planning pay off.

Once you recognize the telltale signs that your organization is expanding, you need to start thinking in terms of your next step. What are your goals, longer term? How will you best achieve them? What resources are available to help you get what you want to help your company further?

Mitzi Sales (Berkeley Rep) knew how to take stock of her company at just the right time and take it toward the next level. "The first four years I was there, it was scramble, scramble, scramble. Then, in 1976, we realized, 'Now, we get it. We've managed to build up an audience, we're attracting some donors, and in order to keep going, we really need a larger space.' Financially, it doesn't work, 153 seats doesn't work. We needed a larger space, we needed a larger audience, which is potentially more subscribers who become donors. You build people up.

"In order to get a new space, we needed a board of trustees. We needed people who were committed to this particular theater to help us build this community institution. Until that time, the board of directors on the nonprofit organization papers were Michael, me, and Doug Johnson, and I think an attorney friend of Michael's was also on the articles of incorporation. It wasn't the traditional board of trustees of a nonprofit organization.

"So, we looked around at our community, at our supporters, at our donors. When we started, of course, all of our board of trustees were in the neighborhood. Then, it actually grew fairly rapidly after that, because you talk to people, and then they know somebody else— 'I know an attorney, I know a banker,' whatever.

"So, we put together our board of trustees and rewrote our articles of incorporation and our bylaws. The period between 1976 and 1980 was the institutionalization. When we thought we needed a new theater space, all we really wanted to do was stay where we were and just figure out how to expand that space. Really stupid—it was not going to work strategically. That was an organic process of thinking, okay, what do we do?

"Fortunately for us, the neighborhood association was alarmed at the idea that we would be expanding, because it's a neighborhood—the parking situation! The traffic situation! They were not thrilled.

"So, we started having to think beyond this cozy, charming, comfortable neighborhood. We found a site in downtown Berkeley, near public transportation and a parking garage. We bought that space, raised the money to build a theater, and that was 1980."

Networking Know-How

Every form of industry utilizes networking as a useful business strategy, and theater is no different. Theater, actually, is one of those professions that's partially built on hot air. If you've worked onstage or backstage in any capacity, you know all about the dominant role juicy gossip plays in keeping life interesting.

Beyond scurrilous talk, conversation that builds relationships has big value. Getting to know your community, for example, can lead to unanticipated good fortune on a regular basis. Susan Kosoff demonstrates how reaching out to all segments of your audience and supporters can build great word of mouth. "We did a lot of networking in the early years; we put a lot of stock into it, and still do. It's very time-consuming, if it's done right, but it pays off in both the short term and the long term. It's especially beneficial for theaters like us, with a targeted audience and a limited advertising budget.

"We certainly did reach out to the Wheelock College community, but it's a small school. One of the things that we did—we realized immediately that people didn't know where we were. So, we decided to reach out to the alumni, because they had an allegiance to the college.

"Because we had done theater for years together, we did have an audience that we could reach out to. We started building our mailing list very early on. We also hooked up with Arts Boston (a resource group) right away to get the word out. We reached out to the schools where Wheelock had student teachers and other kinds of placement—hospitals, social service agencies, that kind of thing. We used that whole network as well.

"That was really our strategy in the beginning. It's something we have maintained, but we're not as dependent on it anymore. We were lucky—a man came from the *Christian Science Monitor* with his kids. He gave us a fabulous plug for our first show. We also got a nice piece in the *Boston Globe*. So, those two PR things were extremely helpful in the very beginning.

"Right after that, we got a very bad review in the *Boston Phoenix*. It really was devastating. This was incredibly cynical and sarcastic—the fact of the matter was, they were totally wrong. I don't even mean about the show, I mean about their assumptions about who we were and what we were trying to do, like we were some kind of 'Christian Coalition'! But I don't think bad reviews hurt us. I think the fact that we were reviewed gave us legitimacy.

"We weren't able to pay for much advertising, so we did things like posters, and we still do it, because that's how we reach the people we want to reach. We did mailings, hung posters in lots of different neighborhoods, relied on public service announcements and calendar announcements. We tried to take full advantage of all the free things.

"By the second year, we just knew we had to advertise in the *Boston Globe* as well. We wanted to advertise in more neighborhoods, maybe where other theaters wouldn't. At one point, there was a TV reviewer in Boston who loved us. When we were doing *The Miracle Worker*, [the TV station] followed the girl who was playing Helen Keller at school and at rehearsal. We got a lot of different kinds of breaks like that, and we continually try to seek those people out."

If you've lived in your community for any length of time, it's very important for you to weave your company into the fabric of this community you know so well. If you happen to be new to the community your company is located in, enlist the natives to help your cause. It's probable that you have a number of people who've spent their whole lives in the community. Great! Instruct them to talk the theater up to as many locals as possible. Civic familiarity and pride can also really help your organization declare itself.

If you happen to live in a big city, though, you can effectively use a network of friends and business contacts to get your company known. Civic pride is a fact of life in big cities just as well as small towns, by the way. Just consider the groundswell of unity that New York City has experienced in the past year. It doesn't always take tragedy to make this phenomenon occur either—something good (like your work!) can bond and inspire as well.

Lyla White shows us how it's done: "I'm a Pasadena person. This sounds like I'm bragging, but I know almost everybody in town. I know the members of the city council and the city staffs, and I know the donors, because I've worked in this town a long time. I've lived in this town. My children grew up here." Lyla says.

"That combination works well for us, particularly in what I do. I try to raise the donated dollars, manage the ticket sales, and manage the ticket revenue. It works really well."

Unusual Marketing Moves

Thinking in an innovative way about your marketing concerns can benefit your company tremendously, especially if you don't have a lot of cash to make mistakes with.

This might seem to be a bit of a contradiction. After all, don't you need lots of cash to throw at your marketing strategies in order for them to be productive? You really don't. In fact, spending your last dime on an ad that will just be plunked in a tiny box on a page with thirty other little boxed ads surrounding it is just plain bad business planning. You're never going to stand out that way.

Think about ways you can connect more directly with your community, and further your purpose, that cost next to nothing. It might seem impossible, but it can be done if you put your mind to it. Let Jack Reuler (Mixed Blood), who's proven himself to always be ahead of the curve, show you the way: "One of the things we wanted to do, in our initial list of objectives and still today, is to attract a nontraditional audience. Part of what I've hoped to do throughout the years, with varying levels of success, is dilute the notion that live theater is an elitist, white art form. I continue to believe that [it's not].

"The first year, before there were child-care laws, we took a piece of what used to be the hayloft in our space and provided child care to the people who came to the shows. We had the van that the Center for Community Action used. In the evening, we would go to centrally located low-income neighborhoods and offer transportation to the theater. I wish we still did it. It was a great idea.

"Our top ticket price was $2.50, and if you were on public assistance, it was $1. The people not only got free transportation to and from the theater, they paid a buck when they got there. I think we had a total marketing and publicity budget for that five-show or six-show summer season of $300. We made it work.

"The press has been very good to us. If they needed a sound bite about the arts community, I was always good for a quote. I was the longest-standing artistic director in town at about age thirty. A lot of people had left. Somehow, I was catapulted to be spokesperson for the theater community. I think that my ability to interact with the media was great for the organization.

"I would say that there should be a point person of an organization with whom the press, public, and audience members identify the institution. A visible, vocal leader. Some really good artists and artistic leaders just aren't media-savvy, but you need a representative, and one that people buy into."

How to Give Yourself Credit

If you don't sing your company's praises to the universe at large, who will? It's neither boastful nor offensive to let people know about your achievements and the fine entertainment you have to offer.

Major players in the theater game know the value of strong self-promotion and freely tout their company value. Here's Sheldon Epps, speaking about the value of self-promotion to the Pasadena Playhouse: "There was a lot of excitement just on the basis of the kind of programming we were announcing and the reception to that programming. But that doesn't do you a whole lot of good unless you blow your own horn, unless you get the word out there.

"So, one of the things we have concentrated on was to trumpet our success, certainly here in Los Angeles, but also on a national level. To go after stories in *Variety* and *American Theatre* magazine. Beyond just publicizing the plays, we've spent the last three years really publicizing the institution, saying, 'The Pasadena Playhouse is not the place you thought it was. It's not the place it was six years ago. Attention must be paid!'

"After about a year, two years of being here, I was very vocal about that. I was very vocal about saying to the staff, 'Let's not be shy about how good we're doing. Let's be aggressive about blowing our own horn, about displaying our pride in the work that we've done.'"

Offer Something Different

Now that you're feeling all bold and sassy, why not use your forthright promotional attitude to plug a few unique programming ideas? Special programs can be a great way to get the word out big about your company. Used imaginatively, offers, discounts, and special events often will prove to serve as a strong catalyst to build interest.

Do the unexpected—midnight shows, Sunday morning matinees, playwright's forums, get-to-know-our-actors nights. Don't get cheesy, though. Serving beer, for instance, in a desperate attempt to attract local sports fans looking for something different is a highly misguided notion. Gimmicks appear gimmicky for the most part—having costume contests where the audience members dress up as their favorite Shakespearean character borders on the Dungeons and Dragons–esque. Even dance parties à la *Grease* on Broadway are tough to pull off on a smaller scale.

Try something classy, intellectually enriching, and respectful of your audience's needs and interests. Jean Cocteau Repertory does a beautiful job at its special programming. Its programs include sixty post-performance discussion sessions, between the artists who produce the work that has just been presented onstage and the audience that has just seen it; preshow discussion sessions, presented as salons; Club Hector, a cabaret geared toward bringing younger audiences into the Cocteau fold, specifically students and an under-thirty demographic; and a weekly reading series of new works, open to the public.

The Validation of Other Artists, and a Dose of Reality

A Traveling Jewish Theatre has been paid the highest compliment a company can be paid: Other theater artists want to collaborate with its members. This portends very well for the future of the company, in terms of infusing it with fresh talent.

Word of mouth is definitely working in your favor when your talent speaks so loudly, your peers validate it. Many actors, after all, are quite competitive with each other. In a case when all competition is overridden by admiration, you know you're doing something right.

Even when great future work with new colleagues is in the offing, though, things are never perfect. Even a respected reputation doesn't change certain realities of the business. Corey Fischer enjoys the lauded position his company is in, but remains aware of day-to-day challenges. Says Fischer, "We went to New York, and there we really got the idea for our second piece. Soon after coming back from New York, at the end of that year, we began work on our second piece.

"We toured it, began touring larger venues, went back to New York, had a tremendous response there, and so it went. People have to understand, here we are, twenty-three years later, by all accounts a successful experimental theater company. And yet, we still are constantly struggling.

"It's not an easy life. There's no job security. In a sense, we go year by year. Every year, we are again faced with having to figure out how we're going to make the budget. So, it's changed quite a bit from where we were twenty-three years ago, but we're, so far anyway, not at a point where we can relax and know we're going to be around another twenty-three years."

A Strong Reputation Can Sustain You

Even though things can be difficult at times, it's amazing how long you can trade on a solid reputation. In order to maintain your edge, after you've gotten your theater's name around, remember: Pay attention.

Stay objective. Take your community pulse as often as possible, to make sure that your audience is being continually satisfied by the artistic output you are offering them. Even if you employ someone to do your marketing, stay on top of things yourself.

If you sense that your reputation for quality is starting to erode or that your patrons are unhappy with something, like a higher ticket price or seats that aren't comfy enough, take care of the problem. Susan Albert Loewenberg (L.A. Theatre Works) says, "No matter how bad it is, you can never let yourself panic and be discouraged.

"Figure out a solution. I'm a good crisis manager. I can figure a way. Sometimes, there's no way out, but I think as you get older, you put things in perspective."

Every experience, either good or bad, teaches you and makes you stronger. Use your experience to keep striving and building your name even further. Keep soliciting audiences and critics. Seek out new funders. Present work of only the highest quality.

Don't rest on your laurels. Your reputation is your currency. Work hard to get the image you want, work hard to preserve it, and even harder to further it.

CHAPTER 7

THE BIGGEST PROBLEM WE EVER FACED

Usually, once a theater company achieves some measure of progress, a gigantic, disturbing, hulking crisis will rear its ugly head, at the worst possible moment.

Sometimes, in retrospect, such a crisis doesn't turn out to be so terrible after all. I directed a musical in Boston many years ago. One Friday night performance, the house was packed, the cast was hot, the show was playing the best it ever had—and then the power went out. No lights. No juice to power equipment. Nothing.

I must admit that I freaked out in those first, dark moments ("dark" meant in both its literal and figurative definitions), but cooler heads quickly prevailed. The audience was digging the show so much, they volunteered to go out to their cars and get flashlights. Our stage manager ran to a nearby deli and bought batteries. A friend of mine in the audience happened to have a battery-operated keyboard in the trunk of his car that the show's music could be played on. Mind-bendingly, the audience trained their flashlights on the cast in unison, and the show indeed went on.

Needless to say, that was one of the greatest nights of theater I've ever been privileged to be a part of—and it started out looking like a complete and total disaster. Lots of theaters have weathered similar crises, which appear large-looming at first, but thankfully, can be taken care of effectively.

Other times, problems are more complicated. If you don't handle them the right way, they can spell the end for your company, worst-case scenario. To a less severe degree, they can cost you time, money, and energy, three important things you can't have enough of when you're maintaining a theater company.

In this chapter, our experts will discuss the biggest problems their companies have faced and how they coped. Their big issues span a very wide gamut, but the common lesson we can learn from the experiences they relate is this: every problem ultimately has a solution. Sometimes, the solution is one you're delighted with; sometimes, it's not the end result you want at all; and sometimes, you end up with mixed results. But everything does indeed pass. If you throw your smarts and strengths—both as a businessperson and as a human being—at a hairy problem full tilt, it can pass a lot faster.

Some of the problems our experts have faced are quite concrete, while others presented themselves in a more abstract form, but all were tough. I'd like to give our subjects extra thanks for their honesty in sharing these problems in the first place. It's easy to talk about good times, but not a lot of laughs to go back over the bad stuff.

Talent in Transition

No company can stay together in its entirety forever. Theater is a transitory business in general, and there are also opportunities for talented people popping up.

Actors, as a general rule, relish the chance to play as many different parts as they can—that's one of the big reasons most choose their profession in the first place. Sometimes, actors will become known through the work they do with a company, and the heavens will rain offers down upon them.

Other times, personal issues—such as the desire to change one's life in some major way—lead to a job departure. Hopefully, one company member at a time elects to leave, but there are scenarios in which you can lose two or more company or cast members at once. This can throw your organization into unexpected turmoil.

Beyond the obvious recasting hassle, keeping your creative purity can be tricky, as new blood will change the company dynamic. It can also be painful when friends and coworkers you've loved working with leave. You may develop some serious nostalgia for the way your company was—until the day your new people deliver you some magic. Paul Zuckerman reflects back on the ramifications of personnel problems Chicago City Limits has had to deal with:

"One of the biggest was, there was a point at which the original cast left. It started when one actress decided to have a child, another got an opportunity in California, so from 1985 to 1988, the cast turned over. I think the biggest challenge was going from individuals—because in some sense, the five of us were Chicago City Limits—and making it an organization.

"You have fundamentally different orientations among the participants. The first group was the fundamentalists, the religious zealots, the crazy ones ready to die for the cause. The second group are people who are in love with improvisation—and that's always been the bottom line. If they don't love it, I don't want 'em, because they're not going to want to be here. But they also don't have the emotional commitment and connection that the original people did. That was the challenge, to develop a company out of that.

"It's not an all-or-nothing thing. To this day, it continues to be a constant battle as people evolve, as society evolves. Yes, when you have that new cast and that new work, all you can think about is how good it used to be and how do you get them there. Then one day, you're sitting there saying, this is a great show. That's where it is. I don't know if it's a 'one day' thing or if you just kind of reflect on it at some point."

The Issue of Debt

Very few theater companies operate without some level of debt. It's quite hard not to fall into that trap. If you've got a good managing director making sensible decisions, plus you yourself stay on top of your company's finances, your debt load will probably be on the lighter side. It can be very rough, however, if you've inherited the problem of debt from somebody else. Say your managing director suddenly leaves the company, and you check out the books and find a mountain of unpaid bills you thought were taken care of.

Terrence Dwyer (La Jolla Playhouse) walked into a debt problem, but pulled his company out in better shape than ever, thanks to some crafty planning.

"In 1992, I got a call from the search committee. Des [McAnuff] had put my name in for the job," Mr. Dwyer recalls. "I walked in knowing the theater's great artistic reputation and that the organization had the finest artistic director in the country.

"Once I got to work here, I discovered that basically, the organization had accumulated a debt of about $1.8 million by the end of the 1992 season. It was a very, very difficult circumstance. There were huge cash flow problems.

"The debt was eliminated in 1997. The easiest challenge in doing that was budget watching. But to come out on the other end in strong shape, we needed to fix long-range planning problems, so we'd reach that outcome of no accumulated debt. So, we began a capital campaign.

"When you have solved debt, as we did through this campaign, your credibility improves. This affects how well you do with fund-raising, and your marketing is affected positively, because you can more effectively plan it."

Artistic directors can feel particularly at sea when faced with the challenge of grabbing hold of any financial problem, but your smartest move is to get involved from day one. Don't be intimidated at the prospect of keeping track of money coming in and going out. Don't pretend you are so busy changing the face of dramatic art as we know it, you simply can't be bothered hearing about cash flow difficulties.

If you act like you're above caring about money, people will believe you, and they won't tell you what's going on within your own organization. If you bite people's heads off when they try to approach you bearing unpleasant financial news, they'll avoid you in the future. As a result, a hornet's nest of money problems can quickly accumulate. My mom always told me to face the truth about a problem head-on. If you know the true circumstances of a situation, no matter how dire things are, you've got a fighting chance to solve it. But if you duck the reality of a difficult situation, you'll never be able to see what you're dealing with clearly, and then you're sunk.

Rick Lombardo of New Repertory concurs with this sage advice: "I think the most difficult time was the first year after I came here. We had an operating deficit. We had lost a significant amount of cash, and things were difficult for a time.

"I think an artistic director needs to think like a producer about the financial aspects of his or her company. I solved the problem by doing that. One of my greatest achievements has been that ever since then, every season has had a surplus. Running a small to mid-size theater company means you have to jump on every angle of a problem and seize every opportunity, short-term, long-term, operating by the seat of your pants. There's always extra pressure."

Goodbye to a Friend

The personal relationships that develop between the people in any theater company become quite intense. You forge a very close bond with your partners in crime—you laugh with them, cry with them, and ride on the same extreme emotional roller coaster of exciting performances, financial terrors, and one-of-a-kind magic moments.

The pain of having to let go of someone you've been through so much with is indescribable. Sometimes, though, it just has to be done. Michael Leibert, the dazzlingly brilliant founding force behind Berkeley Repertory, struggled with the problem of addiction. In the early eighties, he tried mightily to regain his health, and Mitzi Sales, in addition to the rest of the Berkeley Rep family, tried to support him.

Says Mitzi, "Michael was getting sicker and sicker, and it was very hard. Basically, he was put on disability, an opportunity [for him] to go get well. We had an acting artistic director, a member of the acting company. There was a hope that Michael could enter a program and could come back. That wasn't possible.

"One of the strengths of the company throughout those early years was the core acting company. As Michael was declining, the acting company and directors were actually doing a lot of the artistic choice-making. So, it was interesting that during a particularly difficult time, artistically, the theater was continuing. It wasn't a marvelous high point—there were some high points during that time, as fate would have it.

"But it was a period of time of stopping and needing to regroup, having then made the decision to find a new artistic director and creating a search committee of the board of trustees and hiring someone to manage that process—hiring an outside professional to help us find an artistic director.

"I agreed to serve on the artistic search committee, but I said I'd never vote, because I felt like it needed to be the board of trustees' decision. They needed to utterly support whoever they chose. I had a very, very good, very close relationship with the board of trustees, and I didn't want my personal opinion to color who they might choose. I felt the artistic director needed their complete support. Very, very difficult time.

"I sort of helped the process, and we got down to a final three candidates. They made the final decision and hired Sharon Ott, which was a terrific decision.

"Basically, the hardest challenge was the final realization that Michael was not going to be able to come back to who he was."

Susan Medak continues the story, touching on the stress this situation put on the organization from a business perspective. "Michael's problems were a real issue. He drank. During those years, the company had a solid, respected reputation, but was not at the forefront, as ambitious companies in the Bay area were, companies like the Magic Theatre, ACT, plus upstarts. Berkeley Rep was user-friendly theater, tangible theater, not theater on a pedestal, which was great, but in the late seventies, the company members began to aspire to expand.

"With the help of the city of Berkeley, we planned a move to a space on Adams Street. This was a $3 million space with a shop, offices, a rehearsal hall, a deep thrust stage. So here, we could go from the audiences practically on top of the actors, from having very little scene shop space, very little costume shop space, from having to move empty seats, to having a large audience. It was thrilling and terrifying to expand to a second theater like this, profoundly impactful.

"Some people would say, 'We loved the days where you could smell the actors!' because they were so close to the audience! Michael had personalized the theater by standing among the crowd during performances, talking to them after the show, putting faces to the subscribers. We still talk to them all the time, by the way; people can't love an institution if it treats them impersonally.

"And we made a lot of room for opinion within the company. Many people felt we should conduct our growth with the artistic director, that it should not be solely them, what they think. But Michael's personality, although a very charismatic personality, made the decision to expand very difficult because of his alcohol problem.

"Michael was fired by the board of directors in 1983. That creates insecurity within an institution, when a board of directors fires the leadership. But also, hiring and firing can galvanize an organization.

"Sadly, Michael died three years after he was fired."

When You Come to the End of a Road

It can be very hard to know when it's time to change your focus and priorities within the scope of your company, for a number of reasons.

You may not see certain warning signs coming. Economic conditions may change and make the kind of production you want to do impractical. Perhaps you can't afford to do *Nicholas Nickleby* during a recession, for example. If you don't see the recession coming, and you've already started work on such an epic, work that you've already committed lotsa dollars to, that investment could very well be down the drain.

Another possibility: Even if your company proves to be successful and long-lasting, as times change around you, you may find that the company has to change in order to continue to exist. This could mean that you have to update the original founder's "old school" approach to the business.

David Fuller has been leading the Cocteau Repertory in that direction of late.

"We're in the midst of the biggest problem the company's ever had. We'll see where that takes us. Single-ticket income right now is very slow to come back [following the World Trade Center attack on September 11, 2001].

"We have a very low number of subscribers—our subscription base is about half of our ticket income. The rest comes from single-ticket sales. So, I think people coming back to the theater, here in New York, is a big problem, and I think that's going to take some time to overcome. Aside from that, I think the biggest problem I've overcome, or am beginning to overcome, is not from the outside, but the inside. We have changed the culture of the Cocteau from an inside perspective, to make it a forward-thinking company. I think that's why I was brought in. That's something that's happened and continues to be in the process of happening.

"I think it was in the twenty-ninth season—[there was a sense that] you could either move forward or go backwards—I don't think you *can* stay the same; if you try to, I think you go backwards. So, changing the thinking of an institution that's thirty years old is a big endeavor. I likened it to, if you're on an ocean liner going in one direction, if you want to go to the left, you don't immediately make that turn. It takes a while to make that turn. It took us a while to get things shifted.

"We're still changing. In terms of altering how the greater New York City theater community views the Cocteau, that is going to take a long time. It's a perception—we need to upgrade the perception of the company. We get a lot of good press, but we're still seen as the little theater down on the Bowery. Our budgets don't reflect that anymore, but that's what a lot of people perceive us to be."

Go with the Flow

Many companies suffered a forced reworking of their sensibilities when September 11 hit. Suddenly, doing shows replete with violence was seen as a dicey move. Likewise, super-frivolous, silly, navel-gazing material wasn't right for the times either.

Perhaps your company has earnestly promoted a particular playwright's work, and the audience is staying away in droves. Or perhaps you've heard audience feedback that is most unflattering, bordering on verbally abusive—your production values stink. This actor needs to be shown the door. That play was so long, I fell asleep, and now I want my money back, and so do these sixty-three friends of mine.

You might know there are serious problems that keep your company from doing its best work and getting a better audience response, not to mention a better critical response, but you just don't want to admit it. You're in denial. You believe so strongly in your own bountiful genius, nobody can tell you anything. With that attitude, the odds are, your company won't be long for this world.

You've got to be flexible in order to achieve longevity. You don't know everything. Sometimes things change, and you don't see that coming, and that circumstance gives you only two options: quit or adjust. Quitting is beyond lame, isn't it? So, that means you're going to adjust, and you're going to be glad about it, because changing artistic oars in midstream may be the best thing that ever happens to your company. A fresh perspective, trying new things, letting what doesn't work just fall away—it's all good.

Susan Albert Loewenberg (L.A. Theatre Works) says, "I think it's looking at something and saying, you know what? This is a dead end. It would be a crisis point—a point where you feel a dead end. You feel it isn't going anywhere, you need some invigoration, and you figure out where you need to go.

"I think that's been the salvation of this company. It's enabled the company to move and grow, and it's sort of kept my interest."

Changing Your Name

Sometimes, perception problems can be based on something as simple as a company's name. Leslie Jacobson was faced with this type of confusion, and she cleared it up quite thoroughly.

Says Leslie: "Until 1983, we were Pro Femina Theatre, until we moved into our new space. When you hear about Pro Musica, as a chamber music group, you never think that it's 'anti-dance.' But when people heard the name Pro Femina, they did make this assumption that it's 'anti-men.' Which it is not. At all.

"Changing our name was a positive statement to us. We're a woman-identified theater, but we're not anti-anything. So, we decided that what was more important than making people understand the name was having people come to see the work. We wanted to find a name that seemed more inclusive and accessible—but we also wanted to keep the woman-identity.

"So, we changed the name to Horizons—Theatre from a Woman's Perspective. We had a meeting that probably included about twelve people at the time—it was board members and artists who were strong stakeholders in the organization. We'd come up with a variety of names and had sort of narrowed it down to, I don't know, maybe four. Everybody voted, and the first vote, everybody voted for Pro Femina Theatre. So then, we had to say, okay, now you have to vote for a name that isn't the one we already have!

"So then, Horizons—we thought that just opened things up. But we wanted 'from a woman's perspective,' because we wanted to keep that identity. And also, we said we wanted to call it 'from a woman's perspective' as opposed to 'from women's perspective,' because we didn't want to make it sound like we were speaking for every woman in the world. Because we're not. Each playwright gives us a woman's perspective. If you came and saw all of our shows over twenty-five years, maybe then you could begin to understand what a feminine aesthetic might be.

"We're not here to tell people, 'This is it, and it has to be this way or that way.' What we're really interested in is the range of artistic voices and experiences that women have. We've done some highly politically charged plays, and we've done some plays where people say, 'Why are doing that?' and everything in between."

Problems with Perception

A similar hurdle has faced the Pasadena Playhouse—not in regard to its name, but instead, in regard to people's perception of the theater.

It's extremely important to have not simply a clear idea of what you feel your theater is about, but a clear idea about what your community, indeed, the world at large thinks you theater is about, especially as it grows and changes.

Sheldon Epps has been expertly evaluating the concept of perception since he took over as the Pasadena Playhouse's Artistic Director. Epps has been focused not only on preserving the legacy of the Playhouse's rich history, which is no secret, but also on the way that the theater's material has been stereotyped—it's far from old-fashioned!

Epps has also been analyzing the incorrect assumptions people make about the Playhouse's surrounding community, again, with a view toward innovation and progression. To this end, he's been choosing some really intriguing material.

"The biggest challenge, I think, was fighting perceptions of the theater, both those that were true and those that were not true," says Epps.

"There's a perception not only about the theater, but frankly, about Pasadena. That Pasadena's overly conservative, that it's all white, that it's all little old ladies. That's what we've heard about for years. There's a perception that that's the truth about the place itself, and also about the theater, that it was a theater for little old ladies from Pasadena.

"That has not been true for quite a while. The theater has done some very audacious work, certainly during the time I've been here as Artistic Director, but it had done that before. However, it is true that the theater's subscription audience was older, was primarily white—still is. So, we had to fight the perception [that] that was all the theater was and that was all the theater wanted to be, even though that had not been true. The theater had great success with things like *Sisterella*, which was kind of a funky urban musical, and *Twilight of the Golds*, which was about genetic testing for homosexuality in unborn children—very cutting-edge.

"Nevertheless, despite the fact that the theater did that kind of material, there still was this perception. That was a tremendous challenge. The way to beat that challenge was, right out of the box, do some programming that said, 'If you think that's the case, it is no longer the case and is not going to be the case'—and to continue that type of programming, even now and into the future."

No matter how sure you might be of what your audience thinks of your company, keep taking their temperature. Stuff your programs with audience surveys. Plop a comments box in the lobby. Keep up personal relationships with your subscription base, chatting with them at performances, and introduce yourself to new faces. Go as grassroots as possible with this stuff, and you'll be surprised to find a lot of the ideas you thought your audience had about who you are and what you're doing are actually outdated.

Staffing Traumas

You have no staff, so you have to do everything yourself. You have a staff, but nobody shows up, so you have to do everything yourself. You lose great people. These are just a few of the many staffing upheavals every theater company has to face at one time or another, sometimes for years and years.

The ultimate compliment, of course, is that you build such great relationships with your staffers, and offer them so much creative opportunity, that they stick with you for a very long time. It's also a wonderful tribute to your company when actors return to job in with your company again and again, because they so enjoy the experience of contributing to your vision.

Wheelock Family Theatre has been paid these compliments and more. They've also dealt with much staffing drama, as has any long-term, successful company. Susan Kosoff goes back to the beginning: "We had a very, very small staff. Tony and I never went to sleep. We literally stayed up, doing everything, and it was exhausting. So, we came to the point where we able to say, okay, we have to have more help, and finding ways to do that. We still are probably understaffed and still trying to come up with ways to fix that.

"I think in terms of staff development, that's how we've worked, and it's been really hard. We can't pay our tech director what a place like ART [the American Repertory Theatre, located in nearby Cambridge, Massachusetts] can, so it means that every few years, we're having to get a new tech director and adjust to that. I think we develop ways to deal with it, but it's a concern.

"The woman who worked on our business plan with us left after three years. She really wanted to help us get started and continues to be helpful; she did a million things. We're never going to be able to hire someone who's going to be able to do a million things the exact way she does. I think losing her, and losing Tony Hancock [who passed away], were two of our biggest challenges.

"We've had those individual crises, like when we did *The Wizard of Oz* and one of the actors, who was playing the Scarecrow, didn't show up; we had to cancel the show. That's the only time we had to cancel a show, but there was nothing else we could do. We've had those kinds of problems; I think every theater company has those kinds of problems.

"The second season, we did *The Phantom of the Opera*, and the guy who was playing the lead—his lungs collapsed. That's one of the fun things about theater!"

Ignorance Is Not Bliss

Sometimes, a theater's problem has nothing to do with what it's about at all, but is due to a larger problem in society as a whole.

In Jack Reuler's history as the Artistic Director of Mixed Blood Theatre, he has certainly had many more victories than difficulties. Reuler, however, has been rankled by a certain ignorance on cultural issues, specifically one that affected the perception of what he was trying to accomplish within his company.

Jack Reuler certainly wouldn't call this the biggest problem he ever faced, but he did consider it to be a significant issue at one point. Here, he talks about the problem of the phrase "multiculturalism."

"The expression that became identified with Mixed Blood was 'color-blind casting.' We were doing what we were doing for three years before anybody put a label on it. When we took that label on, and when I found out what it meant to other people, we stopped using it, because it didn't define what we were doing. What we do, we've come to call, needing a label, 'culture-conscious casting.' How people are cast is a 'something,' it's not an absence of something. I think they bring that to the role. 'Color-blind casting' meant you did it with disregard, paying no attention, rather than positive attention to people's differences.

"I don't think we changed what we did. We just changed what we called what we did. It was really an issue of 'multiculturalism,' a buzzword we tried to avoid. In education, business, philosophy, philanthropy, we saw it right from the beginning—it was going to be a passing fad. We needed to stay doing what we were doing before it came and after it was gone."

Things Won't Change Overnight

There are other areas of ignorance about theater as a whole, of course.

People mistakenly believe that theater is elitist, exclusionary, and highbrow. Small minds, and closed minds, think that theater is stuffy and boring. We know how many fabulously exciting and interactive productions have blown this theory out of the water, but still, old myths can persist.

In this pop-culture period rife with boy bands, dumbed-down movies, and lowest-common-denominator television, theater doesn't really fit neatly into the landscape. For the past few years, in fact, theater has been treated like Britney Spears's ugly, unloved stepsister.

Corey Fischer, of A Traveling Jewish Theater, says, "The biggest problem is that our culture and society does not value theater as much as we do, or as much as most European countries do. The support isn't what it could be."

Will things change and improve? I believe so. Why? Because entertainment culture is cyclical. Eventually, people will get sick of the stupid swill they've been force-fed and look for fresh alternatives, and theater just may prove to be a very viable and attractive option.

Things won't change overnight, but there are signs that things are getting better. So, keep on keeping on. Then, when the masses are ready, you'll be there, ready to give them the thrill of a lifetime.

CHAPTER 8

THE BIGGEST VICTORY WE EVER ENJOYED

Now, get ready for the good news!

A life in the theater is really, really fun. The adrenaline rush that washes over an actor right before he takes the stage is only one reason why. It's electric to be in your space on opening night, after you've worked so hard putting together a show, no matter what role in a theater company you happen to play. If it's your very own company, the excitement is amped up to its highest power. (As is the nausea you are concurrently experiencing, perhaps. But I digress.)

Opening nights that go well are one great payoff, but there are so many ways victory can present itself. It can be that moment you recognize your cast is working together like a well-oiled machine. It can be a cash windfall at the box office. It can be consistently beautiful reviews. It can be catching sight of the collective joy on your audience members' faces as they watch the work you're presenting. It can simply be the moment when you know your company has made it over the hump and is going to survive.

At the point you may be at right now, you probably think such positive proof of success will never present itself to you. But life can change in a second, you know. Also know this: There is a secret ingredient you can use when you're trying to cook up some victory. It's simple stick-to-itiveness. Hang in long enough, and you'll see results. Make a daily commitment to refuse to let your company go away. Always find a way to keep going. When you ask somebody for something and they say "no," go ask somebody else, until you get a "yes." Sheer willpower applied to any endeavor produces success sooner or later.

This chapter will survey our subjects to find out what their respective big victories were like. Sometimes, these events occurred immediately following a very difficult period in the company's history or after a particularly sticky situation. Some victories were happy accidents. Some victories encompass the realization of a company goal. No matter what the victory might be, each of our experts deserves credit for hanging in long enough to steer his or her organization toward achievement.

We'll discuss these big successes, proudest moments, and most exhilarating achievements, too, in order to inspire you. Just imagine yourself in the same glorious position of accomplishment and satisfaction—it's closer than you think. Just keep working hard and dreaming big.

When Somebody Really Gets It

In that magical moment when an actor finds the truth onstage, the immediate reward that follows belongs to a number of people. First of all, to the actor himself. If he's been hesitant or nervous, then suddenly finds his groove, it's a major personal affirmation. Then, to the show's director, here's validation that his skills and support have really helped in a big way. For the actor's fellow cast members, the unit is now more cohesive, and creativity can flow between people much more easily. If the playwright is present, his or her material will now be able to be interpreted more ideally. And for a theater company's leadership, it's wonderful to know that all of this is happening, not just before your eyes, but under your auspices.

Paul Zuckerman always hires great people for Chicago City Limits, but he realizes that even the most terrific actors sometimes don't have improv experience. He's seen actors break through many times, and every time it happens, he regards those moments as a major validation, not simply of his own ability to nurture a performer, but of the entire troupe's strength and unity.

"We always talk about the ability to anchor a show," says Zuckerman. "If we take our great cast members, I can take someone who's never improvised, put him onstage with us, and you might not notice it. If he follows what's going on and keeps his mouth shut, generally he'll be okay. But that person can't be the leader—he doesn't have the skills. That's sort of the individual affirmation—this guy who maybe a year ago took second billing because he was tentative or whatever, all of a sudden, he's in command, he's dragging a scene along, he's leading it—that's a very satisfying feeling."

Shows That Stand Out

It's not unusual for a theater company to recall a particular production as a most memorable moment, and why not? It's a rare and beautiful thing when all the elements of a production come together perfectly—dramatically, technically, in every way. Those times when it's exactly the way you envisioned, it deserve to be remembered, so you can use them as a sort of divining rod, to help you catch lightning like that again.

Not that Rick Lombardo needs any help catching lightning. His determination to expand the reputation of New Repertory Theatre has fueled the company to huge achievements, and the stamp of high quality that he's helped put on so many New Rep projects is most evident. Rick says: "Artistically, last season [2000–2001] was the biggest, huge! We did the New England premiere of *King Lear* with Austin Pendleton, which was untried, a challenge, but a success.

"The Boston-area critic Ed Siegel once noted that one of the things lacking in this area was a midsize theatre—a 'Steppenwolf' of Boston. New Repertory Theatre has clearly cultivated a literate, sophisticated audience."

Likewise, David Zak recalls with pride a particularly jubilant and sweet moment, when a Chicago critics' poll took notice of his Bailiwick Repertory's fine work: "Our production of *Pope Joan* by Christopher Moore beat out all of the big Equity houses as Best Musical in our eighth season."

Upheaval Leads to Triumph

At Berkeley Repertory, as well, one production, in a long line of tremendous shows, stands out historically as exceptional. This play was not simply well done, but very key in terms of the fact that it came in the middle of significant upheaval and seemed, in many ways, to define the positive results of this sea of change. In Berkeley's case, the show led to a new strength of determination, which subsequently led to the theater creating for itself a new facility.

This anecdote brings up a very interesting point about change as well: It's rarely not chaotic, especially if it is truly needed. Oftentimes, change within a theater company will come about because there is really no choice but to have it. Events and issues start to converge and snowball, to the point where things are changing whether you want them to or not, because it's never just about you—it's always about the communal force of your company's energy as a whole.

So, you shouldn't stand in the way of change, even if you didn't want it in the first place yourself. The only thing you should do is try to guide your organization's shift in a positive direction and make sure something really good comes out of change you can't prevent or control.

Susan Medak explains how this dynamic worked within the changing times at Berkeley Repertory:

"In 1990, I came on as managing director. It was a big transition period, from the founding board philosophy—I was an agent of change. The perception was that I was somebody who was an activist. It also became interesting between me and the community—I wanted to build my long-term, external relationship with it.

"So, a very large signature of this time period happened when we did *Woman Warrior* in 1991. It was a $1 million project, and it broke us out of the box, expanding the universe we were in. It also changed our ambition, gave us an enormous appetite, illustrated our commitment to working outside of the mainstream.

"The production was visually spectacular, and it was about our community—it came from a local writer and would sing here as it would not sing in other places. It pushed us as artists, and as a theater, and made us see that anything we decided to do, we could do!

"Building a new theater was a huge touchstone as well. The building renewed our sense of community. When we first began to talk about building a new theater, people were enraged! But we couldn't remain the same and still grow to be all we wanted to be, to be all our audiences want us to be. I see myself as an interpreter for the layperson—I interact with the city, and we make ourselves indispensable to it. So, once people got that we would open up the building to other organizations and events, all that we as a company were about to experience became something that was for everyone, and the community got that sense of ownership, not stewardship. Urban pride is a linchpin in this city. Thinking about the new building in terms of urban revitalization—downtown Berkeley had declined— made everyone seize the moment and start a new way of thinking.

"We received $4 million from the city, and we were all so proud—we as a community had done this, placed this theater as the new center of our community. So, not only did the new building expand our vision artistically, it redefined what our relationship had been to the community."

The Importance of Ideas

Theater often starts out as one thing—an entertainment form, with a strong philosophy powering it—and develop into something much larger.

For Horizons Theatre, great productions have sparked great responses from audiences and critics, yes. But what has grown to become equally important to Leslie Jacobson is the fact that the work Horizons has done has sparked great discussion. Good theater speaks to its audience, so its audience should be able to speak back.

Bold material choices, such as *A . . . My Name Is Alice*, have sparked the imaginations of audience members for Horizons and have led to many confirmations of the fact that the company's ideology is both vital and fertile.

Says Jacobson: "One of the big victories was, we produced *My Name Is* in our space in the church—it was a huge hit, ran for three months. Then, we moved it to a commercial venue, and it ran for another five months. So, that was an eight-month run, and that was pretty exciting. So, that's one triumph.

"Another was winning an award from the Dramatists Guild, which is the professional organization of playwrights. The women's committee of the Dramatists Guild gave Horizons an award in 1988 for outstanding work in producing plays by women playwrights. That was extremely gratifying. We've won other awards, but I think that [one] is so much of what we're about.

"Going to Copenhagen was a thrill, producing over sixty fully produced plays. Out of that, around five were written by men—because there are some male playwrights that we feel have a feminine aesthetic—and fifty-five or so were written by women. By and large, those were by women who had not been produced in Washington before. These were all either world or area premieres. So, you do feel that these are playwrights people wouldn't have known about if we hadn't done them.

"We've also done some panel discussions about whether there is a feminine aesthetic or not [and] how violence against women is treated in film and theater. We like to think of ourselves as more than just a theater. We're a place where ideas get exchanged and shared.

"In the last five years, we've also revived a series we call *In Good Company*. We're going to do one on sexual icons. I'd say that has some relationship to returning us to the kind of work that we did in our early days. These kinds of productions are developed with improvisation, but ultimately set. So, in some ways, we're working similarly to the way we did in our early years."

Smart Moves

For Steppenwolf, intelligent moves made at key moments have brought big dividends. Physically, in terms of taking their work out to new audience populations in the world, the company's movement led to greater acclaim.

Artistically, as well, the initiation to tackle some magnificent material translated that material into legendary Steppenwolf stage works. Michael Gennaro elaborates:

"Probably in '82, they had done *True West*, and they got the chance to go to New York. That was a big, big conversation within the company, because it was kind of like, 'Well, we're moving from Highland Park down into the city, and now we're moving out of the city? This is too big of a thing, it will splinter the company, that's not why we did this.'

"They ended up making the decision to go, and of course, that really set them on the map. It kind of led to the ability to make the move, in '91, down to the space we're in now.

Clearly, the moving into the city was a big step; clearly, the move of *True West* was a big step; the move here (to our current space) was a big step.

"The other thing that probably set them on the map—there are probably three plays, in my opinion: *True West, Balm in Gilead,* and *The Grapes of Wrath. Grapes* got the Tony, and then, they got the Tony for regional theater. It was a long journey, but one of the things it did was took us to London. When we've gone back now to London, people have never forgotten *The Grapes of Wrath.*

"At the same time, all of those moments have their challenges and their victories, because they all influence and affect the company."

Theater That Touches People

A theater company that strives to specifically address the human condition in positive, proactive ways can enjoy unique affirming victories.

Wheelock Family Theatre is one such company. How Wheelock uniquely operates is from a humanistic standpoint, in terms of being especially conscious and considerate of its audience members' needs. Some of these needs are specialized and, in general, are as diverse as the many different types of people who love the company's productions.

Susan Kosoff expresses her delight at Wheelock's creative successes, then goes on to mention some memorable highlights confirming that Wheelock really cares about its audience:

"I think there are shows that are emblematic, when everything comes together well and we're proud of the results. The audiences like them, the critics like them—they go well, and it's fabulous.

"Some of the individual accomplishments of some of the kids [Wheelock works with] are heartwarming. Some of the recognition we've gotten—we received an award from the White House for one of our programs. We got an Actors' Equity award. We've really gotten some important recognition nationally and regionally. Just this year, we got an award from the African-American Theater Festival in Boston.

"What can I say? It's affirming! I think about people in wheelchairs who have never seen live theater—they are seeing it and loving it. It keeps you going. The first few times I was there to see blind people, people with seeing eye dogs, in the audience, it's such a great feeling for them to be there. It's just great."

The Magic of a Message

Then, there are those nights when you're memorably validated as an artist. David Fuller, of Jean Cocteau Repertory, experienced this phenomenon in a quite unexpected way:

"There have been lots of triumphs, I think," David says. "I would say a personal one that comes to mind . . . Coincidentally, one of my mentors, Harold Prince, happened to be in the audience, with his wife, for a performance of *The Cradle Will Rock*, which I directed. It just so happened that night that there were some members there, too, of a fairly left political organization.

"After the show, somebody stood after the applause, after the actors had left the stage, and said, 'I'd like to invite you all to join me to sing the "Internationale,"' which was not initially a call-to-arms for Communist Russia. It was originally written as a workers' anthem. Knowing the story of *Cradle Will Rock* . . . the entire audience, almost, stood up and sang the 'Internationale' a capella. I mean, the play is a pro-worker play, and it was just nice to see the message carry through.

"We get these things almost every day. I stand and say 'thank you' to people as they leave the theater, and most of them are very happy to have been here. It makes me feel like I'm doing the right thing."

A Breed Apart

Lots of theater companies claim that the work they do is groundbreaking, but not as many can preserve it with as many different forays into creative expression as L.A. Theatre Works.

Says Susan Albert Loewenberg: "In the beginning phases, we broke new ground. We did a lot of the kind of work that's lauded today, but we were really pioneers, creating plays organically within the community, targeting specific populations, and really being creative within that.

"We actually made a film in 1976 about creating a play inside the prison walls, a documentary. We got a grant from the [National] Endowment [for the Arts] to do it, and we actually followed ourselves doing a production from start to finish. It was interspersed with talking heads—people would actually interview people in the workshop about their lives, who they were, and what they did. You'd see this person doing this fabulous vignette, being perfectly charming and wonderful, then telling you how they did a bank robbery. So, it was an interesting film that basically celebrated the human spirit and the ability to find creativity everywhere, how positive an experience creativity is.

"I think that when we did our prison work, we achieved our highest level within that work. We really did it well, and we were recognized for it. We were financially rewarded by major grants; we had critical recognition. We achieved the highest level of excellence, and we were recognized for that.

"When we started producing professional theater, working developmentally, discovering new writers, doing highly theatrical work, we also achieved a high level of recognition. We received the highest award for several of our productions from the L.A. Drama Critics Circle. It was not easy for a Los Angeles theater company to get money from the theater program of the Endowment.

"Through the years, I think the Endowment has supported us incredibly. We've had major, major grants from the NEA for all of our endeavors, which is, to me, the highest recognition. It's really your peers judging you, and it isn't filtered through corporate objectives and who you know. It's really about merit.

"When we started our radio programming, I think we've achieved a unique position, in that we have the only library of its kind in the United States. So, I think that at each level, we've done quality work and fairly unique things.

"I think, in general, we have a very good reputation for quality."

A New Lease on Life

It can get frustrating, waiting out the months and years it sometimes takes for your company to become more financially stable. You're working your tail off, but you never feel like you're really getting anywhere, because money is perpetually so tight. It takes a lot out of you, because you're a human being before you're a worker bee, after all.

What's super is when money materializes out of the blue, money that will allow to you really obtain something that gives your company stronger legs to stand on. This kind of miracle does happen; it happened to Berkeley Rep.

Says Mitzi Sales, "There's the story that's been told over and over again as a high point. Here we are, a 153-seat theater, a fledgling, neighborhood-based theater, and we're going to try to raise $1.2 million, or something silly, to build a theater and move downtown.

"We actually got word that Mark Taper, who was a banker—the Mark Taper Forum was named for his philanthropy—had heard that we were building a theater up in Berkeley, and he might be interested. The negotiation, and the final getting of $250, 000, was unbelievable. It was just breathtaking, it was celebratory, it was, 'Oh, my gosh, I guess we can do this.' I think our largest gift up to that point had probably been $10,000.

"Revenue was coming very, very slowly, very painfully. We thought we'd never make it. I think we were feeling downhearted, so this gave us a great shot in the arm, a great impetus to go forward. So, that was probably the high point.

"Let me just also say, on an extremely personal level, every time we opened a new show and I read a great review, that never got old. Opening night, being in the theater! I would actually stay away from most rehearsals, and part of the reason I did that was because I felt like one of my own values to the company, to the artistic director, to the director, was to come as fresh as I could to the final production. Not that I ever really could—who was I kidding? But I would come to the opening night and watch the show, feeling those feelings, seeing if it's working, cringing every time a prop fell apart!"

No Limits

For a theater with a traditionally staid reputation, branching out to do more controversial work is always a risk. You have to prime the pump first—get your community base ready for the chance you are about to take and the ride you are asking them to jump on with you.

The Pasadena Playhouse positioned itself expertly for an immersion in more daring work by dipping its toes in the water before taking a big plunge. Sheldon Epps slowly, but surely programmed shows with more contemporary social themes into his first seasons at the company. The theater's audiences loved it, and so now, he feels he can safely go even further.

"The greatest indicator of success is that perception of the theater changed so quickly," Epps says. "The fact that we were able to do the L.A. premiere of *Side Man*, that we've announced for the 2002–2003 season David Hare's *The Blue Room*, without a whole lot of consternation, indicates that we are now expected to do that kind of material and that there's recognition of the fact that this is as cutting-edge a theater as any large theater in the country."

The Rewards of Teamwork

Lyla White feels that many of her most successful enterprises at the Pasadena Playhouse have worked out so well because of the contributions staff members and friends have made to their execution and success. She believes strongly in the concept of teamwork and is eager to give credit where credit is due.

"We have enjoyed tremendous growth and recognition from different stakeholders— the artistic community, the community, the donor base. But we have always been a very successful theater company. Things have changed, but there are people who think we were better before. I don't want to give the impression that we did it all; the theater has a long history of being successful."

Lyla continues, "I think it is different now in that we've become more involved in the national network of theaters. We've joined LORT and TCG and different things. I think, for me, my personal victory? Fund-raising. A $1 million gift, a $2 million gift. Those are the real peaks.

"We had a wonderful Executive Director before me, but a very different style. Much more autocratic. What I feel like I've done is to really build the staff as a team. When we read the plays ahead together, we talk about them. People come up with creative ideas of how we can promote them in different ways.

"For instance, the play *A Life in the Theater*. A woman who works with us part-time in artistic development came up with an idea of inviting people who have lived their lives in the theater to come and talk to the wider community—high school students, members of the community—about their life in the theater. We said, that sounds like a good idea, so she sent out a letter. Gregory Hines said he would come and he'd bring his tap shoes and talk about his life in the theater. Sheldon said, 'All right, I'll ask Michael York.' Michael York said, 'Well, if Gregory Hines is going to dance, I'll sing a little and talk about my life in the theater.' He had a book coming out, so there'd be a book signing on the patio; we'd make that kind of a day. Carol Lawrence agreed to come and talk about her life in the theater.

"So, we had three weeks of that six-week run where, on the weekends, three weeks in a row, we had a program. The important part of that program is, [this idea came from] a woman who usually sits at her desk and sends out e-mails. Everybody got behind this; we decided to do it together.

"The play before this—*Do I Hear A Waltz?*—another staff member, a publications editor, said, 'I think we should roll the prices back to what they were when *Do I Hear A Waltz?* came out in New York in 1965.' We did some research, and that was $9.60. So, for one day only, we sold tickets for three of our previews for $9.60. We had a line around the block, and we were all involved with it.

"That is a grassroots idea, and I get excited about building a staff. I regret they're highly underpaid—although we do fall under the TCG guidelines, I'm just thinking about what people could make. My assistant is a paralegal. She's wonderful, but she makes half the money she made as a paralegal—she loves theater. I started my life as a high school and junior college teacher, so I can really celebrate how those younger people are growing in their jobs and at what they can do. I'm very proud of them."

It Shouldn't Have Been a Contender . . . But What a Contender!

Sometimes, you hear about a particular show and think, right off the bat, that's a sure thing. You look over the list of elements it boasts—experienced playwright, gorgeous house, and more—and you just know the thing is a go.

There are other scenarios when nothing about a show shouts success remotely, at first glance. Then, it turns out to be fabulous. Who knew? Nobody did, but one thing you can bet on is that lots of people who weren't involved will leap right up on the old bandwagon and claim they called its genius before anybody else.

Now, Jack Reuler is a guy who can honestly lay claim to recognizing a number of diamonds in the rough. Yet, even he was flummoxed by the success of one show that never should have worked. This show came up in Jack's mind again recently, when he was asked about which productions Mixed Blood had done that he'd list among its biggest successes.

"It's like asking a parent which kid they love the most," Jack laughed. "There have been so many things that I just go, this is fabulous that this happened.

"Here's one: In the big picture of the history of the organization, it's somewhat minor, but there was a guy, he's Chicano, and he wrote this play called *King of the Kosher Grocers*. He'd never written a play; he's a successful restaurateur. I saw him, and I got him to be in a couple of plays, and he was really good. He wrote this play like in two weeks. I said, 'We should develop this and do it.' It was so much about the north side of Minneapolis; every city has a part of town like this, that became the 'bad part of town.'

"We rented this abandoned supermarket and turned it into a theater and did it there, so we could try to convene the people who'd left the north side with the people who'd come to the north side with the people who'd stayed on the north side. It was a huge hit. Marion McClinton, who's gone on to have a great career, directed it.

"There was no reason it should have worked. It was a first-time playwright, doing a play in a space that had never been a theater, in a part of town where generations of people had never gone to that corner, who would do anything to avoid going to that corner.

"The ridiculous part of it was, I thought it was so important to do it there, because who else would care? But [then] the Old Globe [in San Diego] did it. It's been done all over the country. I kept second-guessing myself—is this the right thing to do? And it ran for months. It couldn't have been righter."

It's Called Survival

The biggest accomplishment any theater company can hope to have: that it doesn't go away. In Corey Fischer's opinion, keeping his A Traveling Jewish Theater alive, with a purity of mission, is what it's all about: "The biggest victory is that we're still here and still doing the work we started out to do.

"Another huge victory was getting our own theater and raising the money to renovate it. It's considered one of the best theaters in the Bay area. There have been other victories along the way—awards, grants.

"No specific production comes to mind—I mean, we all have our favorites. But it's not so much about individual productions as it is about having created a body of work. Another success was two years ago; for the first time, we incorporated a new member, a performer/director/writer. We were able to get funding to finance our position. The whole notion of bringing in a younger generation begins to become a sign that the theater will keep going."

Survival is the ultimate victory.

CHAPTER 9

ADAPTING TO GROWTH

Signs of success and longevity are what every theater company strives for. When you start to realize your hard work has paid off to the point where you've outgrown your best-case, big-picture scenario, it's tremendously rewarding.

A savvy theater head is never satisfied, though. She wants to keep going for it, accomplishing more goals once original ones have been achieved. This can be a fresh motivator for staffers and company members, sure, but it also can be a little daunting. How is a company really affected or changed by growth and success, after all?

You have to assess a number of factors—business planning, material choices, marketing, and more—to make sure these things are serving your expansion as effectively as possible. If you need to make changes in these areas, you make them. However, you have to make sure you're not biting off more than you can chew. Over inflating the importance of your position in the market, your financial situation at the present moment, or your creative influence on the universe can be hard traps not to fall into when you're feeling a little power. Yet, to do any of that would be most unwise.

In this chapter, our experts will relate their strategies for adapting to growth intelligently. Sometimes, their particular situations called for taking on a little risk to keep moving forward—but even that risk was strategic. Sometimes, adapting to growth meant diversifying as an organization. Sometimes, it meant a revamping of finances or a realization that the organization has become a little too loose, so more structure needs to be added. Every organization has faced different challenges.

The common denominator among them, however, is courage to push their individual organizations to the limits of being the best that they can be. Long-established company personnel are not afraid of much—they've been through so much on the way up, a certain self-assured defiance in the face of change tends to develop. Rather than worry, they just get on with business.

Another trait these successful companies share? There came a point where they refused to be comfortable. A lot of less ambitious troupes would be satisfied with staying at a certain level that offered few surprises, but was never going to allow for greatness. Our subjects dared to be great.

Let's Go

Paul Zuckerman knew his group could do so much more than its geographical boundaries dictated. So, his group made a radical move, taking a fateful road trip that changed its destiny for the better.

Paul tells of Chicago City Limits' early growth: "Chicago, all of a sudden, didn't seem like the ultimate goal anymore for us. We needed to keep evolving. The bars in Chicago weren't gonna do it for us. So, you've kind of got this sense that, 'We've got something!' The aspiration becomes, well, what's next?

"The way we handled it? We went on tour. We went on the crazy tour, seemed pretty crazy at the time, out west in 1978. We were basically a bar group at this time—I don't think we'd worked anywhere except bars. We go to Las Vegas. Joan Rivers was performing in Las Vegas. At her show, George [Todisco], our founder, slipped a waiter twenty bucks to send a message back to Joan: 'Hey, we're from Chicago'—she's a Second City alumna—'we'd love to meet you.' She sends a note back: 'Where are you performing?' George immediately writes back, 'The Jockey Club tomorrow at 9:00.' We had no gig there.

"So, we called the Jockey Club and said Joan Rivers wanted to see us there; got a spot? Of course, they had one. She walks in, she sees us, and boom! There's a buzz about us in Las Vegas. That gave us a momentum, an aura.

"We were invited to go out to Los Angeles and perform at the Improvisation and at a club called the Ice Palace. We were doing pretty good! So, about getting your foot in the door—there's hundreds of doors, most of them locked tighter than a drum. You've got to be ready, but once you're ready, you've got to act.

"Bud Friedman, who owned the Improvisation in Los Angeles and the Improvisation in New York, had been divorced, and I think his wife got the New York club. He said, 'Why don't you go to New York? You'd be great at the Improv there.' So, we drive to New York from California. We're from New York, a lot of us; we just walk into the Improvisation, let them know who we were, lo and behold, ten minutes later, we're opening the show that night. It was unbelievable. We didn't expect it, and we killed! There was this instant buzz about 'these guys from Chicago.'

"We spent about a year performing in the clubs around New York. At this point, we kind of, in quick succession, cut with Chicago. We quit jobs, a couple of relationships fell apart, and we relocated.

"This solidified us—and almost destroyed us. The problem with the clubs is, you can't develop material. You have to be doing your A material at all times. No club owner wants you to come in and sort of work something out. He wants you to come in at ten o'clock, at Catch a Rising Star, and those twenty minutes better be the funniest twenty minutes you can do.

"So okay, we were good at that. But a year into it, we haven't developed much material; we're working three, four, five clubs a night, not making any money.

"The realities start to hit you. 'We can't do this.' We started looking for a space. Not that we got our inspiration [there], but years later, reading Stanislavski, one of the things he really talks about is that an actor, more than anything, needs to find a situation where he's working, not looking for work. That's how you develop your craft. So, we have a need to find a space. We want to be able to develop material. We want to flourish as a theater company. We find a space on West 42nd Street.

"Now, at this point, we start to expand as a company as well. We need to train people for the future. They were not out there—quality improvisers just weren't there. So, we start workshops, at some level to raise some cash, but really, to develop what turned into our national touring company, so we can start to develop a business and start to get people trained to come into our show and evolve our show over time. That happened probably the first year we had our space. We started the workshops, we had some very promising students. We had very few understudies; people would perform in those days under incredibly bad physical conditions. But once in a while, if we needed to cover somebody, we could use one of these people.

"By 1980, our national touring company was actually performing shows at colleges and regional theaters; that continues till today. It's been almost a constant source of cash replenishment for the resident company over time. And the workshop program, which has evolved and been developed, is basically where most of these people are trained.

"There was no active desire to infuse new blood, but there were a couple of changes in our casting. George, our founder and Artistic Director, died at the age of thirty. Very tragic, but in some strange way, further solidified this odd commitment and religion, if you will. We added our stage manager to the show, who was an actor, but at the beginning, did not have the stage skills he later developed. But pretty much, that ensemble, barring George's situation, performed together as an ensemble throughout the mid-eighties. One cast member had a child, one eventually moved to California as a writer, but there was a very slow attrition. People did develop and evolve their careers, yet stayed a long time.

"Evolution becomes a challenge over time. It's like anything: What have you done for me lately? It's like a restaurant—you can go ten times and it's great meals, then go the eleventh time and it's lousy, and I think theater is the same thing. So, the constant challenge is to evolve the show in a way that reflects the skills of the current cast, doesn't throw the baby out with the bathwater, but doesn't hold on to something that no longer should be held on to.

"You might have a cast that's very strong vocally, which will naturally take you into doing more musical kind of things. When that cast turns over, and maybe the next group of people aren't so vocally gifted, you're hitting your head against the wall to try to develop music with them. You make your adjustments. I've always felt the strength of the group is diversity, but you have to see it, acknowledge it, and utilize it."

That Age-Old Challenge

Even when your company is known and established, giving your creative work and your business concerns equal weight and attention can still be hard to do.

Certain decisions can tend to provide you a shortcut to solving this imbalance. For example, some companies make a great effort at an obvious point of growth to rework their financial plans, in order to create more stability in terms of consistent income. That solid financial base can allow you the freedom to get a little crazy artistically.

Other organizations hire more people to keep an eye on fiscal growth, so key personnel can be free to focus more attention on creative output. Such a plan has its pluses and minuses. On the plus side, if you hire great money minds you can trust, the company can quickly become more organized and profitable. On the minus side, if you make a dumb move like hiring your stage manager's cousin Bob, who was reputed to have attended a top business program, but in reality, proves to you he couldn't manage the profits from a Girl Scout Cookie fund drive, you've got more headaches than ever.

If you're used to hand-to-mouth survival, it's possible that deep down, a part of you likes a little struggle. Maybe you're still a little split-focused on merging your creative and financial sides seamlessly because you don't want to get too "professional." This may sound totally beside the point of why you would go into business in the first place, but it's a very, very common attitude. It's almost a point of pride for some theater companies, in fact.

If this is your outlook, you've got to know something: You've peaked already. You can't grow any further. You've got to be willing to merge your creative concerns and your business concerns to attain a larger profile, which probably sounds all corporate and boring and smacks of becoming part of the establishment and all of that. Yet, it doesn't have to be that way at all—you can retain your artistic principles and still make more money.

David Zak has done just that with Bailiwick Repertory. No one can say that his company hasn't done work that's among the most challenging in its history—such as Terrence McNally's *Corpus Christi*—in recent memory, after Zak took great pains to settle his company physically into a prominent space, a location that would help bring in more dollars.

Zak says, "I still feel the hardest part of my job as Artistic Director is balancing commerce and art. Only when we moved into our most recent home—the Bailiwick Arts Center—could we program things on an annual basis that we knew would generate revenue. Our annual holiday show, *The Christmas Schooner*, and the summer's Pride Series generally are successful. The rest of the year, we love to gamble."

Maximizing Potential

La Jolla Playhouse is known for its smart and entertaining franchising strategies. Very few regional theaters can claim the track record the Playhouse has, in terms of sending so much quality work out into the world and having its investments, both artistic and financial, come back tenfold. Huge box office, critical raves, Tonys, long smash runs—you know the successful end results.

Another priority for the Playhouse is, of course, meeting the ongoing, welcoming challenges of constant growth on the home front. Terrence Dwyer has an expert eye for recognizing not simply how to maximize the potential of the Playhouse's many assets to complement its ongoing artistic and business expansions. He also knows just the right moves to make to create growth movement wherever the organization wants it to occur.

"Improved staffing in 1993 enabled us to grow," Dwyer explains. "Before that, there had been fairly limited progress in terms of growth and meeting financial challenges. A staff must also remain constant in terms of belief in the artistic mission of a company. So, recruiting more staff, plus adding more members to our board—sustaining and building with good people, everything flows from that.

"Another piece of the puzzle: We do a lot of musicals, and entrepreneurially, to get rid of our debt, their success positioned us well, was leverage for us, and very strategic in terms of driving a subcategory of productions we are involved in—shows that go beyond our company, to Broadway, etc.

"Artistically, another strategic move was to get rid of our old menu and try 'flash performances.' Flash performances are artistically exciting show runs of one to seven performances, and we scheduled them at times when things were dark. These works have integrity—they feature such artists as Sandra Bernhard, and they've been very successful.

"More visibility, a broader artistic scope, and good cash flow produce growth."

Taking Material, and Business, in a New Direction

After Michael Leibert's tenure at Berkeley Repertory ended and Sharon Ott was selected as the company's new Artistic Director, it was natural that adjustments and changes would be made.

In such a situation, when a new leader takes over, it's always smart business sense to retain those parts of the company's artistic mission and day-to-day operations that are working. It's also very important that the company's new leader express her creative self. A new face at the top should mean that the company's work feels new and fresh and that this leader can put her thumbprint on the theater's artistic offerings. Audiences rarely reject this—they want to know how the new company head thinks. They're interested in being challenged and don't want to be bored or disappointed by a company playing things too safe after such a major change.

Susan Medak came into Berkeley Repertory as such artistic adjustments were happening, and she felt inspired by the atmosphere of change. In her position as the company's new Business Manager, Medak wanted to deal with the issues of financial expansion in a new way. She explains how Ott's new look at the company's creative scheme, plus her own business philosophy, took the company in a new direction:

"Sharon Ott was interested in the development of new works, in eclectic programming. She used short-run shows, collaboration with companies, as a way to begin to introduce the idea that new work could be as interesting as classic work.

"The company began a parallel season of works that played with form and structure, in addition to the regular season. The subscribers were offered a 'grazer's package,' for those who saw themselves as more adventurous and wanted to sample the more eclectic work in addition to the more traditional productions. It blew up! Out of six thousand subscribers, more than 50 percent were attending both seasons. We now have two theaters.

"Sharon was not interested in a resident pool of actors. She wanted to work more with artists of color, to have much more of a director's theater, more focused on physical design. The shows were things like *Eureka*—gritty, intensely politicized, very vivid, very elegant approaches. Sharon's hallmark and esthetic sensibilities matched the core values of the company, though—quality and flexibility.

"We came to understand that you deal with artists on their own rhythm for finding the truth of the material. We found our own rhythm for producing work, too. Our intention is for artists to do their best work within our theater, so they must be surrounded by support. Support from the production staff—you must assume that duty for each member of your company. Your job is to help them do their job the best they can, to be respectful and responsible for the work the artist envisions. And as far as jobbers are concerned, they are also invested in this company, whether they're with you for two weeks or ten weeks. It all goes back to those core values.

Oh, and here's another core value to add to those I mentioned: comfort with ambiguity. People who want absolutes do not always feel comfortable here. For us, living in the gray area is most interesting. Because with Sharon, we became much more of a risk-taking organization, taking risks onstage and taking financial risks, too.

"Mitzi [Sales] resigned eventually, because even though she was flexible and prudent, she couldn't solve the fact that our budget was not reflecting the expansion—not because of anything to do with her, but because the resources weren't immediately there. Since 1985, we've lived with a degree of financial risk. We've had years with surplus and years with debt. But without risk, without taking large leaps, you can't grow. That's a price I choose to pay.

"You've got to always think you can do it. Leaps of faith and acts of will! Every day, I come into work, open the doors on the first day of rehearsal for a show, and I believe that show will be great."

Increased Support Leads to Good Things

The progressive, exciting work Horizons Theatre was doing made its name and got the attention of state funding sources. In turn, that support has allowed the company to grow in terms of the audiences it reaches.

Leslie Jacobson says, "In 1993, we found a home sharing space with a group of other arts organizations in Arlington County. We were then supported by the Arlington County Performing Arts Division and the Arlington County Commission on the Arts. Since '93, we don't have a permanent space, but we do have access to county spaces and have been able to produce two- or three-show seasons, or an abbreviated season.

"This year [2001–2002], we're going to do four productions. Two of them will be in spaces in town [Washington, D.C.], one of them is going to be in Arlington County, and then, one is going to be in the fall of 2002; we're not exactly sure in what space that's going to be yet. Theater can go to people; it's not just about people coming to theater.

"Of course, the obviously disadvantages [to moving] are there, too. People aren't always sure where they can find you. It's got its pluses and minuses."

The Importance of a Board in the Growth Process

The members of the Steppenwolf ensemble have, of course, always been ahead of the curve. The Steppenwolf board is also brilliant at foreseeing the future and the changes that must be made to meet it.

Choosing Martha Lavey and Michael Gennaro to head Steppenwolf was one such well-strategized move. Another very important step the board took was to completely examine where the company could go next, in both artistic and business aspects.

The board then handed its proposed plans to its two new hires, who deftly carried out the changes and took the company on to even greater achievements.

But what's most unusual about this story is the way the board reevaluated itself to benefit the company as a whole.

"Six years ago now, in the process of bringing Martha Lavey and myself on," Michael Gennaro relates, "the board worked on a strategic plan to get a sense of what they wanted [us] to change, expand upon, whatever. All of those [things] were accomplished in just about three years.

"At the same time, things started to happen, like getting the National Medal of Arts and the Illinois Arts Legend Award. A number of things mounted on top of each other from just doing the work. We've also expanded the spaces. We've also expanded the amount of real estate we have to support what we're doing. About the last two years, I think what's interesting is, the board kind of looked around and said, 'Wait a minute—we challenged the administration and the artistic office to do a bunch of things, and now they've done them all. We've kind of fallen behind. Now, we need to step up and regovern ourselves, put a plan on the table to change the structure of the way we do things, so we can catch up and get back on course.' Which they did. So, there was a kind of stepping up of everything around us, and I think to get to that place, for the organization as a whole, was a great accomplishment."

Diversification

Sometimes, in order for a company to be at its most productive, it has to be willing and eager to wipe the artistic and business slate clean and start over.

Susan Albert Loewenberg explains how her company (L.A. Theatre Works) has progressed through her willingness to fully embrace changes, in her environment, as suggested by her esteemed collaborators, and as a unique means to an end in order to secure the organization's ultimate longevity and excellence.

"I think the reason I've succeeded is because I've kept moving. By my nature, I'm a tenacious person—you'll notice I've been with the same company for twenty-seven years—but I've reinvented the company. I think that, rather than go off and do something else, I stayed within the same structure and just made different businesses.

"I think that my skill is, I'm able to see an opportunity and go with it, move on. Producing theater in a 99-seat situation was a great learning experience, but it's not something I'd want to devote my life to. I mean, in Los Angeles, it's silly. It's for young people to stretch their wings. It's not a lifetime career. It's just not.

"We were never really able, for whatever reason, to fully realize this company as a theatrical performing company. Not because of the actors—we just couldn't raise the money. That's part of the problem with Los Angeles. Los Angeles, particularly at that time and probably just as much today, just doesn't step up to the plate. It just doesn't.

"To me, the fact that [much of Los Angeles theater] never professionalized was its death knell. The fact that we don't have a coterie of general managers and advertising agencies—it's impossible to advertise in the *Los Angeles Times*. There are all kinds of reasons why, until recently, it's been a one-show town with the Taper. It's been too difficult. Too many things conspire against being taken seriously.

"Plus, if you see what's happening in New York [after the World Trade Center attack], you realize how dependent even that city is, frankly, on the bridge and tunnel traffic and the real tourists, the out-of-towners. You can't support the theater just with the people living in New York City.

"People don't come to Los Angeles to go to the theater. We don't have that advantage, so we have to depend entirely upon our indigenous population. And it just doesn't work.

"But be that as it may, we continued as a group. The fund-raising for this idea was kind of languishing. We had actually built a beautiful, gorgeous space for a workshop. We would meet regularly and work on pieces and stuff, and Richard Dreyfuss said one day, 'You know, I've always wanted to work on the radio, do a radio drama.' I said, 'I'll go and see Ruth Seymour.' She got very excited about it—she's a very adventurous [radio] programmer. She thought it was a fabulous idea and said 'Let's do something big.' I said, 'Why don't we do a book?' We then began the search for a book, and my idea was, all thirty-four people have to be in this thing. We came up with Sinclair Lewis's *Babbitt*. It took us a year and a half to record and edit. We did it in the studio, put the whole book up on a computer, and figured out which characters were in which scenes. There were ninety characters played by all thirty-four actors; the main characters, of course, were only played by one actor, but the minor characters, they doubled. We split up the narration. It was a twelve-and-a-half-hour recording. Lynn debuted it in 1987 on Thanksgiving day as a marathon, all day long, and it became a huge hit and instant cult classic.

"National Public Radio picked it up and ran it all over the country. It is still a magnificent recording. I mean, we had absolutely no idea what we were doing, but we had a fabulous editor who was a real radio pro. And Gordon Hunt, Helen's dad, who still works with me today, a terrific guy, and was the head of recording for animation for

Hanna-Barbera at the time. The BBC heard us and contacted us. They came over—it was the occasion of the U.K.-L.A. Festival 1987. We did two plays with them—*The Crucible*, starring Stacy Keach, Richard Dreyfuss, Hector Elizondo, and Michael York, and *Are You Now or Have You Ever Been?* as a companion piece. The BBC, Martin Jenkins, came over, and it was a big task. We were doing it on a soundstage, not in front of people. And the programs came out brilliantly—the BBC paid for everything. Ruth aired them, the BBC aired them, we got paid for our time, all the actors got paid, and it was a fantastic launch.

"We have since done twenty-five or thirty programs in collaboration with the BBC. They usually come over—once, we went to England, to the BBC studios. Some of the best work we've ever done, we've done with them.

"This began slowly taking over—we were still doing a little theater production, but by 1992, I think I did my last [stage] show, my last regular theater piece. We had a little program of play readings that we usually did in our office. It was becoming too crowded— it held about seventy people. Ed Asner called me—I was on vacation in Europe—and he said, 'You've got to meet with these guys! A partner of mine is staying in this new hotel, and we should do something in their ballroom!' I thought, 'Yuck, Ed, I don't want to do something in a hotel ballroom.' But he kept insisting.

I came back, and I said, okay, it's Ed, I've got to do this. So, I went and met with the hotel manager of the Guest Quarters in Santa Monica, which later morphed into Doubletree and then became part of Hilton. Long story short, we're having this meeting, and they wanted to build up the hotel, because they'd just opened in Santa Monica. Suddenly, a light bulb went on in my head, and I thought, 'I could record plays live in performance, just like we did at our benefit.'

"I had no idea whether this would fly. I contacted Ruth, and she thought it was interesting. We agreed that we would do six plays, send out a little brochure, and see if anybody was interested. We got a terrific response back. We did each [play] over one night, no idea what we were doing. We hired a recording engineer who brought in equipment.

"I remember the first show we did was a Molière play. The actors were all grouped around one microphone—it was terrible! But people seemed to like it. Over the course of those six plays, we actually began to figure out how to do it, and we were stunned—people loved coming there. They loved coming to the hotel, having dinner there—it was a package deal, it was easy to park. It worked for L.A.

"It was very strange, because everything worked. You had famous actors, you had a limited time frame for them, you had a kind of interesting, car-culture-friendly venue.

It was a very odd thing. We actually started, by the second year, doing some good work. We figured out how to record, we figured out what to do.

"The thing about Doubletree was, they were a fantastic corporate sponsor. They paid for everything. All of a sudden, hundreds of people were coming to their hotel. We were with them for ten years—we went from one show to four shows; the ballroom held about four hundred people. They paid for the brochure, they really got us going, and we got a grant from the Irvine Foundation, which also helped us.

We built a subscription audience. By the time we left the Doubletree in 1998, we had a huge subscription audience and a fantastic program. By that time, we were doing fourteen shows a year, four performances each, so we could make good recordings, but we realized we had to do a lot of performances to get a good recording. Now, we do five or six, so we cross-edit and get a very superior product. We built this incredible reputation; we were on KCRW, the centerpiece of KCRW Playhouse. We were on twenty, twenty-five times a year; we were promoted every week. If you said 'L.A. Theatre Works,' everybody knew what it was, because we were on the radio all the time.

"Around 1994, I began to realize, we ought to sell these things. So then, we had to go back and get all the rights for audio sale, which was an interesting process, and start another business, which was the audio publishing business. We got a great start-up grant from the Endowment for about $100,000, developed a catalog, developed packaging. We basically started a whole, huge other business, which was an enormous undertaking, I cannot begin to describe it. I mean, we are audio publishers, and radio has been a very interesting vehicle for us, but it's not the end of the story."

When Faith and Fortune Collide

Sometimes, when faced with whether to take a risk in the name of growth, you just have to believe it will work. Even when you're not sure it will.

In the early days of Berkeley Repertory, Mitzi Sales and Michael Leibert both believed in the future growth of their organization against very high odds. They made a move despite the risks, and it paid off in spades.

"A very interesting experience, actually, a wonderful, sort of alarming, funny thing: There was a minor joke when Michael first looked around and found the space on College Avenue; my comment was like, 'build the space, and they will come.' When we built the space in downtown Berkeley, that actually happened!" Mitzi Sales remembers.

"We had this subscriber base; we were practically sold out at 153 seats. But when we built this four-hundred-seat theater, I thought, 'Oh, boy'—based on my experience of how long it took us to build up the audience in the College Avenue space. We built the theater, sent out a subscription brochure, and the unbelievable number of subscribers! It grew—kabloom!

"People were buying subscriptions who had never seen a show. It was like, 'What?!' It was remarkable.

"You've got to prepare yourself for a lot of lean years, to build your reputation, to make your mistakes. But it did help, in those early years, that there was a foundation for the expansion and development in theaters in those days—it actually did help that there were those organizations, that they would have meetings, and we could come together with other people who were struggling. We could all figure out where to go to get some money, how to market with no budget and no money. There are resources."

Partners in Progress

Speaking of fruitful partnerships, you can't find a better example of a complementary team than Sheldon Epps and Lyla White at the Pasadena Playhouse.

They couldn't be more different, in terms of backgrounds and sensibility. Yet, Epps and White's two disparate halves make up the perfect whole. It's preferable, in my opinion, to team up with people who are very different from you. That way, someone is always bringing a new and needed perspective to the table when there's a difficult problem to solve or planning to do.

Lyla White explains: "I came to the Playhouse five years ago, a year before Sheldon, although Sheldon had been an associate with the Playhouse before that. In March of 1999, the executive director left, and Sheldon and I became partners. We worked on a more traditional organization, which isn't always clear to the rest of the world, but seems to work in theater. Sheldon became the Artistic Director, and I was, for a while, the interim Executive Director, because I see myself as a fundraiser. Little did I know that being the Executive Director is just the same as being the fundraiser! It's just a different title on the same page.

"Our team has worked really well. We're very different. Sheldon is newer to Pasadena, he's younger, he's African American. I'm an old white lady who's been here a long time, and I know this town! We get along very well, and we enjoy working together. We are both committed to the growth and the enrichment of this theater, both in the short-term and the long-term, and we're both committed to what theater brings to a community. He comes at it more from the art, and I come at it more from, 'This community deserves and needs this beautiful, historic theater, and it needs to have on its stage an art that's worthy of the beautiful building.'

"We come at it from a different way. I don't want to do Sheldon's job. I am not the theater person. I don't want to pick the plays. And he doesn't want to do my job, although I talk to him about what we're going to be doing; I am our demographic, so if I like it, it's a pretty sure thing that the audience will. If I don't, then for sure, the audience won't. That doesn't mean we don't do it anyway. It just means we need to prepare the audience.

"Sheldon is willing to help with the fund-raising, but he doesn't really want to do the fund-raising. He doesn't really want to manage the staff. He doesn't really want to attend the board meetings; he doesn't really want to work the board. I do that. That division works really well, yet we're both really collaborative. I think we're both really easy to get along with. Sheldon has a very good business sense. He does not pick plays that would necessarily be his first choice. He picks plays that will move the theater along, so that our audience will grow and come to appreciate some of the wilder things he comes up with. Practical, though. He doesn't try to offend our audience.

"The other thing that he has done for us, that he might not say himself, is that he has built a relationship in the national artistic community. He's very well-respected out of the Theatre Communications Group, he had a fellowship to work at the Old Globe, he's asked to direct in New York and Washington, and that's very good for us."

Epps appreciates the opportunity to work with White and sees it as his responsibility to progress the theater artistically, on a daily basis. Additionally, a great interest of his is his company's profile expansion. One of his top priorities, in this vein, is to up the Pasadena Playhouse's national recognition factor.

Says Epps: "This is a theater that has a really long and illustrious history. It's one of the oldest operating theaters in the country. There have been producing companies in Pasadena for, I think, a little over eighty years. The theater we now operate in just had its seventy-fifth birthday in 2000.

"It's been a very, very long history; it has, however, been something of a roller coaster history, including a big gap in the middle, when the theater was closed for twelve or fifteen years in the seventies going into the early eighties.

"I came here in 1997, after a period when the theater had not had an artistic director for about five or six years. Because of primarily economic forces, the company had just been in survival mode. It had been about just keeping the doors open and keeping something on the stage. The idea of resurrecting the position of Artistic Director, and bringing me in to fill that position, was about, once again, revitalizing the theater artistically, which, if you do well and correctly, also revitalizes the theater economically.

"Certainly, in terms of perception, both in the theater community in southern California, Los Angeles in particular, and in terms of the theater's national perception, if I had a goal when I decided to take the job, it was to once again have this theater considered, on a national level, one of the best LORT theaters in America. I think that we have certainly come close to or reached that goal, in a short amount of time."

Job Satisfaction

A good artistic director wants to make his employees happy—every employee, including actors, directors, technical staff, design staff, administrative staff, the lot. A good managing director helps the artistic director make this happen.

When your company has a high job satisfaction percentage, the company moves forward. This can be tough to accomplish in the theater, by the way. As you probably know, theater folks love to be dramatic and complain. Some live to be long-suffering.

So, know this in advance. When it happens to you, stage a preemptive strike: when you hear rumblings of discontent; address them directly with an employee, before the discontent starts to spread. Often, employees will try to enlist other coconspirators to agree with their complaints, and you don't want to have mutiny on your hands. So, try to give in on little points when you can. Make a pleasant working environment for your actors.

Still, don't be a pushover. You can't allow your people to go diva on you. You also have to make sure that folks don't get too comfortable after a while in the routine of working for your company. Find novel ways to discourage laziness.

In addition, a smart company head is always moving forward with unique ways to keep all aspects of the organization's agenda fresh. As a managing director, Dona Lee Kelly sees this as a key part of her job at the Cocteau. "David has a vision of an acting company really being able to be flexible. He is expecting a certain level of artistry and technique; they have to be able to speak really well and have to be trained well classically. They have to have a range, to be able to be that flexible.

"He would hope, at some point, to find someone to do master classes, so [the actors] keep up with their craft. One of the biggest things in an acting ensemble, sometimes, is that they stop working on that. He doesn't want them to be lazy or go back into doing their schtick.

"As we do have a classic reading series, I'm also encouraging him, okay, maybe every other year, to also have a commissioning arm where you're doing a new translation, or adaptation, or stage adaptation of a novel, something that is classic. To always encourage that side. It also will encourage American writers to hone their craft at doing new translations and adaptations. So, all of those things have to be defined, because ultimately, it's art that's going to bring people into the theater, not how well you manage, even though I'm saying you'd better manage impeccably well. But that's part of management, making sure that the art is very focused and everything it's saying is prioritized.

"People have to understand that management is not just crunching numbers. It's really making sure that the organization is defined, handled well, and positioned artistically well within the community. That's part of being a producer."

Small Steps Forward Mean a Lot

When charting the growth of your organization, you may feel a bit discouraged if you only see small improvements happening slowly. You've probably got your heart set on big, explosive, visible changes you can brag about to your family and friends, like four-star reviews in the *New York Times*, riots breaking out in the unruly patron lines that routinely ring your block, and Dame Judi Dench calling every hour on the hour, dying to know when you'll be casting her in a classic.

Okay, back down to earth. That stuff is very nice, indeed, but much more realistically, growth should be measured in small increments. Set mini-goals you can meet fairly quickly—it's a real boost, plus every drop in the bucket gets you closer to your ultimate dreams fulfilled.

The best way to make early progress, which carries you through to the next level, is to decide what is important to you to achieve within your company. Susan Kosoff followed a slow-but-sure strategy at Wheelock. The company began by focusing on its interest in theatrical education.

"In the second year, we started having classes. That program has grown tremendously over the years and has become a substantial part of our budget. But we only started it as an educational enterprise.

"It took us a long time to get a full-time educational director—it's only been in the last couple of years that we've had that.

"I think in the beginning, every power tool we bought was a big deal! But I decided early on that we were going to put money into permanent equipment rather than rent it, and that way, we built things up. There are always ways that you want to build up a space, and I think that there continue to be. But it's a very different facility, much more current, certainly, than it was twenty years ago. This year, it improved. Some of that is that, over time, we've worked with some very good designers, tech directors, people who make that happen."

Marketing Milestones

There are as many theories of how you can use marketing to power your company along as there are members of the Osmond family. Yet, I feel there's only one way that really helps you determine whether you are on the right horse: Don't compete. That's when you make true progress.

Crazy? Not at all. When you're marketing something at your theater while looking over your shoulder to see how the guy next to you is marketing something at his, you've already lost your edge. You've stopped paying attention to what is great about the show your company has to offer.

Pay attention to the reasons you love the play you're presenting. Why did you choose this material in the first place? Review your enthusiasm, and when you figure out what you loved originally about this work, and continue to love, use marketing to tell your potential audience about it. It's that simple.

The key to marketing progress is to polish each product you offer your audience, as you go along, into the best product it can be, then tell the world about it, and collect your money. Not every show will be a winner, but if you're trying your best to make each current offering the most it can be, you will be learning more with each show you do.

Jack Reuler (Mixed Blood) has this very healthy take on marketing: "I don't believe that we're competing with other live events. I think if you go to a live event and have a good experience, you're going to go to another live event. In terms of subscription, what we've done is say, you can come and see all these shows that we're doing, but then you can go see culturally specific programming at these other institutions. I'm real excited about the possibility of that. I don't know if I have the marketing chops to get enough people to buy it, but I'm sure going to try.

"We're getting a good audience—it's who we want to have. We're getting a good mix of audience members. So, that's looking good. I think we've had really good luck, in a city like ours [Minneapolis]. A number of theaters in different cities have done bilingual work. We do a show each year in Spanish and English—some nights it's in Spanish, some nights it's in English—and we've done very well with that in terms of attendance. This last year, we actually did a show where the characters were bilingual, and depending on who they were talking to, they actually kept switching during the course of the production. It worked out really well.

"We're sort of finding our way in that area. My current intention is to become the theater, in our area, of new populations—primarily immigrants and refugees, of which there are many. The programming reflects that.

"So, between doing new work, which I feel strongly about, giving the voice of the great writers and others the place in which they can be heard, and trying to reach these new audiences—again, whatever we do, it's the very nature of doing race-based things. Whenever anybody who isn't white gets onstage in America, there's some political statement made. Because of that, you need to be that much better than everybody else doing it. So really, to maintain high-level standards of quality, while doing what we're trying to do in terms of substance and content, is really important.

"The eighties, in many ways, were a huge success for us. I think that a couple of those theater critics who completely bought into us were directly responsible for that. It wasn't genius marketing; we'd open a show, we'd get a rave review, then we'd get more support and word-of-mouth. I thought that's what marketing was."

Jack's right—that is, in a nutshell, what marketing is supposed to be.

Jack defines his idea of progress very personally, and so should you. Your company is not like anybody else's, so to compare yourself to others is a futile exercise. Don't do something if it doesn't mean anything to you.

To really make the most of your company's growth, that growth has to be for a purpose. Every step that forwards your company's mission is the growth that counts.

PART THREE:
NOW AND
FOREVER

CHAPTER 10:

OUR CURRENT PROFILE

Theater companies need to stay very objective about how well they are doing.

This doesn't mean companies need to be relentlessly self-critical. That isn't useful. Yet, it's important for a company to step back and take a good look at where it stands from time to time. You don't need to do this on a daily basis. But every six months or so, it can be very helpful to sit down with your season paperwork—your financial records, your reviews, audience surveys, and comment sheets, if you have them—and see what's really going on.

It's also helpful to have regular bull sessions with your staff and company members about how they feel the company is doing. Giving everyone a forum to air their joys and grievances can make for a closer, more productive company.

Perhaps the most important tool in the evaluation process is your gut feelings, though. As a leader, how do you instinctively feel that things are going? If you had to describe your company's current situation to an outsider honestly, what would you say?

Our experts have been frank enough to do just that. In this chapter, they discuss where their companies stand at the moment.

What's the best use you can make of this chapter? Well, read it and enjoy it, of course. Then, use it as inspiration. Turn the tables on yourself. Pretend I'm asking you how your theater company stands right this second, and you have to answer me right off the top of your head. Answer honestly, then use your own valuable information to feel the pride in your company you know it deserves or to give your company the shot in the arm it needs.

Stuck in a Moment You Can't Get Out Of

The world changed one day in the late summer of 2001, and it's probably never going to be the same again, in countless ways. We all realize that.

We know how devastating the World Trade Center attacks have been to the economy of New York City as a whole. Particularly devastated has been the arts community. One of the largest segments of the arts community, of course, has been the theater, which has traditionally depended on the massive tourist dollar to stay afloat. Initially, those tourists stayed away in droves.

Even though things are not as dire as they were—theatergoers have returned, at least to Broadway—many shows have been shuttered. So, how does a Manhattan-based theater company proceed? How does it ultimately survive? Paul Zuckerman (Chicago City Limits) has been formulating ideas about just that. Says Zuckerman: "You know the beginning—September 11, 2001.

"What do you do? If they're not going to come, that's the one thing that can stop us. We've been challenged. We're looking creatively to the future. The first two weeks [after the World Trade Center attack], we didn't do shows. Cancel, cancel, cancel—groups of one hundred, one hundred and fifty canceling, oh, my God! And this is coming after the summer, which is our traditional slow point. Just when the season should be in full gear, right now, it's hold your breath every night.

"So, we've been having meetings, and we're in the process of enacting a lot of things. There's lots of ideas over the years that we've back-burnered—thought, 'Gee, wouldn't it be nice, but . . .'—and things like that, I think we're going to enact sooner than later. With the business model here now of, 'x is the number of people that potentially will come,' it's a smaller x than it was a year ago. So, anything we can do to encourage that x to visit us more often is, I think, where it's going to come from. For instance, we're starting silent comedy films with a live accompanist. We sort of had that in motion anyhow, but we're accelerating that, and I think it could be very exciting. It's obviously going to be a very low-ticket item, but right now, I'm trying to pay rent.

"Children's theater—we've done great interactive things with kids. We don't really have a program—now we're trying to develop a program again, something that's been in the works that's maybe being accelerated. Perhaps inviting other groups on our off nights, to make us more of a center, relying less, if you will, on the core of our show and giving the audience more opportunities to have fun, to participate in our theater. It's perhaps, more so than ever before, our business plan.

"We had more corporate events on the schedule before, more group sales, and that part of the business has not completely vanished, but evaporated drastically. You have to be able to change your business plans as conditions change." CCL's post-9/11 survival is a testament to how well Zuckerman's approach is working.

A Sense of Security

Outside of New York, things have not been that peachy either, from an economic standpoint. During periods of belt-tightening, the unfortunate thing is that attending theater and other entertainment events can become a less frequent diversion. As people become more cost-conscious, they are forced to become more selective about which performances they attend.

What can a theater company do to keep perspective? Outside of paying close attention to box office and dreaming up new and effective advertising tactics, it helps to have a healthy dose of confidence. You have to know exactly who you are and what it is that your company does best. Says David Zak: "We are confident of [Bailiwick's] position in the Chicago market. We know what the Goodman, Steppenwolf, etc., will and can produce. Our theater can be more daring, diverse, and in some cases, left of center. Being a leader in the off-loop movement is a position of responsibility to our artists and our audiences, and we are most excited when we know the city is talking about our work."

Controlling Only What You Can

Berkeley Repertory is currently at a place of exciting physical and artistic development.

First of all, the company is still breaking in its freshly built space and learning all of its possibilities for creative utilization. The theater is also monitoring its audience response to this space, which is fantastic.

Administrative changes are also being mulled over, plus more. Susan Medak addresses these issues, plus offers us a very sage piece of wisdom. Susan suggests that, as a theater administrator, you should do as much as you can with any given situation, but know when it's time to quit. "Tony Taccone, our current Artistic Director, is an artist of the highest caliber," Medak continues. "At this moment, we fill at least 600 out of 850 seats regularly. Our new space is really totally redesigned, and audiences love the perceived intimacy of it. You have to know your strengths—I was scared, walking people through the changes, but people love it! Tony has opened the doors even further with his artistic leadership and his complete support of this community. He is not in conflict with anything or anyone.

"We are on the cusp of another change. We want the building sometimes to be filled with work that is not ours—we want it to be filled all the time. We will also change the way our board works and thinks. How? That sensibility will have to emerge. I do know, however, that we all have to let go of control, find a way to manage all sorts of human emotions and opinions. The challenge is to build the organization around individuals' knowledge and strengths.

"I think that the greatest challenge for me is learning when to pick my battles—when I should impose myself and when to step back and pick up the pieces. It's easier to build a building than it is to run a company. You have to make as many choices as you can up front. You try to fix the things you can control; there's a point at which you have to let go."

Empowering Ourselves for the Future

A Traveling Jewish Theater's three founders have decided that it's time to make a few changes, to empower their company for its next level of accomplishments.

To do this, the company has been actively looking to involve a new generation of actors, writers, and directors in the very specific type of work that they do. The founders have been gratified by the interest and availability of quality talent in this respect.

There is also the philosophy that it's best for the theater to make some very significant changes to the way decisions are made within the company structure. According to Corey Fischer, "Young artists who are coming into our theater bring a new energy, a new perspective. What's particularly gratifying is that we're finding more and more young people who want to do what we're doing. It feels like it almost had to skip a generation—we're in our fifties, and now we're meeting people in their twenties and thirties, whereas people in their late thirties and forties we don't see being drawn to this so much. The opening production of this season (2001–2002) is a new play by a new playwright who's not yet thirty.

"There's a big change that we're right in the middle of trying out, and this gets into some very interesting and challenging issues. The whole question of how to run the company, how to govern it, who makes the decisions. For many years, one of the things that's been unique about us, in the broader context, is that we've always been an artist-run theater. A lot of regional theaters, resident theaters, are really board-run, and we've never been that, never want to be that. So, the way we've functioned is really on the basis of consensus between the four co–artistic directors.

"In recent years, especially since getting our own theater, we've been discovering that this process is getting unwieldy. So, with a lot of consideration and strategic planning with an organizational planning consultant, we have finally come to trying the model of having a single artistic director, who, with a lot of input from the others, will be responsible for making final decisions and for being a single artistic voice in terms of relating to management.

"In the early days, there was no management—we were the management! We did it all ourselves—we did the promotion, we did the grant-writing, we did the tech work. Then gradually, out of necessity, we began to expand. For a while, we just had one staff person, we had a managing director and a development director, we added a marketing director. Gradually, the position of managing director has become more and more important as a partner to us.

"That's a big change, and it just happened, so I can't really tell you how it's going to work out. To delegate, to empower one of us to be the artistic director—it feels like a relief to be giving up some of the ultimate responsibility. It also feels like it's going to be a challenge, as is any change."

Back to Our (Grass) Roots

For a company that thrives on experimental, alternative work as much as Horizons Theatre does, keeping the structure of your organization—even your location—mobile fits the aesthetic like a glove.

Leslie Jacobson has always smartly operated her company by keeping its purpose in the forefront. She understands that to some people, that purpose is unusual, but that doesn't dull her desire to do fine work.

For these reasons, Horizons has often found itself operating best from a grassroots kind of model. "Probably the period when we were organizationally the largest, in terms of board members and staff, was around 1990, right before we thought we were going to be moving," Jacobson remembers. "With moving to a new space that was going to be ours, and with fund-raising and other financial commitments, we were really starting to worry, since we do all this new work, which is always such an experiment and a risk.

"We had a great board and a great staff. But with *A . . . My Name Is Alice* having been such a great success in 1989, we were looking for musicals, things that were still focused on women, but things that would be commercially viable.

"We were never all that mainstream to begin with. Now, I would say we are more grassroots again. I'm not sure if that's good or bad; that's just sort of what it is, because we don't have a permanent space, and funding is difficult.

"It's hard to get people to give money to arts organizations in the first place. If it's between arts and cancer research, oftentimes cancer research wins. We are a theater with a very strong and definite mission, and when you're an arts organization that has this focus, it's great for people who really believe in women, but it also can be off-putting to people. Even though we're a humanistic, open, accessible, wonderful organization, people may not always understand that.

"We're living in increasingly uncertain times, and I'm not sure that's such a bad thing, necessarily. It would have been great if we had some permanent space, but right now, if we did, we'd have some permanent space we'd have to pay rent on.

"At various times, we've worked with management consultants, really wonderful people. One helped us through what we thought was going to be our move to a permanent space. He warned us—he helped us try to make the move a reality, but he actually didn't think the move was going to be a good idea. He'd worked with a theater that had done something similar, and the entire character of the theater changed—the artistic director, who'd had the vision and kept that theater going in the first place, left, because it wasn't the theater he visualized anymore."

Cultivating New Relationships

Steppenwolf has always been a haven for the most brilliant theatrical talent. The company is going through somewhat of an exploratory process at the moment, in regard to searching for new artists to work with.

If there's any challenge in this endeavor, it's in the fact that Steppenwolf is so sought-after as a nesting ground for talent, it doesn't want to find itself overrun with it. Collaborating with artists whose sensibilities best fit the company's style of working is really the preferable way Steppenwolf likes to do things. Michael Gennaro says, "Right now, there is a structure, at least a loose structure evolving. In the past, in the last couple of years, we've brought on Tina Landau, who is, interestingly, not an actor, but a writer and director, I think the first person of that nature—everyone else had basically been an actor—Amy Morton, who is a longtime actor in the city, who has worked with all these folks, and Martha Plimpton. So, there's been more women of late.

"I think what the look-towards is, is people who are actors, but also director-actor-writers, so that there's more breadth to what the company can do. I think that one of the things we instituted, when Martha Lavey and I got here, was that we started inviting companies into our studio space. In '91, we built basically one space, the 511-seat theater. We expanded that [to include] a roughly 200-seat studio space, in which we've produced some new work, as well as invited companies in, basically local companies, usually ensemble-based companies who share the same kind of aesthetic we do. There have been repeatable relationships that have come out of that that may or may not evolve into ensemble people or not.

"At the same time, we also created a space in our garage, which is basically sixty seats; that kind of returns to the number in the original space at Immaculate Conception. We also have a school, which originally started for high school students years and years and years ago, which has evolved basically into a professional school in the summers. I think the hope is to draw talent for the future.

"Between those repeatable relationships with other companies, as well as the school, I think that's hopefully the pipeline that will bring in new people. But there's no question, I don't think anybody wants to sit around with an ensemble with sixty people. It will be interesting—we're kind of at a point of time where we're looking at that. More than anything, it comes from repeatable relationships and an affinity for people working together. That, more than anything, has driven how [the company] works."

Boosting an Already Prestigious Profile

David Fuller's hopes for Jean Cocteau Repertory are many, but he's got an especially keen interest in more fully expanding the company's highly lauded image. "I think that the company is, for the most part, respected in New York in the theatergoing community," says David. "We're respected nationally in the theater community, which is different than the theatergoing community.

"We have toured internationally before and would like to do that again. I would envision that this theater becomes more famous—that we have a higher name recognition. That's a long-term goal. That means more touring.

"We're going to have to upgrade our theatrical facility somehow. We're not a union theater—I expect the theater to be a union theater. Right now, we work in a 140-seat theater, and we're limited to 185 performances a year, but I see this theater growing and making inroads in that way."

Something for Everyone

L.A. Theatre Works doesn't simply offer great theater to its many satisfied audience members or great roles for its actors to play. It also produces its work in many different media, truly offering something entertaining and significant for everybody to enjoy.

Such branching out can't occur overnight—you've got to plot out a move into multimedia. Susan Albert Loewenberg has figured out how to pounce on good business prospects when she's seen them. She explains: "We're kind of a hybrid organization. We're not really a radio organization—we're a media organization. We have this very peculiar niche. We're members of the Audio Publishers Association, a very small group, twenty or thirty book publishers. It includes Random House and Simon and Schuster and Time Warner, but it also includes small people. We are the only people who do plays.

"We have our own niche—it only works for a nonprofit. It would not be practical for a profit-making commercial organization, because it's too expensive. The sales are modest. They're limited. It's not like doing Tom Clancy—it's different. But it's an interesting, steady business. It's a great library business—libraries love us.

"It's been interesting, it's been difficult, it's been a money-loser, but I think we're seeing the light at the end of the tunnel. We now have recorded over three hundred plays on tape. We have a unique library—nobody in the world has this library. It's a pretty good representation of the best writing of the American canon in the twentieth century. It's the best state-of-the-art technology—this year, we're recording everything multitrack. We've done two new American operas, we've done several musicals, we've worked with major theaters all over the country. We expanded this project to Chicago for ten years—I did recordings in Chicago under the Doubletree corporate sponsorship, because they had a flagship hotel [there]. I've recorded plays by Steppenwolf, Goodman, Second City, Victory Gardens, and Organic.

"Then I started a project in Washington, D.C., with the Smithsonian and the Voice of America, in working with the local theaters. Basically, I work under the sponsorship of the local theaters, but I'm really bringing in my own production. Those recordings are aired over the local NPR station and the Voice of America.

"I did one year in Boston with WGBH and the leading theaters in that area, always bringing in my guest stars from Los Angeles and New York, bringing in my people. We now have a core acting group of fifteen hundred people. Of the thirty-four people who started with us, there have been two deaths, and of those remaining thirty-two, I'd say twenty-eight still work with us on a regular basis.

"We now have two really fabulous outreach programs. One is called Alive and Aloud. We're in twenty-two hundred schools in every state of the union. Through an initial grant from the NEA, with additional support from a number of foundations and corporations, including the Capital Group company's charitable foundation and Sony, we distribute ten tapes, five literary tapes and five docudramas, and study guides. Teachers use these tapes to teach English and social studies. They really are fabulous teaching tools, much better than video. They're great for concentration and reading skills, critical listening skills. The goal is to get them in all thirty-four thousand public high schools in the United States. We've done teacher training workshops, and we're expanding the program this year to do a formal evaluation, a lot more interactive stuff, bringing artists into the schools, and having the kids come and see a show on a local level. They're completely free—you can download the study guides on our Web site, so we save some costs there on printing.

"This year, we're going to distribute *The Crucible*. We never had the rights to distribute the audio, but now we've done six Arthur Miller plays and have the rights to distribute the audio. We've also gotten involved, of course, with the Internet. We're with a company called Audible.com, and you can download our stuff—you have to pay for it, everybody gets royalties—but you can download about a hundred of our plays onto your computer or MP3 device.

"Now, we're in bookstores all over the country. We were leery—the publishing business is a crazy business, and the fact that people can return everything is unbelievable. We were not prepared for that. We did not want to go into the bookstores; we were very cautious about it. We kind of tiptoed in by licensing our stuff to a company called Listening Library, the people who do the Harry Potter books. I was on the phone one day, met this guy on the phone, we ended up licensing various pieces to him, so we didn't have any risk, and they did very well with us in bookstores. It was the right thing to do.

"Last year, we ended up taking the plunge and going with a major distributor in bookstores. We're in Barnes and Noble and Borders and all the bookstores all over the country and have been working very hard at building our library business, because we knew that was our business. We send one hundred fifty thousand catalogs a year—very expensive. We're in about two thousand libraries. Some libraries have bought the entire collection—UCLA, Harvard, Princeton, Fordham, NYU—so that's been very impressive. We just went with Books on Tape—they think they can increase our business in libraries tenfold, something we couldn't do on our own. We need to concentrate on individual customer business.

"We're learning how to do it. One of the big challenges for us has been, because we have so many products, figuring out how to make them inexpensively enough so the cost of our products wasn't so high, we could never make any money at it. It needs to be a revenue source; it can't be a losing source. One of the things I did as an administrator was, when we started, we were almost 100 percent dependent on contributed income, as a young organization, and I decided to try to reverse that trend. We did reverse it, so we were going from 30 percent earned to 70 percent earned. That's been very important.

"Like everybody else, I'm very, very worried, because these events in the last year [2001] have really severely impacted everybody, and we just don't know what's going to happen. It is very hard to sell radio drama on public radio. It's been basically dead for years, [and now] they have officially closed down NPR Playhouse. Program directors are not interested in ninety-minute formats; they're wrong, they've never known how to market it, it's bad conventional wisdom, it's all of those things. But be that as it may, it is reality.

"The good news is satellite radio. They bought eighty programs from us and paid real money for them. It will be like HBO, like if you're a subscriber to cable television. It's perfect for us. We're going to be on a channel that's called On Broadway, and we'll get to our listeners. It will also help us publicize our audiobook sales, and so on. We're very excited about that. It's a perfect arrangement—our relationship ended with KCRW this year, which was unfortunate, but this is actually going to be more powerful, put us on fifty-two weeks a year, which is actually better for us."

Bringing New Works to the Table

Lyla White and Sheldon Epps are working in tandem to put the development of new plays on the front burner at the Pasadena Playhouse. They have found that staying in constant touch, to regularly brainstorm the planning of that development and all of the theater's operations, is very wise. It helps that they have a very good personal rapport. Lyla White says: "Sheldon and I really like each other and respect each other. We get together sometimes on Saturday mornings. We spend two or three hours having breakfast and talking about the future, where we want to go, so we're always on the same page about that.

"It sometimes happens that people feel competitive with one another, and that ruins it. There are other things we're competing with, but not one another."

Epps and White have already formed a general strategy for shepherding the original work they hope to be doing in the future.

Says Epps: "What we really have to concentrate on is a stronger development program for new work. I think that we've had tremendous success doing existing material that's unexpected for this theater and in expanding the diversity of the programming. Where we are not doing as well as a theater of this size and current reputation should do is in the development of new material.

"That takes additional money. That takes the space to do it. So, we're really concentrating a lot of effort now on developing a second space where we can produce, number one, new material, but also a greater diversity of material, both in terms of scale and content. Material that might be a bit more cutting-edge than is comfortable in the mainstage theater. Because of the huge success of *Side Man*, we are involved in ongoing talks with Warren Leight about doing a new play of his. Selena Houston—we did a new play of hers last year. She's an African American–Asian writer, and we have an ongoing relationship with her. Cheryl West, the woman that I did *Play On* with, we continue to talk with her about premiering one of her plays. So primarily, we're trying to continue the relationship with writers we've already produced, with the hope that as they develop new material, they'll give it to us first, give us a shot at working with them to further develop it and, hopefully, premiere the material."

Corporate Clientele

The message of cultural pluralism espoused by Mixed Blood Theatre has been long appreciated by culturally aware audiences. Avid fans, plus the Minneapolis community at large, have always been positively affected by the company's thought-provoking work.

So, imagine what good could be done if you dropped Mixed Blood's personnel into corporate environments, where issues of social misunderstanding have, unfortunately, been rampant at times. Jack Reuler thought that prospect sounded like a much-needed infusion of education about social understanding.

He set about making the corporate world aware of Mixed Blood's message back in the 1980s. Now, Mixed Blood's corporate outreach work is in high demand in many different fields of occupation. A lot of thinking has been properly adjusted by Mixed Blood's innovative efforts. Jack Reuler explains: "To me, the most interesting part of the organization: in the late eighties, diversity initiatives were everywhere. People looked to us, and we developed, by happenstance, this section of the organization called EnterTraining. It used theater as a voice to address barriers to people succeeding in the workplace.

"The last dozen years of this program have been unbelievable, in terms of what doors they've opened for us. When we do plays at the theater, we hope by osmosis we are able to change the audience's mind. But here, you're actually being invited in to create new works, which is what we like to do, with people saying, 'We know that we have issues, and we also have the wherewithal to do something about them.'

"So, we go in and do a series of focus groups and find out the very specific issues of places. Some of them were corporations in the earlier years, which were a lot less interesting, but a lot of them are in the legal profession, a lot of them are in health care, in law enforcement. Really interesting areas in which the subtleties, and not-so-subtleties, of race play a major factor.

"We've been able to do some unbelievable theater for some unbelievable audiences with very tangible effects, that can really be quantified, and in qualitative ways, measured. I can tell you more success stories from that program than from any of them. You can not only change minds, you can change policy. It's sort of three-pronged—policy, behavior, and attitude. We can change somebody's attitude, but they might not do anything about it. Yet, if there's a policy change, they don't have any choice but to do something about it."

Living in the Moment

For Ralph Remington, it's all about what his company stands for at the moment. Remington is, perhaps, doing more company evaluation than most artistic directors at this time, because he has been presented with the challenge of updating a number of old-school traditions at his company.

Remington understands that the audience he wishes to reach—young people—simply aren't going to respond to antiquated theories from many years ago. He's working hard to blend elements of today's hip-hop culture into The Living Stage's most effective existing features and hallmarks. To do this, he's paying close attention to what kids want. "Living Stage was founded in 1966, and aesthetically, it's really kind of, over the years, stayed in a 1960s, 1970s style," Remington says. "The music used, the particular philosophy behind the workshops—a lot of that is good, but I think it was at a place where it was ready to go someplace else from tie-dye and bare feet.

"So, that's what I'm trying to do, in a nutshell—bring the core, the spirit of the work, up to the present day. Look further into the future. Earlier, Living Stage was famous for having a bold use of primary colors, and I'm doing away with that. What Living Stage had a reputation of being, over the years, is being all things over [the course of] thirty-five years. At any given time, these things could be ascribed to Living Stage: children's, hippies', educational, therapy theater. Not all of the time it was all of those things, but all of the time it was at least one of those things, and then over the years, maybe at one point, it was all of those things. To the good and to the bad.

"It inspired hundreds, if not thousands of theater companies across the nation to do similar work. In the earlier years, the theater used to travel a lot, nationally and internationally as well. It would go into these communities and do residencies of three to five days, and by the time it would leave, it would plant the seed for people to create their own companies. In actuality, if Bob [Alexander], or Living Stage, or Arena, had franchised, they would have made a lot of money! What I want to take it to is a hip, underground resident theater company with Arena. The audience, I think, I'm going to skew a little older, because typically, over the years, the education lobby has done really well with getting a lot of programming at the theater to young kids. So, there's tons of things for kids from pre-kindergarten all the way to fifth, sixth grade, but at that point we drop them off and kind of just leave them. What's happened in the past is that's been left to athletic departments, or whatever's happening at their junior highs or high schools, extracurricular school activities. We, as a society/community, kind of left them to their own devices at that point. But I want to hold on to that audience, because these are the kids that are blowing each other away at school. These are the kids that feel a sense of alienation because of separation from their community.

"That's key. So, I think what I'm going to do is start gearing toward seventh grade and up. Seventh grade, eighth grade, high school, college.

"What Living Stage has done is work for pre-K to geriatric. You kind of get to the point where you're jack-of-all-trades, master of none, and I think [the theater's work] had a danger of going in that direction. Focus is really important, in what you're trying to do and what you're trying to work on. For me, it's listening to those kids.

"For instance, spoken word and poetry will play a big part, because that's what young people are interested in, whether it's rap or spoken word over a beat, poetry slams, absolutely. Midnight shows, a lot of late-night stuff, work that really kind of pushes the envelope.

"There are business changes, too. In the past, Living Stage had almost carved out a separate identity from Arena Stage. What we're doing, and emphasizing, today is that this is Arena, and with regard to that, Living Stage actors are also world-class actors at Arena Stage. So, they come from that pool and have those skills. We want artists that are interested in the community, and I'll be working with the artistic director at Arena in charge of play development. We'll be working closely together, so we can do some plays that are relevant work here, a new play lab. I'll be directing at Arena as well.

"So, it's more of an all-in-one situation, rather than Living Stage as a satellite, separate entity. It never really was, but people perceived it so, so getting the word out is not only good aesthetically, but organizationally, for board involvement and for the community to know."

Getting the word out about what you are—a great mindset for any company to adopt, once you know exactly where you stand.

CHAPTER 11

A DAY IN THE LIFE

When you're running a theater company, you don't have a whole lot of time to fritter away. You always have to have your eyes peeled on the many doings and goings-on around your environment—you need to supervise those working for you; watch rehearsals; keep up to date with your supporters, funders, and board (if you have one); monitor audience responses; pay bills; wash dance tights; and refill the Coke machine (at least when you're starting out)—you get the picture.

Because there are just twenty-four measly little hours in a day, it's important to pace yourself correctly, if you want to accomplish everything you need to accomplish. You need to prioritize correctly. Multitask expertly. Delegate, when that's appropriate. In order to maximize your energy and efforts, it can help to hear how the pros manage.

This chapter asks our experts to walk us through a typical day in the life of their respective companies, from their perspective. They explain to us what exactly it is that they do with their work time. This is not only interesting and absorbing information, but remarkably helpful. This is because our experts have, of course, distinguished themselves professionally long ago, and so, they herein allow us individual glimpses of what it means to operate from an advanced position of knowledge, experience, and success. You may be feeling like quite the novice at the moment, overwhelmed about how exactly you should put one foot in front of the other on behalf of your company. These professionals, in letting us in on exactly how they get their jobs done, will clear up some of the mystery for you.

Jam-Packed Days

For the members of A Traveling Jewish Theater, there's much variety in the company schedule. Sometimes, the group tours its running productions. Sometimes, they are deeply immersed in the rehearsal process for upcoming shows. Then, there's fund-raising, administrative concerns, and business meetings to deal with. What activities happen from day to day can be very diverse.

There's just one constant to the company's daily planner—it's jam-packed, literally from morning to night. Sometimes, in fact, a typical day at ATJT can encompass all of the above activities that the company puts its attention to—literally, a completely new activity every couple of hours! Each activity is as important as the last, too, so they all must be given equal attention. For this enclave of excellent artists, taking care of business is never a problem.

Corey Fischer says: "I can give you a quick example what a day will be like next week.

"We're going to start rehearsal on the first project of the season—I'm performing in it, so I'll be showing up as an actor for the first day of rehearsal. Earlier that day, Naomi [Newman], the one who's taking over our artistic directorship, will be having a meeting with our Managing Director, Helene [Sanghri York], and the Assistant Artistic Director.

"Then, we'll all meet at rehearsal. At some point in the afternoon, a playwright is going to arrive, and one of us will go with him to an interview at a radio station.

"After, hopefully, a short break, I will have to drive down the peninsula, about forty miles, to do a kind of a fund-raising event, an audience development event, at the home of one of the theater's supporters. I'm going to do a report on a recent trip to Israel, where I was part of a theater conference. So, that's one day!

"Meanwhile, of course, Albert [Greenberg] and Helen [Stoltzfus], the other two members, are working simultaneously on the development of what will be the second production this season. Having our own theater and a four-play season has necessitated that."

Getting Your Mind Around It All

ATJT's extremely busy days bring an interesting question to mind. You're probably reading such a dizzying list of activity with incredulity, thinking, "How could anybody possibly cope with switching mental gears so quickly, in order to get so much done? And do it so well? And make it look so easy?"

How exactly can you compartmentalize your thinking process correctly, so you're handling everything you need to handle with equal and proper attention? You do this the best when you think in terms of effective troubleshooting.

A good troubleshooter learns to stay on an even keel emotionally at all times, because he never knows quite what crisis is about to emerge that will need solving. You have to literally decide to be unflappable. It's a choice you can make—you don't have to give in to nerves or insecurity, you know. Every problem has some form of solution, and if you apply yourself calmly, you can work most things out faster than you'd ever have imagined.

Rick Lombardo uses a dramatic metaphor to explain this approach, which has come to serve him quite well in his work as artistic head of New Repertory Theatre. He doesn't waste time trying to predict what might come his way; he saves his considerable brain power for what needs attention most, when that attention is actually called for.

"I've never had a typical day," Lombardo explains. "I can best explain why by using the metaphor of directing a play. Directing is problem-solving. So doing that, I learned not to plan the day too much. Let the problems emerge.

"Rigid people don't do well in this type of job—you can't simply get your cup of coffee at the same time every day or open your mail at the same time. Like directing a play, running a repertory company is like, first day to the last day at the end of the rehearsal process: What are the issues I'm faced with right now, while I'm keeping an eye on the long term?

"I need a staff that can function in a fluid environment."

Lombardo's partner agrees with that hypothesis. She likes to work with self-motivated individuals herself as well.

Harriet Sheets, New Repertory's Managing Director, says: "I agree with Rick's opinion—that you have to go with the flow. The staff must work as a team, but it's also important to have people who can move and do things on their own as well within the day and can handle their own area."

Stay in Touch

Another frequent challenge many companies need to deal with head-on: how to actually stay in regular and productive contact during the day.

This sort of dilemma most often presents itself in situations where a company is made up of a lot of part-time members, who are busy working in a variety of other capacities, many times in far-flung locations away from company headquarters. Most organizations actually struggle with the issue of scattered personnel—actors might be working on more than one project at once in the same city, the office manager might be running errands most of the day, people might have day jobs—you know the drill.

If everybody's running in different directions like chickens with their heads cut off, how do you schedule meetings that people can actually attend at the same time, on the same day? How do you touch base on important decisions that can't be made unilaterally? How do you keep track of how people are handling important duties? How do you coordinate all of this, plus make progress plowing through your own formidable work load?

You must simply accept communication as a top priority of your leadership position. Make up a daily communication schedule, preferably on your computer or in your date book, and stick to it. Plan who you are going to call to say "hello" to on which days. Figure out who needs to deliver which project's work when, and check up when necessary.

If your staff sits in one big communal office, make open discussion a way of life. In some professions, this is not the norm, but in the theater biz, as you probably already know, it's common, accepted practice for coworkers to chatter away like magpies. Use this free exchange of conversation as a forum for work discussion, above all else.

If your staff is spread out around the building, walk around frequently to see people. Encourage people to be able to drop in on you at any time as well. (Be respectful, though—neither you nor your employees should intrude on important meetings, phone calls, and the like. Obvious, of course.)

Leslie Jacobson describes how she runs Horizons Theatre effectively in this manner, plus dedicates her time to operational matters.

"We do have a small office, and that's great—our wonderful, decentralized organization. A lot of my day is spent on the phone or on e-mail. But I actually like to talk to people. When you e-mail somebody something, it goes out over the Internet, and do they get it or don't they, and what happens when they get it? So, there's a lot of phone calling involved.

"Today, we had a PR meeting, not with just the person actually doing the PR, but with our managing director, myself, and another member of the company—although she's primarily an actress, she has writing skills and marketing ideas, so we wanted the opportunity to meet with her. It took a while to get everybody's schedules coordinated. I mean, if you were in your own building, you'd walk down the hall and say, 'Okay, we're going to have a meeting now.' When you're in a decentralized situation, it's not always quite that easy.

"Some of the time is spent reading plays. Some of the time is spent working with various subsets of people committed to the organization. Some of the time is spent looking for places to do things in. When you've finally got all of those other things together, then you're rehearsing."

Art Is What Counts Most

When you're very busy concentrating on the details of your administrative work, your worldview can get pretty small. If you're working hard writing up a budget, it can quickly become all about number crunching in your head, not about the amazing rehearsal that's going on down the hall right this second. You've forgotten all about art, in favor of calculation. You might as well work at H&R Block, my friend.

Sure, you've got to keep your mind on important technical tasks while they're at hand. We all know that the boring practical stuff is what keeps a company afloat. It's also important, though, that you keep your peripheral vision trained on the beauty your company is creating. Isn't art what inspired you to crunch those numbers in the first place?

Stop and smell the roses within your organization's walls, often. Don't allow business concerns to make you uptight and forget all about the reason you're working so hard. Art is what counts most.

Steppenwolf's administration has never forgotten this. Their art is their utmost priority, and it informs every communication transacted within the company. Otherwise, what's the point? Michael Gennaro says: "I think from the artistic side, a lot of it for Martha [Lavey] is communication with the ensemble—just saying, 'What do you want to do?' Then, them thinking about different ideas and who they want to work with. That's part of creating the season. I think one of the things she's been doing more and more of is looking farther into the future—I mean, we're already thinking about the 2002 and 2003 seasons.

"The second thing is, on that side of the operation, they've built up a much stronger base of artistic folks to really hone in on new work, working on new work, and developing local writers. Once more going back to the community—taking the wealth here of people who can write and working with them. That's a typical day over there.

"On the administrative side, I think it's probably not unlike most other places. Most of the departments here operate on their own, but they're all hooked together. Communication here, between e-mail, and just walking down the hall, and back-and-forth memos, that's probably the most important thing any place can have.

"One of the things that sometimes happens—and you have to fight against it, I've seen it everywhere I've been—is the fact that you sometimes can lose the connection between administration and artistic, during production in particular. You've got to keep in touch and in contact and embrace those folks who are making the work every night. If you lose touch with them, you lose touch with what's going on.

"All we're doing is getting to the point where we put the show on at night. That's what everybody here knows that it's about. You can never forget that. You can say, we gotta get out this subscription brochure, we gotta get out this grant or that grant, but why are you getting it out? If you keep thinking back to that—when someone calls me up and says, 'I've just read your grant, and it's phenomenal because of the explanation of what you're about,' then I know we've made sense."

24/7

If you take on the mantle of artistic director or managing director, you have to accept, and relish, the responsibility of working, at least in your head, on pushing your company forward twenty-four hours a day, seven days a week.

You may not be behind a desk all that time—frankly, if you were, you'd be unconscious eventually, and what good would that do your company? Please remember to take care of yourself, no matter how hard you're working. Get lots of fresh air. Eat well, and sleep regularly (although while you're sleeping, there's the perfect opportunity to dream up fabulous new plans for your company, so feel free). You don't have to be physically present at your theater to work out plans, read plays, and make work contacts.

Keep your mind open to the possibilities of artistic and business inspiration, which can strike anywhere, any time. And use your time well. David Fuller explains the way he has learned to operate most efficiently at Jean Cocteau Repertory:

"When you run an organization—I don't care if you're running a small theater company in Queens, or running the United States, or running a theater—you really don't ever *not* work. There's always a part of your brain that's working on something having to do with running your organization."

Fuller continues: "When you're in charge of people, and responsible for their livelihood, that's a big responsibility. I'm fortunate to have a good staff, and I have a managing partner, Dona Lee [Kelly], who's a big help. I think we work well together—her presence allows me to be more artistic than I could be if I didn't have her.

"My normal day starts at home, because I do work at home before I come into the theater. It primarily has to do with Internet stuff and some computer stuff, because I have, frankly, a better computer at home than I have at work. I don't get to the theater till about noon, which is good for me, because I stay up late. So, when I'm not directing, the afternoon consists of correspondence, mostly. That runs the gamut, because I'm on the phone most of the time. Usually, this correspondence has to do with fund-raising; most of my time has to do with working to raise money for the theater, in many different aspects.

"I do try to temper that with reading plays, because I have a lot of reading I have to do to plan the season. I'm now trying to look two, three seasons down the line, so to get things together, there are a lot of things that have to do with that. There's some correspondence that has to do with rights, royalties, planning a season, that sort of thing.

"In between that, I attend meetings, if we have them here, that are with our marketing staff, or we'll have meetings with our development staff; I'll attend those as well. When there's rehearsal, I'm often watching a rehearsal in the evening.

"On performance days, I will, at this time of the season, greet the audience, make sure my presence is known, so they can look to me if they have any questions. We're still selling subscriptions to the season, so I try to get my face out there, be the face of the theater.

The subscribers like it. We have some subscribers that have been with us for thirty-one years, and they appreciate a little personal touch, so I try to do that.

"You do wear a lot of hats, but the thing is, when you are tantamount to being a million-dollar theater, you have some help, so you don't have to wear so many hats. I think a few years ago, the producing artistic director here wore more hats than I wear. Sometimes, when you're young, you can do that, but you can only do it for a certain amount of time. Then, you burn out. I'm past that stage. I don't have that kind of energy anymore.

"I just rely on the people I hire. That's the important thing to be able to do. Learning to delegate, I think, is one of the hardest things for young people to understand. It's very freeing to be able to finally say to somebody, 'You do that. I don't want to do it.' You have to know what you're good at and know what other people are good at. There's a kind of a constant shifting thing in this theater. We still have a small staff, so we play to each other's strengths—we're able to do that."

Sometimes, Things Are Just Crazy

A sure sign of success is having more work to do than you think you are humanly capable of doing. The good news is, when push comes to shove, if you're good, you always rise to the occasion and get everything done.

Surprise yourself, and take on more than you think you can handle, as soon as your company is working well on its feet. This trains you, and your coworkers, faster in the fine art of multitasking than anything else. This is not to recommend you knock yourself out with overwork, but it's okay to take a lot on and have confidence that you'll complete it.

David Zak has come to accept that sometimes, things just get crazy. Still, he's learned to handle frantic times with finesse and a grain of salt. "The day-to-day varies during the times of the year," Zak says, regarding Bailiwick's schedule. "Last summer, for example, there were thirteen full productions during a twelve-week period for the Pride Series. Six of these plays were world premieres. That meant that most days were highly stressed, with lots of production work and preproduction work going on."

Always Keep the Future in Mind

No matter how absorbed you might be at any given present task, at any given moment, in order to be a good leader, you must always be planning future endeavors at the exact same time. This is an absolute.

Why? Because for a theater organization, the future is now. Many elements of next year's season need to be locked in now—performance dates, development issues, business details that must be sewn up. You should resist the temptation to procrastinate on such issues, or next season will get away from you fast.

Sheldon Epps, of Pasadena Playhouse, says: "What's interesting about the artistic director's job is that you're sort of a split personality as far as your time goes. Today, and this week, I'm working on getting the play into rehearsal that will open a month from now. At the same time, I'm working on selecting the creative staff for the play that will open a year from now.

"Literally, talking with the director of the current show and talking to directors about the shows we're going to do next year. Put out the fires, or encourage the fires, maybe, of whatever's in rehearsal, and then try to get the fire going for what we're going to do. Trying to carve out the time in your day so that you give equal time to both of those things, because everything is always upon you sooner than you think it's going to be. Opening night will be here faster than I think, but also, opening night of the play that's going to be in the July/August slot next year is going to be here faster!

"Because of our subscription cycles, and the fact that we sell things so far in advance, I'm almost constantly in the selection process for new material. Having just announced our season for 2002, I don't get a breather, because this theater, unlike many other theaters, produces full year-round, from January to December.

"The moment that I announce the selections for the upcoming season, I have to start looking for and planning the season after that."

Starting Fires . . . and Putting Them Out

Now, let's take the opposite point of view. In addition to generating new projects. you have to pay attention to what's currently on the front burner at all times, too.

As the head of the company, you have to know what's going on in every corner of your business. Does this mean you have to become obsessive-compulsive or micromanage like crazy? Not at all.

You simply have to care. Be detail-oriented. Understand how the workings of your organization interlock—in an organization that's running properly, everything is connected on a base level and should be working in tandem.

Susan Albert Loewenberg (L.A. Theatre Works) gives us a peek into her day, into which she incorporates a detail-driven philosophy in order to manage both present and future concerns.

"I usually get up between five and six. I work at home until 10:30, 11:00 sometimes. I'm on the phone a lot, with New York, with London. I do a lot of homework at home, I do a lot of thinking at home, I do a lot of reading, because I'm always looking for new - material.

"Then, I come in. I don't take lunch; I'm not a lunch person. I just work until six o'clock at the office. I'm basically doing a lot of things—I have to fill seventeen slots a year at minimum. I'm always looking for plays. I'm kind of planning ahead and dealing with imminent crises.

"There are times when we'll book actors, and they'll get a movie. That's part of the deal, because we work under an AFTRA contract, but it's nothing, it's basically a very minimal public radio contract, and if you're working with Richard Dreyfuss and he gets a major movie, he's going to ultimately back out, and I'll have to replace him. So, there's a lot of forward planning, six months in advance. You're into one season and you're already planning the next, you're coaxing agents to get them to send you material. You're looking for material frantically all the time; you're trying to book actors.

"I have a personal relationship with a lot of people, but a lot of it is also finding new people to work with, working with agents, working with directors, working with other actors, coming up with ideas, coming up with projects. So, you're planning the long term and dealing every day with a crisis—something fell through, you've got a marketing problem, a play isn't selling well. You've got to deal with all of those issues while you're forward-planning. I'm sort of the new business development person, so I'm always looking for new opportunities.

"It's somewhat dynamic, but everybody has their jobs. The positions are pretty well-defined. I'm looking over everybody's shoulder. I'm doing the long-term planning on the audio publishing business with my audio publisher person. I'm working with my associate producer, overseeing the season. I'm working with our managing director and our development people—I have my hand in all the development stuff, brainstorming how we approach development challenges. I'm into every single thing, and I try to let people do their jobs, but it's a small organization.

"I'm also traveling to Washington to oversee my Washington shows. At one point, I was traveling to Chicago and Washington, and it just became overwhelming—I felt Chicago had played itself out. You have to be not fazed by multitasking. You have to put one foot in front of the other, and if you've got an immediate problem, just focus on that and don't worry about other things. Those have to wait until you can get to them. At the same time, you can't let them slide too long. So, you've got to be comfortable with having a million balls in the air."

Get Your System Down to a Science

Your operation simply must run like clockwork, if you intend for your performances to go smoothly. There's no way around that.

A traditional rotating rep model is probably the most demanding of all theatrical schedules. One show is going up as another strikes, then vice versa. Many of the same actors and crew members, if not all of them, are dually involved with both productions. This mode of performance must be planned to the second, but it can be amazingly beneficial to your company on multiple levels. Your actors will stretch their abilities to their limits; you make more money with two shows running simultaneously; your company will enjoy double the exposure. So, if you're up for the challenge, why not go for it?

Jean Cocteau Repertory has its rotating schedule down to a science. Dona Lee Kelly tells us how her company pulls it off, night after night: "We are basically never down. We're always rehearsing another show. Everything is here, which is unusual among companies. Usually, you have your sets done outside, but we have ours here, the box office is here, the office is here, we have production all happening here. We don't really have a load-in. All the set building is pretty much downstairs.

"Fridays, we also have what's called a changeover. That means they take the set down. Say we have performances Wednesday and Thursday for *The Merchant of Venice*, and Friday, they take the show down and they put up *Oedipus*. Then, they have Friday, Saturday, Sunday, *Oedipus*. Then, Wednesday and Thursday, again, *Oedipus* continues. Then it comes down for *Merchant of Venice*. So, our sets have to be able to fit in the stairway. They have to be able to be broken up and fit in the corner, and we have a black curtain around them. It's a really tight schedule.

"Rotating rep is a tough system. For many companies, it's a challenge. For us, it is, but it's the lifestyle."

Have Hats, Will Travel

Another taxing challenge is constant mobility. Some companies really know how to cook with gas. This morning, they're doing a show here. This afternoon, another show across town. Tonight, a third show two towns over.

A touring company, or a company that works out of a base of operations, but also regularly moves its work into the community, learns quickly how to perform on the fly. Leadership duties for such a company can be bit jarring though. You might feel like you've got mental whiplash, having to zip your thought process back and forth from this show to that show, all of which are being performed this very day. You don't even have the luxury of forward-thinking about next season, while you work on this slot's show! It's all in-your-face, immediate stuff.

Ralph Remington (Living Stage) makes a fast-moving day look easy: "Every day is different; there's not really a typical day. But if there could be such a thing, it's rehearsing from nine to six. The actors are here by nine, they're expected on the floor at nine-thirty. Then, it will be a full rehearsal day, preparing work in our space or work to go out.

"The smaller a company is, the more hats you've got to wear. The larger it is, the more help you get, but—maybe I'll have a show in the morning, so I'll have to go out. Then, I'll have rehearsal for a couple of hours. Then, I'll have to turn that rehearsal over to an assistant director, because then, I have to go to Arena for meetings with the production manager over there or about how we're going to market a show."

The Big Picture

Of course, the best way to handle a quick pace is to know what's coming your way. How you avoid surprises—and by now, it's probably clear to you that you can't avoid them entirely, but you can damage-control—is by having your season planned scrupulously. This sort of big-picture thinking should cover what's going to happen every single day of your preseason, active season, and postseason. Sounds elementary, but stunningly, many companies leave lots of their time completely up in the air. A very dumb move.

Structured time answers your company members' questions and reassures them. A good company knows how to perfect a big-picture game plan and encourages their people to learn it like the back of their hands. Susan Kosoff tells us: "Some of the staff [of the Wheelock Family Theatre] reconnoiter August 1. I will have just put the season brochure to bed with the printer; that goes out mid-August. As soon as I get back in September, we'll have auditions for the first show. Our fall offerings for classes start in early October, about the same time that we go into rehearsals for our first show.

"I've been meeting with the designers for the first show over the summer; the tech people will start working on it. One of the challenges for us is that we build our sets, we rehearse, and we perform in the same space. So, we always try to have the basic set ready for rehearsals. That's particularly helpful for the people who aren't as trained; they actually work on the set, and it makes them very comfortable. So, we don't have a load-in. It really helps.

"All the technical stuff will start in September, and we'll gear up, go into rehearsal in October when classes start. In a day, they're working on a set onstage, our rehearsals are evenings and weekends, and our classes are late afternoons and early evenings. As soon as the show goes up in early November—it runs through the month of November, and in addition to weekend performances, Friday, Saturday, and Sunday, we have student matinees—we have as many as seven shows in a week—while the show is up, we're beginning to work on the second show. Meeting with the designers, we'll have auditions in November, early December, for our February show. We try to give everybody a little time off for Christmas. Then, we come back, and we go right back into rehearsal first of January for the next show.

"The first session of classes ends in December. We started intense, one-week classes for young people and teenagers over school vacations, which we run in February and April. In February, we open our second show, and that comes down the end of February. During that time, of course, we're starting to work on the next show—the turnaround time between the February show and the next show is faster than in the fall.

"In March, we start our second session of classes. Then in April, we open our third show. We're working in schools all the time—we have partnerships. Although we do some programs within the schools themselves, and we have two satellite sites—one in Newton, one in Framingham, Massachusetts—we also try to work with teachers. We're not necessarily just doing classes for kids ourselves in the schools—we're helping teachers learn how to do it.

"What makes us different from other educational programs is that we are a professional theater, one that is connected to productions. We have Q-and-As with the partner schools. In July, we have hundreds of kids. It's a pretty intense schedule—we're never out of good ideas!"

Do What Feels Right to You

There are practical ways to manage a day that you always can do well to use, as we've learned. Still, theater is a business with a lot of wiggle room. If you eschewed professional freedom on principle, after all, you'd probably be working for IBM.

If you're like most artists who've chosen to blend their love of creativity with making a living, though, you like to keep a few options open. You should, definitely. Do what feels right to you, in terms of time management. Work out a system that you like best and that your company members like. Observe whatever hours within which you work best. Be a little abstract at times. It's okay. It might just spark a surge in more creative thinking.

Base your system on a structure, but add your colors, and you can't go wrong. Jack Reuler discusses what makes up his working day at Mixed Blood:

"I think it really varies. I remember when that Rodney Dangerfield movie, *Back to School*, came out, and he was saying, 'Here's how you really do business: You grease the palm of this politician, and you talk to that inspector.'

"I had the opportunity two school years ago to teach a class called The Artistic Director at UCSD's M.F.A. program. It was really good for me to realize I've learned something in the twenty-odd years of doing it. I brought in some of the artistic directors from San Diego to talk to this class; they sort of did it by the book and understood the value of directors and artistic directors. These students were around thirty; they weren't right out of undergraduate school, and they really did sort of buy into my live-life-on-your-own-terms approach to artistic directorship. To not be, for lack of a better term, starfuckers, by really wanting to be like the Globe or the Playhouse or the San Diego Rep.

"I'd say that one thing that differs about me: I've never had a managing director, in terms of classic relationships of artistic director-managing director. I don't know if that's right or wrong, but I never have a managing director saying, 'We can't afford this,' and I never have an artistic director saying, 'We need to do something bigger.' By being both, it's actually worked out for me pretty well, but I think the art, I've done less, because I've been both."

You Gotta Love It

A spontaneous attitude toward what may happen in the life of your company, in any given day, will get you farther than anything.

Also, remember this: If you're not enjoying your day, something isn't right. Figure out what it is that's bothering you about your work, and fix it. You have lots of control. You work for yourself, remember? That's a lot of responsibility, sure, but it's monumentally rewarding, too.

Strike a balance between the work you have to do and the joy you've got to experience. Mitzi Sales did this in her days at Berkeley Repertory, and she's never regretted it.

"As in most jobs, and certainly in a managing director's, there are certain routine things that have to be accomplished in any given week," says Mitzi. "One of the great appeals of a job working as managing director in a theater company is, there are also unexpected things that come every week, sometimes every day.

"One of the reasons I was able to stay in the job as long as I did was because it was fun. It was challenging. There were unexpected things that happened, and it was engaging. What was my worst fear? Being bored. I was rarely bored!"

CHAPTER 12:

THE PROCESS OF PLANNING

In order to get to where you want to go, you have to adopt some sort of long-range planning model. This is accepted, conventional wisdom in most corners of the business world.

Usually, this planning model is broken down into manageable time increments—frequently, you have a one-year plan for what you hope your company will accomplish and/or a five-year plan. So, does this type of traditional model work for the sometimes very nontraditional business of theater?

Some of our experts speak from a very calculated, strategic point of view. They are using traditional business practices and thinking to realize their company's intentions for the immediate future. Other subjects are a bit more apt to see where events will take them and have always operated quite successfully from keeping a looser hold on the reins.

I've come to believe that both of these approaches are right on. Why? Because planning is a totally individual process. How you do it best depends completely upon who you are, as an organization and as a human being (business people are, after all, human beings first).

Planning scrupulously and effectively is a talent. So is eyeballing a situation and trusting yourself, and your company, enough to go with the flow. Both of these mindsets have merit. My advice on how you might plan your company's future? Figure out who you are, and use that to dictate the steps you wish to take.

To be in charge of a theater company means you are automatically following some kind of "yellow brick road." Either it's a road you've carefully constructed inch by inch yourself, or it's a road you're happy simply to wander along and see what comes up ahead of you. No matter what, you're in forward motion. It's up to you how to pace your steps.

Creative Goals

By nature, most companies actually employ a one-year plan without even realizing it. They do this by setting their next season in advance.

Even if the choosing of material and announcement of slotted offerings seems like a necessity rather than a careful plot, it instantly determines a company's direction in the shorter term. Your next season's selections speak volumes about where your company currently aspires to be—to your audience, funders, and especially, those who work within its structure, whose professional futures are tied intricately to these selections.

The nature of Chicago City Limits and its performance work, as we know, is completely spontaneous, not preset in a traditional season slot format. Yet Paul Zuckerman makes a strong case for setting creative goals: "I honestly don't believe so much in the business plan model, so much as kind of knowing what you want to do. Maybe that sounds contradictory—right now, our business plan is probably clearer than it ever was. That is, to diversify the offerings of the theater. That is going to happen, or we'll go out of business making it happen, one way or the other."

People Like It When You Know What You're Doing

Another strong argument in favor of formulating some sort of solid plan—it's professional. People admire professionalism, even in a creative field.

This isn't to suggest you need to start faking business acumen you simply don't have familiarity with or start tossing off million-dollar SAT vocabulary words to dazzle people. Just make sure you can discuss where your company is going in the longer term with simplicity, clarity, and a sense of command. Make sure you can both verbalize this and write it effectively, as no doubt you'll need to do both.

Corey Fischer (A Traveling Jewish Theatre) explains his feelings about this issue of clear expression, plus talks about his company's future goals:

"As anyone working with a new company will quickly find out, you're probably going to want to become a nonprofit as soon as possible—you almost have to. And you're probably going to want to start applying for funding. To do that, funders want to know you are thinking beyond the day-to-day and that you have at least a three-year plan. That's not only important for the funders, it's an important tool for decision-making. It becomes a rough guide, not written in stone, but you need to have a sense of, what do you want things to look like in a year, two years, three years.

"Our goals are to continue expanding the company, bringing younger artists, in and developing a process in which to do that that makes sense, prepares the younger artists for taking more and more responsibility. We, of course, are always looking for increased financial responsibility, so a lot of our plan is administrative and developmental.

"We're at a point where we'd very much like to see some of our work produced by another theater. That would be a new milestone."

Growing beyond All Expectations

When has a theater company defied all conventional wisdom? When it grows to the point where its growth becomes an actual challenge for the future!

In Steppenwolf's case, not only has the company surpassed its artistic zenith, but it has grown financially beyond its wildest dreams, to the point where this issue must be addressed on several fronts in the immediate future. Michael Gennaro discusses this:

"We're now at a place where, the last three years, we were completely sold out in terms of subscriptions. We've been building a subscription base successfully, so we have that going on. And we've been trying to do more and more new work. The next steps, if you want to look to the future, are threefold.

"One is ensemble growth—which there may or may not be. Number two is, what do we do in terms of physical expansion? There's been a lot of talk of, 'Okay, over the years, every time you come to this point in time, you build a bigger theater.' What that does, though, is question intimacy. We've got a space that provides the most intimacy possible, yet gives us the ability to do anything on a stage, because of the size of the stage and the resources we have. We have a huge vacant lot next to our building, between our building and our garage space, which we've been parking on, and we keep spinning around what would we do there. So, that's a question that's out there.

"The third thing is, we've danced around the idea of film and TV development for ten years, because so many people in the company are involved in it. We finally, in this last year, have really taken an aggressive approach to it. We've got a couple of projects now that are going to get somewhere. They're now going to do an American Masters special, on PBS, on Steppenwolf. It's being filmed as we speak. Number two, we've started to work on and adapt stage product into film development. We're working on an adaptation of *The Winter of Our Discontent* by Steinbeck—the obvious connection [we have] to Steinbeck. And secondly, a piece we did last year called *The Drawer Boy*, which we are going to develop into a film. These are the next steps toward potential growth.

"It's interesting, because we're also at a point where—the budget—we're running out of room to grow, because you can't really bring in any more ticket income. There's only so far you can go in contributor income. So, we've kind of reached a plateau there, too. So, that's a challenge."

A View toward Stability

The psychological relief that accompanies true stability will carry you far. When you have a bit of money set aside in case you need it, a staff you can count on, and actors who take their work seriously (they stick with you, cheerfully doing the same role over and over for months, happy for the steady gig), then you have an organization that's matured and stabilized. Horizons Theatre has a long legacy of stability and success. Leslie Jacobson has built her organization wisely, drawing upon stable management as a key component.

"I guess where I'd like to see us in a year is with some really good, stable management," Jacobson says, regarding the future of Horizons Theatre. "Artistically, there are some people who've worked with us over ten years—a couple of people have been with me almost since the beginning. It's ebb and flow—people flow into the organization, they flow out of the organization, but they're around. But I think from a managerial standpoint, we have had a number of people over the years. The period we were in Georgetown, we had myself and two other people who were the kind of artistic/managerial team for an eight-year period. That was a period of incredible growth. But then, one person adopted a baby, and her life completely changed, the other person had other financial pressures and had to make more money somewhere else. Things happen.

"So, I'd like to see some real stability on the managerial side of things."

When It's Wise to Stay Fluid

There are a number of extremely good reasons not to seek too much stability at the wrong point in time, however.

Sometimes, it's simply not in the makeup of a company to work from too rigid a point of view. If a company is very young and very based on collaborative thinking, there isn't that much to lose yet. So, that's why making decisions in a fluid, group-think, brainstorming kind of way may serve the organization best. As this company grows, it will eventually pay off to appoint a theoretical "head" to deal with more structured decision-making and as a liaison to the outside world (i.e., funders, press, and the like).

Other times, circumstances completely out of the realm of your personal control make it essential you don't lock in any ideas you can't change if necessary.

David Fuller (Cocteau) says: "I think in the current climate of New York City [immediately following the attack on the World Trade Center], you can't be too rigid in your plans, because then you're just setting yourself up for disappointment. I think you have to be fluid.

"I am by nature a very patient human being. Because I happen to be patient, my ideas, I know, can't happen overnight. It's just a question of having a vision and moving forward. It took me over two years to assemble the staff that I wanted, and that's normal."

The Specifics of Good One-Year Planning

The specifics of a one year-plan for your company are, of course, going to depend largely upon your company. Its size, what you want and need, why you need it, and by which specific date are all factors that must be taken into consideration.

It can be very helpful in mapping whatever your individual plan might entail, however, to take a look at how another company tackles their issues. Dona Lee Kelly of Jean Cocteau Repertory offers up a very strong example of one point of a one-year plan.

Kelly addresses the company's fund-raising goal with directness and clarity. Notice, too, how she stresses not only the specifics of her initiatives, but correlates that to an expert and necessary grasp of larger issues that come into play in terms of planning:

"There are a number of different fund-raising initiatives I've started," Dona Lee explains.

"What we're doing is called the Capacity Building Initiative. Essentially, it was a $200,000 budget, really trying to improve internal management, get money for printing materials, marketing materials, and specifically, to strengthen the development, so that we could cultivate individuals. We've so far raised about $50,000 of it.

"So, that is this year. We have to earn income and contribute an additional $100,000 over this year. We can do it, but it's going to be difficult. Midsize companies and middle class companies are probably the most difficult companies to go and manage. A small company doesn't have the overhead; they can cut really fast. A big company can absorb any losses in earned income. A midsize company, you have expenses—no matter how you cut them, you have them. There's a certain amount of staff you need to run the company well. Midsize companies are in the most dangerous position. I have to really be very careful how we give raises and how we streamline. Cash flow is always a problem—you can never get enough money fast enough."

Do Your Own Thing

Jack Reuler learned the dangers of trying to fit Mixed Blood into an institutional model when he was putting together his early organizational planning. His experience has made him determined ever since to operate on his terms.

Says Rueler, "I really took things for granted. In 1984–85, things were humming along.

"You've got to understand that the maturation of the philanthropic world sort of matches the history of the regional theater movement. There was a major IRS tax change in 1964 that really changed giving across the country; that's about the same time as the regional theater movement is recognized as beginning. But there was a lack of sophistication in the giving world.

"There's this notion of an institutional model; if you look like this, we know how to evaluate you. For one year, I pandered into that and got certain administrative staff I'd never had. In 1980, we went from one to two, then in 1984, I think we went from two to five.

"The problem wasn't that we got these people; the problem was that for that one year, I found myself pandering to what someone else wanted, not to what I wanted. Within a year, I was back down to three.

"The NEA had this advancement program. We applied and got in. We said, 'What we really want to be is the best Mixed Blood we can be, not the best institutional model by somebody else's definition.'

"We worked with a good consultant they provided and developed a three-year plan. It came with $75,000 that we strictly used as a cash reserve. Before that, zero meant zero; suddenly, zero meant $75,000. To me, it was quite freeing. Up until then, if the show was a bust, we had zero and went out of business. I still, to this day, have never had a deficit. Not because of any great wisdom—I just don't know how to spend money we don't have. I think one time, in the years we've had that money, we have dipped into it, just for cash flow purposes.

"In that year that we had that staff of five, instead of saying, I can relax, I did ten shows. Which was just nuts. We'd do three shows in one night. I just got zealous. I forgot that rule of producing in the nonprofit world—the more you do, the more you lose. So by doing ten shows, you're losing not only technically and artistically, but financially.

"The key thing that came out of that was to do things on a long term. To be the best Mixed Blood we can be. I don't care how the rest of regional theater does it. I don't care what funders think. Let's do good work. Do it well. When we went through that advancement process, I think it reminded us of something we probably knew, but had let other people talk us out of."

Strategies That Surprise

Long-term planning can be very useful in preserving the artistic freshness of your organization. You can, and should, actually strategize the creative curve balls you intend to pitch to the public. In addition to planning for practical matters, La Jolla Playhouse's major strategy seeks to prevent its artistic reputation being pigeonholed in any way.

"Longer term, we want to enhance our name in the field nationally," says Terrence Dwyer. "We want to be building an endowment as well and utilize a new building. A certain sense of artistic unpredictability is also a priority—doing a different set of productions than people expect, so that we defy description."

Administration Adjustments

Sometimes, a five-year plan is based primarily on one facet of a company's growth. Maybe you don't have a long-term eye toward material choices, for example, as much as you are precisely transitioning an aspect of your administration, such as staffing, by utilizing specific methods of intention.

This is the mode of adjustment Wheelock Family Theatre has elected to go with. Susan Kosoff's set priorities are human resource–related.

"Over the next five years," Kosoff states, "a lot of how I think about things will have to do with who comes onto the staff, who might be able to move into doing some of the things Jane Staab and I have done.

"I think that's the five-year plan. The steps toward that are really shoring up the theater, so we have good houses for all the performances. That we can underwrite the position of director, that we can maybe have a marketing director who only does that, and who doesn't also have to manage the front of the house. Things like that.

"There are little ways in which we can build some of that, but it's going to have to be done in baby steps. It's not going to all happen at once."

Proceeding with Caution

During his first year as The Living Stage's artistic head, Ralph Remington was already enthused about what he could envision down the road for the company. However, he's proceeding carefully—plunging in too quickly, in his opinion, would be a mistake.

"Second year, I'll look at larger issues," Remington states, "but in three years, I think the theater will look a lot different, because then, I'll have had two years and already have been through that 'I've thrown out a lot, I've added a lot.' I'll kind of see where we're pointing. At the same time, in addition, I'm very interested in doing even more work within schools, and within five years, strip down bare. Make it simple. Dealing with the words, in how we're interacting with the audience.

"Long term, really, the goal is to get eighteen-to-thirty-five-year-olds back to the theater. I want to get them as excited about theater as they get about music. What is it about going to see rock and roll, going to see rap, that energizes people in a way they don't get energized in the theater? One of the things I'm looking at is to make things unpredictable. Make them raw. It has to be experiential, and it has to be unpredictable. Like in the theater, you know you're supposed to sit down, watch something for this amount of time, then get up, and there's an intermission, and then dah-dah-dah-dah-dah, lights go down again, here's act two. But what happens if we explode all of that? What happens if at any given time, you're pulling people out of their element, if the front of the play is now the middle of the play and the middle of the play is at the front?

"NBC had a great advertisement for their TV shows: 'If you haven't seen it, it's new to you.' And it's true! Why has Tony Bennett become so popular again?"

David Fuller has been steering the artistic ship at Jean Cocteau Repertory a bit longer, but he is more reticent in regard to future planning.

"People ask me what I want next, and I say, talk to me after I've been here five years, then I'll know," says Fuller.

"I think in five years, I'm going to know if the potential I thought was there in 1998, 1999, is still there and something that we can use to move forward in this current century. I think it is, still, but we'll see.

"Five years from when I started running the company, I'll be fifty, and fifty is a good point from which I'll be able to look and see where it is."

Two Smart, and Opposing, Viewpoints

You can be extremely successful following a long-term model . . . as well as going in the exact opposite direction.

Here are two differing opinions about whether a five-year plan can work. The circumstances of L.A. Theatre Works and the Pasadena Playhouse are very different, of course.

Experience has shown Susan Albert Loewenberg what isn't right for L.A. Theatre Works.

"I'm not a five-year planner," she says. "We've done a couple of those things, but basically, it's a year ahead. But there's a vision—like the vision of the audio publishing business, we've realized the vision.

"Unfortunately, the reality of a small arts organization is, it's just not going to happen. People telling you to do five-year plans; it's a big waste of time. It's nonsense. You don't have the resources. It's not possible, and it's certainly not possible in the arts.

"You can't spend all that staff time doing that. These corporations and foundations come with their lofty—they're overstaffed, they're underworked, and they're telling you to make five-year plans, and you're wondering where your next dollar's coming from!

"It's unrealistic. It actually makes me mad, because I think that they don't realize how much we put out, and how much we do, with very few people. It's absolutely unrealistic.

"It's very fluid, but at the same time, there are some basic rules. You have to learn to delegate. You have to think big. You have to learn how to diversify. You have to learn very quickly how to build your revenue. You cannot be dependent on the whim of a corporation or a foundation, because nothing is forever. Nobody's going to fund you forever. Your best funder is gonna disappear one day. You can't be dependent on a single source.

"You have to be in constant motion, and you do need to have an idea where you're going, and you have to have some goals. But you can't be thinking that you've got to act like a major corporation thinking five years out. Not gonna happen."

Sheldon Epps, on the other hand, is a believer in strategic visualization for Pasadena Playhouse. "The longer-term dreams are about things like a second space," he states. "About the ability to find the resources to do more classical theater. This theater, for a long time, had a hugely successful and very good training program, and I believe in that. I believe that great training programs attached to great theaters provide a kind of education and preparation for actors, designers, and directors that nothing else can. So, that's something I'd like to see us reinstitute.

"All of those are more in the realms of wonderful dreaming than planning. But it's only by dreaming that you come up with the plans to do those things, and that is something we spend a lot of time talking about, strategic planning for the future. If you talk about measures of success for the company, the fact is, when I first got here, the years just prior to my getting here, this was a theater that was existing day to day. The long-term plan was, how do we survive to the next production? How do we survive until next week?

"The very fact that we are secure and solid enough to start to think about, what are we going to do three years from now, five years from now, is a great measure of success. We feel strong and stable and secure and vital enough that there's no longer a question mark about, are we going to be here? The question mark is about, what are we going to do ten years from now—a great position to be working from. To get there yourself, allow for a bit of trial and error. Try a little forward planning. If it doesn't work, focus primarily on the more immediate. Or mix up your strategy, and try a little of both."

Bottom line: evaluate your own specific situation, while weighing the sage advice of others. Then, follow your gut.

CHAPTER 13:

OUR ULTIMATE GOALS FOR THE FUTURE

You have to earn your legacy in life.

Our experts will all have legacies admired by many people, that's certain. Yet here's an interesting question: How do they perceive their own achievements and the achievements of their companies?

Considering all of the changes, successes, battles, disappointments, and issues each of our subjects' companies have been through, what are their ultimate goals for the future? Have these goals changed from those envisioned at the company's origin? How would these theater personnel like to go down, reputation wise, in history?

In short, what is each subject's definition of complete success?

Here's what they think.

What's Good for the Group

Michael Gennaro, of Steppenwolf, says, "The seamless integration and harmony of the staff, board, and ensemble means a lot.

"I was the one who got to go up and get the Tony Award for *Cuckoo's Nest*—it was very moving for me. More important to me were the feelings and emotions of the staff, board, and actors and what that meant.

"Personally, for me, not only have I had staff members leave and come back, but I have staff members who continually return here to visit their friends and just hang out. That is an important thing, because it means people are happy. These are people who are making choices to do this kind of work for not a great financial reward. If we can be leaders in that regard, in terms of, 'This is a good place to work, and they pay as well as anybody,' if people can go, 'I get a chance to really explore,' that to me is what it's all about."

No Regrets

Paul Zuckerman, speaking for Chicago City Limits, states, " In terms of defining success, I think that's a multileveled question. I've often thought, gee, I've had a pretty good run.

We came out to New York in a little van, nobody knew us, and created New York's longest-running comedy review. So in some sense, if it all ended today, I'd have lots of regrets that it ended, but also have a sense of accomplishment that, we did it—it was a fun job. I can't think of anything I'd like to do more than this sort of thing."

The Rush

"None of us work here for the money," says David Zak, of Bailiwick. "We work here for the excitement, the fun, and the intense relationships we can have as artists in rehearsal, particularly for new works. We know we are successful when our lobby is full of intense conversations about shows people have just seen."

Making Our Mark

New Repertory Theatre's Rick Lombardo has this to add: "I'd like to know that New Repertory Theatre can grow, through civic discourse and the art we produce. That we are the Boston area's finest midsize theater. That our impact reaches a very large segment and that our art serves our audience."

A Major Reputation

Harriet Sheets says: "I see New Repertory Theatre as being a national presence. I see us making a statement at the midsize, LORT theater level."

More Growth

Terrence Dwyer shares his dream for La Jolla Playhouse: "That we continue to grow and expand, simultaneously, in both an artistic sense and a business sense. My dream project? A great production of *Hamlet* or *Richard III*."

Freedom to Make Our Impact

Corey Fischer's hope for A Traveling Jewish Theatre is, "Artistically, to continue to create works of theater that are unique and create a deep need within the audiences and within ourselves—what complete success would look like would be having secured the where-withal to do that. With something like an endowment, we would know that the basics were covered. We would know that the development costs of new works were covered. We could devote more time and energy to the work itself and less to fund-raising.

"We could then know that the infrastructure was there to bring new people on and to engage in collaboration, so that the artistic work would become richer and richer. I think, also, complete success would include achieving another level of recognition and performing at a certain kind of venue we're still not—the Brooklyn Academy, Lincoln Center.

"In terms of audience, it's never about sheer numbers with theater—you're really limited by the nature of the event. You're never going to reach as many people as with film or video. But the impact has to do with how you're received and how you can inform other work that's being done, what people go and do with it—the depth with which you impact people's lives."

The Many Facets of Success

Susan Medak, of Berkeley Rep, says, "I don't mean to sound Pollyannaish, but complete success for me is to do work of the highest caliber—our production of *Oresteia*, which was the opening show of our new theater, is an example. What I mean by this example, too, is, artists have been able to do their most ambitious work here—not always their best, but that will come later. To get them there, you can support them, you can help them.

"Complete success for me as well is when audiences can see great artists producing great work and feel engaged, respected, and challenged by that. Complete success is when an audience feels they've been well-served.

"You learn from the people in your life, too. I've been able to grow within this job and as a human being, because I have a family and a full life away from the theater."

Giving Back

"I want to raise the actors' salaries, so they don't have to work day jobs," says David Fuller, regarding Jean Cocteau Repertory. "We're making inroads. The actors this year are making more money than they ever have in their lives here, so that's a good thing. It just takes a while."

A Lasting Contribution

Leslie Jacobson wants two things for Horizons Theatre: "The first is, I'd like to hand over an organization to other people that isn't in debt, that is viable, so that somebody else could be the artistic director and not just inherit a whole series of problems, as well as opportunities.

"The other thing is, at the end of the day, I feel that one of the most profound changes in the twentieth century for America has been the shift in gender roles—the emergence of women and the exploration of what it exactly means to be a woman, and means to be a man, in our contemporary society. I feel that Horizons' mission has been to contribute to that exploration. I'd like to feel when it's all over that we have, in meaningful ways, made people think, question, and explore what it means to be a woman and what it means to be a man in the twenty-first century."

Changing Kids' Lives

Ralph Remington wants Living Stage to reinvigorate the theatergoing habits of a generation: "A kid can come to see a show here. Let's say they buy a ticket for twenty dollars, and they can see four things for that twenty dollars. Then, they get in the habit of going to see theater, the theater that they want to see. Then, they're there, and it's all a part of the process of Arena Stage; then hopefully, they get energized by those artists. I'm bringing them in through the back door.

"I define complete success for Living Stage as making a contribution. That is success."

Staying Alive

Susan Albert Loewenberg has high hopes for L.A. Theatre Works' most recent endeavor: "I would love to leave L.A. Theatre Works intact with an endowment I'd realized from the audio publishing business," she says. "I would like to build that business. L.A. Theatre Works would never be able to raise endowment money—it's too small. But I've always had the dream, since I started this business, that the audio publishing business would become so successful that we could endow ourselves. Then, I could leave the organization with a small endowment and allow it to continue.

"Whether it continues in the same form, or altered, is not important to me. I would love to be able, when I leave, to have it go on and to be able to leave it in good financial shape. Leave it to someone, or a group of people, who could carry it forward with the same degree of excellence and do better than I. Much better than I, because at a certain point, they'll be younger people who can do this better than I can do it, who can see other exciting things and other directions to take it in."

Encouraging Expression

Mitzi Sales no longer works for Berkeley Repertory, but she has this to say about the goals of that theater and all theaters: "I've always felt like the principal goal of any managing director is to find the audience for the artistic output, for the artistic director's vision. I think that we were able to do that over the years.

"It's that situation where, let's do some theater—what do people want to come to? Well, you don't do theater like that! Hello?! You find somebody who needs to say something, and then you find people who want to do that. I think, largely, that was my goal. That was my role, and I think that we were able to do that.

"I would like to take credit for knowing when to leave. I think that it was one of the smartest things I ever did, because with Susie Medak, Tony [Taccone], and Sharon [Ott], this fresh, new creative energy was able to get this new theater built. I'm not saying it wouldn't have happened if I'd stayed, but it might not have. I was very wise to leave when I did, for the theater as well as for myself. The theater deserved to have somebody that was completely engaged, and not feeling unchallenged.

"So, I take full credit for knowing when to leave and doing it."

Strength and Prominence

"I would hope that I would leave Pasadena Playhouse as a really strong, vital arts institution," says Sheldon Epps. "Respected on the national level, well known for the diversity of the work, the quality of the work, and for taking care of the artists who are involved in producing the work. Compensating them and making it easier for people to go about the process of creation without as many economic restraints.

"I want the theater to be contributing to the national canon of dramatic literature, that fewer artistic decisions have to be made based on the pressures of economic success, meaning box office take. That we're able to be a little more chancier and a little more daring. Not that we don't want to sell tickets, but that we don't want to worry about that being the only measure of our success.

"I'd like to do a revival of the musical *House of Flowers* by Truman Capote, and the score's by Harold Arlen. It's from the fifties, and it made Pearl Bailey a star. Beautiful score! And I'd like to do a production of Shakespeare's *The Tempest*."

Forward Motion

Like many of our experts, Dona Lee Kelly wishes for improved finances for her company. "I don't think you can ever have complete success, but it would be great to have a little bit more financial stability [for the Cocteau]. I want to strengthen the development team. My goal coming in was to professionalize the staff. It had a kind of community theater culture. [That goal] has already happened; the staff members that are on really want to do the best job that they can and understand that anything they do is representative of the organization.

"So, that has certainly changed, and I think that some of the fund-raising successes and support we had this year have given the company a kind of spiritual boost, in a way. They see that it's possible.

"We came from no hope and dysfunction in July to saying, 'Okay, if we keep getting money, we can do these things.'

"You never know—the Cocteau always had surprises. The theater has, too. It's almost like you're riding on an ocean—you can get hit by storms and all kinds of things. Another image I like to use, because it also gives a forward action, is as an actor, you always have to go in one direction, even though your tactics will change. It's truly a campaign. You're here to do a campaign. You get everything set up, and then you do it, and you get focused. If you're going to do it, you're going to really make a choice to do it. Do it fully. That's the way you have to charge ahead—you have to show funders you're aggressive, but you also have to show the community that you understand where your artistic position is at the time.

"You're not more than you think you are; you are who you are."

Hope for the Next Generation

Susan Kosoff hopes the Wheelock Family Theatre has a longevity that outlasts her helmship. "I think ultimate success for me will be, when I retire, that it continues," says Susan. "Part of the impetus for a strategic plan was the knowledge that Jane Staab and I are not going to go on forever.

"Part of what we looked at is, how do we look at the leadership for the future? As a tenured professor at Wheelock, I'm in a kind of unique position. It's not clear whether the college would want to replace me or have the next artistic director be a member of the faculty or not. How is that going to work?

"For me, the tale will be told in whether the theater continues, and continues with the same general mission. That's not to say there can't be changes, adjustments, and new ideas. I think that's healthy. But I also think I'm not going to do this forever. My hope is, the theater will be stable enough, and not dependent on me and on Jane to continue."

Mission Accomplished

On the other hand, Jack Reuler hopes that the need for Mixed Blood will diminish in the coming years. "We'll be ultimately successful when we're no longer necessary. If you have a mission, you've got to be aspiring to realize it. The Polio Society, when it existed, its purpose was to find the cure for polio, and when it found that cure, it no longer needed to exist. I think it still existed to help people who had polio get through life. I sort of see us that way, perhaps farther and farther away all the time. When people, both audiences and other arts organizations, have embraced what it is we're trying to do, more intelligently than we do it, all we can be is another theater doing good work, or maybe there's enough theater doing good work that we don't need to be.

"Closing our doors because we've realized our mission would be the greatest thing that could happen, not a sign of failure."

As For Your Legacy

It will be whatever you choose to make it. Hopefully, that will be glorious. To give you a head start, I'm going to clue you into something. Here now, I will impart to you the ultimate secret to achieving total and complete success in the theater. Get ready—it's Holy Grail time!

Here comes the secret . . . Is your seat belt fastened? Good.

The secret is . . . always have fun.

Having fun as you work in the theater. It's why Carol Channing has been smiling constantly for the past seventy years. It's also contagious. That's why audiences have had such a good time watching Nathan Lane and Matthew Broderick joke their way through *The Producers*. It's also why you never noticed you'd gotten fleas until that performance of *Cats* was over.

Great theater is great because it's infused with joy. Those who make it work directly from the truth that they love what they do. Whether onstage or backstage, they have fun.

I once read a quote attributed to Paul McCartney: He said that doing music should never feel like work—you always want to make it play, and therefore, it will be great. This is one of the best nuggets of wisdom I've ever heard. Creativity springs from our imagination. The same imagination that we developed as kids playing, having a good time. That sense of fun is the purest resource of success a theater professional can draw upon.

A life in the theater is rough, right? So, don't make things any more difficult than they have to be.

Stay loose. If your work feels like fun, trust that you're onto something. Other people are going to respond to it.

At all stages of building your company, work as hard as you can. Learn as much as you can. Allow each and every accomplishment inspire you onward to future achievements. But never forget to have fun.

Enjoy the ride as you go along. Make yourself some great memories. You'll be successful then, no matter whether the show makes you rich and transfers to the Winter Garden or closes opening night.

Don't get me wrong. I wish you millions of dollars and hundreds of Tony Awards. (If you apply the information you've learned within this book, hopefully, you're well on your way.) It's just that you can't measure success materially, not really. You can only measure it through self-satisfaction, creative fulfillment, friendships, and peace of mind.

So, make happiness your goal as you build your own successful theater company. Break a leg . . . and always have fun.

APPENDIX A

**PHYSICAL PRODUCTION DETAILS FOR THE THEATER COMPANIES
PROFILED WITHIN *BUILDING THE SUCCESSFUL THEATER COMPANY***

Steppenwolf Theatre Company
Mainstage Space: 510 seats. Thrust stage setup.
Studio Space: 200 seats. Black box structure.
Garage Space: 60 seats.

The Pasadena Playhouse
Mainstage Space: 686 seats. Proscenium stage setup.

La Jolla Playhouse
Mainstage Space: 492 seats. Proscenium stage setup.
Second Stage: 398 seats. Thrust stage setup.

Chicago City Limits
Mainstage Space: 190 seats. Proscenium stage setup.

Berkeley Repertory Theatre
Mainstage Space: 401 seats. Thrust stage setup.
Second Stage: 587 seats. Proscenium stage setup.

Arena Stage's The Living Stage Theatre Company
Mainstage Space: Workshop, 100 seats, with an adjustably structured stage
measuring 30 by 50 feet.
The company also tours productions to various spaces.

Mixed Blood Theatre Company
Mainstage Space: 200 seats, with an adjustably structured stage.
The company also tours productions to various spaces.

Horizons Theatre
No permanent performance space.
The company performs its season offerings in various spaces.

Wheelock Family Theatre

Mainstage Space: 650 seats. Proscenium stage setup.

L.A. Theatre Works

No permanent performance space.

Records and performs in various settings.

A Traveling Jewish Theatre

Mainstage Space: 80 seats.

The company also tours productions to various spaces.

Jean Cocteau Repertory

Mainstage Space: 140 seats. Proscenium stage setup.

Bailiwick Repertory

Mainstage Space: 150 seats. Three-quarter thrust stage setup.

Second Stage: 99 seats. Black box structure.

New Repertory Theatre

Mainstage Space: 160 seats. Thrust stage setup.

APPENDIX B

NATIONAL ASSOCIATIONS AND ORGANIZATIONS

Here is a listing of some national theater arts assistance organizations you may wish to contact for resources and advice as you establish your own theater company. Arguably, your first stop should be the Foundation Center for grant/funding information.

Alliance of Resident Theatres/New York
575 Eighth Avenue, Suite 17 South
New York, NY 10018-3011
(212) 244-6667
(212) 714-1918 (fax)
questions@art-newyork.org (e-mail)

Americans for the Arts (New York City)
1 East 53rd Street
New York, NY 10022
(212) 223-2787
(212) 753-1325 (fax)
www.artsusa.org

Americans for the Arts (Washington, D.C.)
1000 Vermont Avenue NW, 12th Floor
Washington, DC 20005
(202) 371-2830
(202) 371-0424 (fax)

American Theater Wing
250 West 57th Street, Suite 519
New York, NY 10107
(212) 869-5470

Black Theatre Network
c/o Kuntu Rep Theatre, 3T01 Wesley W. Posvar Hall

230 South Bouguet Street

Pittsburgh, PA 15260

rroebuck@pitt.edu (e-mail)

Institute of Outdoor Drama

CB#3240

University of North Carolina

Chapel Hill, NC 27599-3240

(919) 962-1328

(919) 962-4212 (fax)

outdoor@unc.edu (e-mail)

www.UNC.Edu.depts/outdoor

International Association of Theatre for Children and Young People

724 Second Avenue South

Nashville, TN 37210

(615) 254-5719

USASITE@aol.com (e-mail)

www.assitej-USA.org

The League of American Theatres and Producers

226 West 47th Street

New York, NY 10036

(212) 764-1122

National Endowment for the Arts

1100 Pennsylvania Avenue NW

Washington, DC 20506

(212) 682-5400

Performing Arts Resources

dbradypar@aol.com (e-mail)

http://members.aol.com/perfrtsrc

Theatre Communications Group (TCG)

355 Lexington Avenue, 4th Floor

New York, NY 10017

(212) 697-5230
www.tcg.org

Theatre Development Fund
1501 Broadway, 21st Floor
New York, NY 10036
(212) 221-0885

The Theatre Guild
226 West 47th Street
New York, NY 10036
(212) 221-0885

United States Institute for Theatre Technology
6443 Ridings Road
Syracuse, NY 13206-1111
(315) 463-6463
(315) 463-6525 (fax)
www.USITT.org

University/Resident Theatre Association
1560 Broadway, Suite 141
New York, NY 10036
(212) 221-1130
(212) 869-2752 (fax)
URTA@aol.com (e-mail)
www.URTA.com

Volunteer Lawyers for the Arts
1 East 53rd Street, 6th Floor
New York, NY 10022
(212) 319-2787 (information directory)
(212) 319-2910 (legal matters line)
(212) 752-6575 (fax)
vlany@bway.net (e-mail)
www.vlany.org

APPENDIX C

REGIONAL ASSOCIATIONS AND ORGANIZATIONS

Austin Circle of Theatres (Texas)
4402 Burnet Road, #1
Austin, TX 78756-3319
(512) 454-9700
(512) 454-9988 (fax)
acot@eden.infohwy.com (e-mail)
www.acotonline.org

Baltimore Theatre Alliance
43 West Preston Street
Baltimore, MD 21201
(410) 783-0777
(410) 783-1059 (fax)
www.towson.edu/bta

Greater Philadelphia Cultural Alliance
100 South Broad Street, Suite 1530
Philadelphia, PA 19110
(215) 557-7811
(215) 557-7823 (fax)
gpca@philaculture.org (e-mail)
www.philaculture.org

League of Washington Theatres
P.O. Box 21645
Washington, DC 20009
(202) 638-4270
info@lowt.org (e-mail)
www.lowt.org

Mayor's Office of Film, Theatre, and Broadcasting
1697 Broadway, 6th Floor
New York, NY 10019
(212) 489-6710

Portland Area Theatre Alliance
1017 SW Morrison, Room 505
Portland, OR 97205
(503) 241-4902

Stage Source (New England)
88 Tremont Street, Suite 714
Boston, MA 02108
(617) 720-6066
info@stagesource.org (e-mail)
www.stagesource.org

Theatre Bay Area
870 Market Street, Suite 375
San Francisco, CA 94102
(415) 430-1140
www.theatrebayarea.org

Theatre League Alliance (California)
644 South Figueroa Street
Los Angeles, CA 90017
(213) 614-0556
info@theatrela.org (e-mail)
www.theatrela.org

APPENDIX D

UNIONS

Actors' Equity Association (National Headquarters)
165 West 46th Street
New York, NY 10036
(212) 869-8530

Actors' Equity Association (Chicago)
203 North Wabash Avenue, Suite 1700
Chicago, IL 60601
(312) 641-0393

Actors' Equity Association (Los Angeles)
5757 Wilshire Boulevard, Suite 1
Los Angeles, CA 90036
(323) 634-1750

Actors' Equity Association (Orlando, Florida)
10369 Orangewood Boulevard
Orlando, FL 32821
(407) 345-8600

Actors' Equity Association (San Francisco)
235 Pine Street, Suite 1200
San Francisco, CA 94104
(415) 391-3838

American Federation of Musicians
1501 Broadway, Suite 600
New York, NY 10036
(212) 869-1330

American Federation of Musicians (Washington, D.C.)
Local 161-710
4400 Mac Arthur Blvd. NW, #306
Washington, DC 20007
(202) 337-9325

American Guild of Variety Artists
184 Fifth Avenue, 6th Floor
New York, NY 10010
(212) 675-1003

Association of Authors' Representatives
P.O. Box 237201
Ansonia Station
New York, NY 10023
(212) 252-3695

The Dramatists Guild, Inc.
234 West 44th Street
New York, NY 10036
(212) 398-9366

International Alliance of Theatrical Stage Employees (California)
10045 Riverside Drive
Toluca Lake, CA 91602
(818) 980-3499

International Alliance of Theatrical Stage Employees (New York)
1515 Broadway, Suite 601
New York, NY 10036
(212) 730-1770

Society of Stage Directors and Choreographers
1501 Broadway, 17th Floor
New York, NY 10036
(212) 391-1070

Theatrical Costume Workers Union, Local 22

218 West 40th Street

New York, NY 10018

(212) 730-7500

Theatrical Protective Union, Local 1

320 West 46th Street

New York, NY 10036

(212) 730-7500

United Scenic Artists Union, Local 829

16 West 61st Street, 11th Floor

New York, NY 10023

(212) 581-0300

APPENDIX E

TALENT BANKS

Here is a listing of resource organizations that you may find helpful in terms of locating qualified professional performers for your theater company and for filling administrative staff positions.

ArtsSEARCH

c/o Theatre Communications Group

355 Lexington Avenue

New York, NY 10017

(212) 697-5230

www.tcg.org

Art Job

Western States Arts Federation

1543 Champa Street, Suite 220

Denver, CO 80202

(303) 629-1166

(888) 562-7232

www.artjob.com

Breakdown Services

www.breakdownservices.com

Non-Traditional Casting Project

1560 Broadway, Suite 1600

New York, NY 10036

(212) 730-4750

info@ntcp.org (e-mail)

www.ntcp.org

APPENDIX F

AUDITION RESOURCES

The following organizations sponsor audition conferences for professional theaters, or offer networking opportunities that liaison talent with theater companies.

Florida Professional Theatres Association
P.O. Box 2922
West Palm Beach, FL 33402
(561) 848-6231

National Dinner Theatre Association
P.O. Box 726
Marshall, MI 49068
ndta@aol.com (e-mail)

New England Theatre Conference
Northeastern University
360 Huntington Avenue
Boston, MA 02115
(617) 424-9275
info@netconline.org (e-mail)
www.netconline.org

Princess Grace Foundation
150 East 58th Street, 21st Floor
New York, NY 10155
(212) 317-1470
pgfusa@pgfusa.com (e-mail)
www.pgfusa.com

Southeastern Theatre Conference

PO Box 9868

Greensboro, NC 27429-0868

(336) 272-8550

SETC@spyder.net (e-mail)

www.spyder.net/setc

APPENDIX G

PUBLICATIONS

Consult the following publications for consistently helpful information about the business of theater. Subscription contact information is listed below; also check newsstands for a number of these titles.

Academy Players Directory (**Actors' Directory**)
8949 Wilshire Boulevard
Beverly Hills, CA 90211
(310) 247-3058
www.acadpd.org

American Theatre Magazine
c/o Theatre Communications Group
355 Lexington Avenue
New York, NY 10017
(212) 697-5230
www.tcg.com

Back Stage/Back Stage West/Drama-Logue
(800) 437-3183
www.backstage.com

Black Talent News
1620 Centinela Avenue, Suite 204
Englewood, CA 90302
(310) 348-3944
www.blacktalentnews.com

Call Board
870 Market Street, Suite 375

San Francisco, CA 94102

(415) 430-1140

Dramatics Magazine

Educational Theatre Association

2343 Auburn Avenue

Cincinnati, OH 45219-2815

(513) 421-3900

www.edta.org

Performing Arts Magazine

Performing Arts Network

10350 Santa Monica Blvd.

Los Angeles, CA 90025

(310) 551-1115

www.performingartsmagazine.com

Players Guide

123 West 44th Street, Suite 2J

New York, NY 10036

(212) 302-9474

www.playersguideny.com

Ross Reports (union, TV, and movie coverage)

770 Broadway, 6th Floor

New York, NY 10003

(646) 654-5746

www.backstage.com

Stagebill Magazine

Stagebill LLC

823 United Plaza at 46th Street

New York, NY 10017

(212) 973-3960

www.stagebill.com

Stage Directions Magazine
250 West 57th Street, Suite 420
New York, NY 10107
(800) 362-6765
www.stage-directions.com

Variety/Daily Variety
5700 Wilshire Boulevard, Suite 120
Los Angeles, CA 90036-5804
(323) 965-4476
www.variety.com

APPENDIX H

THEATRICAL SUPPLY RESOURCE LIST

Here is a listing of supply companies that may be able to provide you with specialized equipment for your company via shipping. Most have full catalogs available upon request.

All Pro Sound (sound and lighting)
(800) 925-5776
www.allprosound.com

Charles H. Stewart Scenic Design (curtains and backdrops)
115 Flagship Drive
North Andover, MA 01845
(978) 682-5757
www.charleshstewart.com

City Theatrical (multiproduct stock)
752 East 133rd Street
Bronx, NY 10454
(718) 292-7932

Columbus McKinnon (rigging)
140 John James Audubon
Amherst, NY 14228
(800) 888-0985
www.cmworks.com

Eartec (headsets)
145 Dean Knauss Drive
Narragansett, RI 02882
(800) 399-5994

Kryolan (theatrical makeup)
132 Ninth Street
San Francisco, CA 94103
(415) 863-9684

Pacific Northwest Theatre Associates (multiproduct stock)
333 Westlake Avenue North
Seattle, WA 98109
(206) 622-7850
www.pnta.com

Premier Seating (audience seating units)
4211 Shannon Drive
Baltimore, MD 21213
(888) 456-SEAT

Sapsis Rigging, Inc. (safety inspections)
233 North Lansdowne Avenue
Lansdowne, PA 19050
(800) 727-7471
www.sapsis-rigging.com

Stagelam (theatrical flooring)
173 Glidden Road
Brampton, Ontario, Canada L6W3L9
(800) 361-1698
www.stagelam.com

Stageworks Lighting, Ltd. (lighting instruments)
1100 Capital Boulevard
Raleigh, NC 27603
(800) 334-8353
http://stageworks-lighting.com

TicketMaker (box office software)

(888) 397-3400

www.ticketmaker.com

tools for stagecraft.com (a huge selection of theatrical hand tools and more)

(877) 80tools

www.toolsforstagecraft.com

Tracey Theatre Originals (costumes and props)

(800) 926-8351

www.tracytheatreoriginals.com

INDEX

Books from Allworth Press

The Stage Producer's Business and Legal Guide
by Charles Grippo (paperback, 6 × 9, 256 pages, $19.95)

The Business of Theatrical Design
by James L Moody (paperback, 6 × 9, 288 pages, $19.95)

Movement for Actors
edited by Nicole Potter (paperback, 6 × 9, 288 pages, $19.95)

Producing Your Own Showcase
by Paul Harris (paperback, 6 × 9, 224 pages, $18.95)

Technical Theater for Nontechnical People
by Drew Campbell (paperback, 6 × 9, 256 pages, $18.95)

The Health & Safety Guide for Film, TV & Theater
by Monona Rossol (paperback, 6 × 9, 256 pages, $19.95)

Booking and Tour Management for the Performing Arts, Third Edition
by Rena Shagan (paperback, 6 × 9, 288 pages, $19.95)

Career Solutions for Creative People
by Dr. Rhonda Ormont (paperback, 6 × 9, 320 pages, $19.95)

An Actor's Guide—Making It in New York City
by Glenn Alterman (paperback, 6 × 9, 288 pages, $19.95)

Clues to Acting Shakespeare
by Wesley Van Tassel (paperback, 6 × 9, 208 pages, $16.95)

Creating Your Own Monologue
by Glenn Alterman (paperback, 6 × 9, 192 pages, $14.95)

Promoting Your Acting Career
by Glenn Alterman (paperback, 6 × 9, 224 pages, $18.95)

VO: Tales and Techniques of a Voice-Over Actor
by Harlan Hogan (paperback, 6 × 9, 256 pages, $19.95)

Please write to request our free catalog. To order by credit card, call 1-800-491-2808 or send a check or money order to Allworth Press, 10 East 23rd Street, Suite 510, New York, NY 10010. Include $5 for shipping and handling for the first book ordered and $1 for each additional book. Ten dollars plus $1 for each additional book if ordering from Canada. New York State residents must add sales tax.

To see our complete catalog on the World Wide Web, or to order online, you can find us at www.allworth.com.